STO

FRIEN
OF AC

BC
JA
THE CULTURAL POLITICS OF THE
NEW CRITICISM

D1191656

**DO NOT REMOVE
CARDS FROM POCKET**

**ALLEN COUNTY PUBLIC LIBRARY
FORT WAYNE, INDIANA  46802**

You may return this book to any agency, branch,
or bookmobile of the Allen County Public Library.

DEMCO

In this book, Mark Jancovich concentrates on the works of three leading American writers – Robert Penn Warren, John Crowe Ransom and Allen Tate – in order to examine the development of the New Criticism during the late 1920s and early 1930s, and its establishment within the academy in the late 1930s and early 1940s. This critical movement managed to transform the teaching and study of English through a series of essays published in journals such as the *Southern Review* and the *Kenyon Review*. Jancovich argues that the New Criticism was not an example of bourgeois individualism, as previously held, but that it sprang from a critique of modern capitalist society developed by pre-capitalist classes within the American South. In the process, he clarifies the distinctions between the aims of these three Southern poets and those of the next 'generation' of New Critics such as Cleanth Brooks, Warren and Welleck, and Wimsatt and Beardsley. He also claims that the failure on the part of most contemporary critics to identify the movement's ideological origins and aims has usually meant that these critics continue to operate within the very professional terms of reference established through the New Critical transformation of the academy.

# The cultural politics of the New Criticism

The cultural politics of the new criticism

# The cultural politics of the New Criticism

Mark Jancovich

*Department of American Studies,*
*University of Keele*

CAMBRIDGE
UNIVERSITY PRESS

Published by the Press Syndicate of the University of Cambridge
The Pitt Building, Trumpington Street, Cambridge, CB2 1RP
40 West 20th Street, New York, NY 10011–4211, USA
10 Stamford Road, Oakleigh, Melbourne 3166, Australia

© Cambridge University Press 1993

First published 1993

Printed in Great Britain at the University Press, Cambridge

*A catalogue record for this book is available from the British Library*

*Library of Congress cataloguing in publication data*
Jancovich, Mark.
The cultural politics of the New Criticism/Mark Jancovich.
    p.    cm.
Includes bibliographical references and index.
ISBN 0 521 41652 3 hardback
1. Criticism – United States – History – 20th century.  2. American
literature – History and criticism – Theory, etc.  3. Ransom, John
Crowe, 1888–1974 – Knowledge – Literature.  4. Warren, Robert Penn,
1905–  – Knowledge – Literature.  5. Tate, Allen, 1899–  –
Knowledge – Literature.  6. Politics and literature – United States.
7. New Criticism – United States.  I. Title.
PS78.J35  1993
801'.95'09739041 – dc20  93–19909 CIP

ISBN 0 521 41652 3 hardback

Allen County Public Library
900 Webster Street
PO Box 2270
Fort Wayne, IN 46801-2270

TAG

# Contents

**Part IV: The development of the New Criticism**

**Conclusion: Modernism and postmodernism within the
American academy**

# Preface

In 1983, I took a course in American literature under Dr Richard Godden at the University of Keele. The course was entitled 'The Southern Renaissance', and alongside writers such as William Faulkner, Eudora Welty, and Erskine Caldwell, we read and studied works by John Crowe Ransom, Allen Tate, and Robert Penn Warren, who were influential both as Southern writers and as leading figures in the American New Criticism. At this time I was also interested in structuralist and post-structuralist theory, and I had done a great deal of work on theorists such as Saussure, Barthes, Althusser, Lacan and Derrida. For most of their English and American followers, these theories were seen as a reaction against the existing dominant positions in philosophy and literary theory. In literary theory, these dominant positions were associated with F. R. Leavis in England and the New Criticism in America. What struck me at this time was that the positions which I had identified in the works which Ransom, Tate, and Warren had produced during the Southern Renaissance seemed to contradict the positions attributed to them as New Critics. In fact I was impressed by the similarities between the positions of the New Critics and those of the post-structuralists themselves, and I decided that a major reappraisal of the origins, practices, and impacts of the New Criticism was necessary. This book is a contribution to that reappraisal.

My initial aim was to refute and modify aspects of contemporary criticism by illustrating both that it was largely defined in reaction against the New Criticism, and that it had misread the interests which defined the New Criticism. In so doing, I had intended to argue that contemporary theorists had failed to acknowledge the extent to which the New Criticism had actually defined the institutional and intellectual preconditions for contemporary theory through a politically motivated reorganization of the terms of reference for literary study within the academy. However, as many people pointed out, this task actually included three potential books. I had intended to illustrate that the New Criticism developed out of certain Southern critiques of modern society; that contemporary interpretations of the interests and practices of the New Criticism were largely inaccurate;

and that the New Criticism had actually established the terms within which contemporary theory was defined. Consequently, I was persuaded to concentrate on the second of these arguments. None the less, it is vitally important to bear in mind that these other two theses remain as very important subtexts which give meaning and purpose to the book as it stands.

In the following book, I have concentrated on the work of John Crowe Ransom, Allen Tate and Robert Penn Warren, though I do acknowledge that the New Criticism as a term refers to a far wider group of critics. My reason for concentrating on these three writers is that they were responsible for organizing the New Criticism as a movement. They led the activities which established the New Criticism as the dominant mode of criticism within the academy, and as a result, they had a great deal of influence over the manner in which the New Criticism was defined. My own concentration on these three critics is also a response to contemporary commentators on the New Criticism, most of whom acknowledge that Ransom, Tate, and Warren were central to the emergence of the New Criticism as the dominant mode of critical activity within the academy. It is not my contention, however, that these writers were the only figures who influenced the New Criticism as an activity, nor that Ransom, Tate and Warren constituted a monolithic entity within which there was no disagreement.

I have divided the following work into five parts, the first of which is an introduction in which I discuss contemporary interpretations of the New Criticism in order to clarify the positions which I am arguing against throughout the rest of the book. However, at the end of this part there is a slight shift in emphasis in which I introduce my main argument through a brief examination of Ransom, Tate, and Warren's defence of the South and their critique of modern society. It is my case that the New Criticism developed from these social and political positions. In part two, I examine the way in which the New Criticism was developed during the late 1920s and early 1930s in order to identify both the interests which motivated it, and the specific social and cultural critique which it established. This part is divided into four chapters. The first three examine the individual contributions of Ransom, Tate, and Warren, while the conclusion illustrates my position through a study of their collective analysis of the Southern poet, Sidney Lanier. Part three moves on to consider the political motivations which led these writers to attempt a reorganization of the teaching of English and the various tactics which were involved in this attempt. Part four is concerned with the potentials of the New Criticism, or the way in which it developed after its institutionalization within the academy. In so doing, this part considers the extent to which Ransom,

Tate, and Warren continued to draw on their specific criticisms of modern society, even while they realized different potentials within these criticisms, and began to engage in different forms of activity from one another. The final or concluding part moves on to examine the ways in which the New Criticism laid the foundations for contemporary criticism and to detail the features which distinguish the two from one another.

I am indebted to many people, not least to Richard Godden who gave me the encouragement to pursue these ideas and who continues to be a close friend. Martin Barker, Elizabeth Dawn Barlow, Ian Bell, Patrick Brantlinger, Martin Crawford, David Ellis, Gordon Fyfe, Jo Gill, Richard Gray, Graham Hitchen, Brian Jarvis, Carole and Davis Joyce, Liam Kennedy, Richard King, Brian Lee, Pete Ling, Alf Louvre, Paul McDonald, Pete Messant, Geoff Mulgan, Pete Nichols, Alan Purves, Steve Rigby, Karen Schneider, Bernard Sharratt, Bev Skeggs, Martin Stanton, Charles Swann, Douglas Tallack, Barry Taylor, David Turley, Duncan Webster, and Tim Youngs have all contributed ideas and encouragement over the years. Without my mother though none of this would have been possible. I can't mention everyone, so I don't think I had better try, but it seems appropriate to end with a very special thanks to Keith Carabine, who put up with the awful job of reading and re-reading this book in its different – or not so different – stages, never making anything but sound and encouraging comments.

# Abbreviations

Certain periodicals are abbreviated as follows:

| | |
|---|---|
| *AHR* | *American Historical Review* |
| *AQ* | *American Quarterly* |
| *AR* | *American Review* |
| *AS* | *American Studies* |
| *Bo* | *The Bookman* |
| *JAH* | *Journal of American History* |
| *JAS* | *Journal of American Studies* |
| *KR* | *Kenyon Review* |
| *MVHR* | *Mississippi Valley Historical Review* |
| *Na* | *The Nation* |
| *NLR* | *New Left Review* |
| *NR* | *New Republic* |
| *SeR* | *Sewanee Review* |
| *SR* | *Southern Review* |
| *VQR* | *Virginia Quarterly Review* |

*Part I*

# The New Criticism and its critics

# 1 Contemporary responses to the New Criticism

In his book, *After the New Criticism*, Frank Lentricchia attempts to counter 'two misleading perspectives' which may be suggested by his book's title. He argues that the New Criticism was never a monolithic entity; and that the period defined by the title is not one distinguished by the absence of the New Criticism, but, in a very important sense, one which is distinguished by its presence. In the case of the first argument, he describes the New Criticism as 'an inconsistent and sometimes confused movement'. Unfortunately, while he does acknowledge real differences within the movement, he regards these as the result of weakness or a lack of clarity, rather than the disagreements and discussions which are present in any critical discourse. Lentricchia fails to acknowledge that the social organization of the New Criticism was very different from that of contemporary criticism – at least in its early stages. While the New Critics did share a common reaction against previous forms of criticism, and while they relied on similar intellectual traditions, their social organization was largely that of an informal group which only began to formalize itself in an attempt to reorganize the teaching of English in America. Contemporary criticism, on the other hand, is defined within specific institutional and theoretical structures which tend to make it far more monolithic.

This situation is also related to Lentricchia's second argument. The institutional and theoretical structures of contemporary criticism are part of the legacy of the New Criticism:

If my title suggests, then, that the New Criticism is dead – in an official sense, of course, it is – I must stipulate that in my view it is dead in the way that an imposing and repressive father-figure is dead. I find many traces (perhaps 'scars' is the word) of the New Criticism and of nineteenth century thought in the fixed and identifiable positions we have come to know as contemporary theory. Such traces or scars produce, in turn, another effect, not easy to discern: an intertextual mingling among contemporary theorists. I am arguing not only that the ruptures separating nineteenth-century aesthetic traditions, the New Criticism, and contemporary theories are not absolute but also that the differences among contemporary theories are not clean discontinuities. In my opinion it is the very condition of contemporary critical historicity that there is no 'after' or 'before' the New

Criticism: no absolute presence *in the present* means that the present is opened up
to the 'drift from the other ends of time'.[1]

In this passage, Lentricchia does acknowledge that contemporary criticism
is defined in relation to the New Criticism, but he obscures the continuities
between the two. Contemporary theorists have often misrepresented the
positions of the New Criticism, and the extent to which it defines their own
activities. They have often failed to acknowledge its specific strengths,
while reproducing many of its problems. In fact, Lentricchia himself makes
this mistake in relation to the issue of history. He argues that one of the
legacies of the New Criticism is the 'denial of history' in contemporary
theory:

The traces of the New Criticism are found in yet another way: in the repeated and
often extremely subtle denial of history by a variety of contemporary theorists. The
exploration and critique of this evasive antihistorical maneuver is one of my
fundamental concerns.[2]

One of my own fundamental concerns is to illustrate that while this denial
is part of the legacy of the New Criticism, it is the result of a
misrepresentation of the New Criticism and the way in which it defined
literary activity. Contemporary critics have argued both that the New
Criticism maintained that literary activity was completely autonomous
from other activities, and that the New Criticism failed to account for the
autonomy of signifying practice. In both instances, these critics have
misrepresented the ways in which the New Criticism defined the relationship between literature and other forms of social and cultural
activity.

It is also interesting that Lentricchia never tackles the New Criticism
itself. Instead his book offers a succession of highly interesting readings of
the critical movements which rapidly followed each other after 1957, the
year which Lentricchia regards as the end of the New Criticism and the
beginning of its aftermath. However, one of the questions which is raised
by Lentricchia's book, and by Eagleton's discussion of it in his article, 'The
Idealism of American Criticism',[3] is whether this moment in 1957 (which
is identified with the publication of Northrop Frye's book, *The Anatomy of
Criticism*)[4] was actually the moment at which many of the myths associated
with the New Criticism were generated. Both writers argue that Frye was
concerned with a critique of the New Criticism, and that he claimed that
literary analysis should concentrate on literary and mythological systems,
rather than on the study of the individual text, a practice which he
identified with the New Criticism. They also maintain that Frye's book
introduced a whole series of concerns which would be central to
contemporary criticism. In fact, Eagleton attempts to identify a proto-

structuralist conception of desire in Frye's criticism. For this reason, Frye's criticism can be regarded as the moment at which the New Criticism was identified with the formalist study of an individual, autonomous text which was displaced from any sense of context. It can also be regarded as the moment when the literary context (or that which is 'beyond formalism' as Geoffery Hartman refers to it)[5] was identified with unconscious processes of desire and structuration, processes which were defined as both global and ahistorical: it is therefore interesting that Hartman's *Beyond Formalism* begins with an enthusiastic defence of Frye's criticism.

The misinterpretations of the New Criticism found in Lentricchia and Eagleton are only part of a far more general tendency within contemporary criticism. It has become commonplace for critics to claim that the New Critics distinguished the text from what Wimsatt and Beardsley referred to as the 'Intentional' and the 'Affective' fallacies,[6] and that this meant that it was a form of bourgeois individualism and/or scientific positivism. It is argued that Wimsatt and Beardsley's position – which is close to that of Brooks and Warren in *Understanding Poetry*[7] – regards the individual text as a fixed object which bears no relation to its conditions of production or consumption. As a result, the New Criticism is supposed to have claimed that the literary critic should only be concerned with the interpretation of individual works. Unfortunately, the New Critics did not define the text as a fixed object which was completely autonomous from the contexts within which it was produced and consumed. On the contrary, they recognized that the production and consumption of texts were only moments within broader cultural processes. Their position was that if students were to be taught to understand the workings of these broader processes, it was necessary to focus their attention on the texts which mediated between the contexts of production and consumption. For the New Critics, the critic should concentrate on the formal processes of texts, formal processes within which both the intentions of the author and the responses of the reader were framed. None the less, they were well aware that their attempt to concentrate on the text as that which mediates between the contexts of production and consumption was itself problematic. The text as such never exists as an independent object, but, as Wimsatt and Beardsley stress, it is always an ideal construction.

Despite this there is general agreement that the New Criticism saw the individual text as an objective, self-sufficient object, but contemporary critics have come to different conclusions as to what this position might mean and what is wrong with it. It is generally agreed that the New Criticism was associated with the practice of close reading, and that, as Eagleton and others have argued, this practice did 'more than insist on due attentiveness to the text. It inescapably suggests an attention to *this* rather than to something else: to the "words on the page" rather than to the contexts which produced and surrounded them '.[8] But there is considerable argument as to which contexts are appropriate to the study of literature. For example, while some contemporary critics have accused the New Criticism of isolating the literary text from society and history, others claim that it did not go far enough in this direction; that it failed to identify the autonomy of literary activity. In fact, these criticisms can be present in the same writer. Eagleton, for example, argues that the New Critics separated literature from its social and historical context:

Rescuing the text from author and reader went hand in hand with disentangling it from any social or historical context. One needed, to be sure, to know what the poem's words would have meant to their original readers, but this fairly technical sort of historical knowledge was the only kind permitted. Literature was a solution to social problems, not a part of them; the poem must be plucked free of the wreckage of history and hoisted into a sublime space above it.[9]

Eagleton accuses the New Critics of seeing literature as an autonomous activity, but his own criticism draws on post-structuralist theory and also seeks to defend the autonomy of literary activity. He is highly critical of those who see literature as a simple reflection or expression of either authorial intention or its social or historical context. As a result, he repeats many of the theoretical manoeuvres which he criticizes in the New Criticism. He is also quite simply wrong to claim that the New Critics saw literary forms as merely a solution to social problems, and not as a product of them.

In fact, the American Marxist critic Fredric Jameson acknowledges many of the similarities between the New Criticism and post-structuralism. He argues that they share a concern to disentangle 'the literary system from other extrinsic systems'.[10] For Jameson, the strength of both the New Criticism and contemporary post-structuralism is that they challenge 'diachronic' theories of language and literature, theories which see texts as the reflection or expression of an author or a social and historical context. He does see a difference between the two critical movements, but claims that it lies in a failure on the part of the New Critics to reject 'the tendency to resolve the literary work into a single technique or a single psychological impulse'.[11] This criticism is directed against the New Critical theory of the organic nature of the literary text, but it misses the point that, for the New Critics, the literary text was an organic whole specifically because it could not be resolved into any one element or feature. It was a complex system of interrelated elements.

The issue of literary autonomy is a problem for Marxist critics such as Eagleton and Jameson though. Like the New Critics themselves, while they wanted to emphasize the 'relative' autonomy of literature in opposition to those who see it as a simple expression of social and political forces, they are still concerned to emphasize that culture is related to these forces. Their problem is that post-structuralism has a tendency to isolate literary activity from society and history and define it as 'a system with its own order', a system which can only be understood in terms of its internal organization rather than in its relation to other social activities. This tendency was already present in the work of Frye, and it has two aspects: it challenges representational theories of language and literature; and it defines literature as a system with its own rules, a system which is 'autonomous' from other activities.

The first aspect is particularly significant given that many critics have attacked the New Criticism by claiming that it devalued representational and realist types of literature,[12] or that it denies that literature can offer any form of knowledge. This latter position can be found in the work of Robert Scholes. For example, he argues:

Both Formalist and New Critical schools of criticism tend to deny literary texts any cognitive quality. In terms of the model of communication we are working with, this means denying the access to any context beyond their own verbal system or other texts that share that system.[13]

In fact, the New Critics did not devalue 'realist' types of literature in quite the way that is often claimed. Robert Penn Warren, in particular, was a defender of Theodore Dreiser. What they rejected were those types of writing that Lukacs described as 'naturalism', writing which concentrated on the surface details of social reality rather than on the social processes which produced those surface details. Nor did they deny that literature offered a form of knowledge or cognition. On the contrary, their project was specifically to define literature as a form of knowledge, but one which was defined in opposition to the form of knowledge offered by scientific positivism. It was for this reason that one of Allen Tate's major New Critical essays is entitled 'Literature as Knowledge'. The irony of this situation is that it is post-structuralist critics who have been most instrumental in devaluing representational and realist types of writing. For many such as Catherine Belsey, Terence Hawkes, and even Eagleton, realism is seen as an ideological form which is opposed to a truly revolutionary avant-garde. The notion that language can represent a pre-existing reality is seen as that which must be challenged. They argue that language does not offer us knowledge about a pre-existing world, but structures not only the ways in which we think, but also the objects about which we think.

For these reasons, the most common complaint is not that the New Criticism isolated literature from its social and historical context, but that the practice of close reading concentrates on individual texts in isolation from the context of the 'autonomous' literary system. This criticism has a strong line of continuity with the work of Frye who maintained that the literary critic should not concentrate on the individual text, but on the literary and mythological systems within which these texts were produced, and it can be identified in Robert Scholes' comparison between the Russian Formalists and the New Critics:

The Formalists differed from the New Critics, however, in their extreme interest in devices and conventions of poetic structure. They always sought the poetic in poetry and the prosaic in prose, so that even their studies of individual texts always came to turn on a point of poetic principle that could be applied to other texts in the same genre. Thus, their interpretive strategies tended to move from an emphasis on texts to an emphasis on the codes that govern the production of texts.[14]

It is difficult to see what books such as *Understanding Poetry* and *Understanding Fiction* are seeking to do, if not to identify 'the poetic in poetry' and 'the prosaic in prose'; to say nothing of 'the literariness of literature'. None the less, Scholes claims that it was the New Critics' concentration on individual 'works' of literature, rather than 'textuality' or the system of literary codes, which made it successful. It is argued that their supposed avoidance of the unconscious structures within which texts are constructed meant that they offered no challenge to empiricist assumptions.

A similar position is developed by Jonathan Culler, but he takes it one stage further. For Culler, the practice of close reading which he associates with the New Critics not only fails to analyse the literary system, but as a result, regards the process of reading as natural and unproblematic. It fails to recognize that the activity of reading is also dependent upon the literary system.[15] This argument is similar to earlier criticisms, but it is also part of a general shift in focus within theory away from the analysis of the literary system to a critique of the process of interpretation itself. Writers such as Stanley Fish and David Bleich, for example, have argued that there is no 'meaning' to a text prior to the act of interpretation, but that different groups of readers bring different 'interpretive strategies' to bear on texts. These groups construct texts in different ways depending on these different strategies, and no approach is more 'true' to the text than any other.[16]

While this position might lead to mere relativism, the critique of interpretation becomes a political project for some post-structuralist critics such as Terence Hawkes. For Hawkes, the practice of close reading depends upon the assumption that the subject and the object of study – the reader and the text – are stable and independent forms, rather than products of the unconscious process of signification, an assumption which he identifies as the ideology of liberal humanism. This ideological position is attributed to the New Critics who are accused of attempting to disguise the interests at work in their critical processes. Despite these claims, it was central to the New Critical project that they recognized that the process of reading was not natural. This was the reason they saw literary education as important. They wanted to counter the forms of reading and culture produced by the rationalism of industrial capitalism, and to train the student in an alternative form of reading which would challenge the values of bourgeois society. They were not concerned to disguise their interests, but to present and justify them to the student. It should also be clear from this description that they did not adhere to the principles of liberal humanism, but were opposed to them.

Hawkes is not simply stressing that the reader inevitably brings certain values to the critical process though. He is arguing that language is such a complex process of interrelations that the 'meaning' of any text is always in process; that any attempt to identify a 'unity' or 'meaning' within the text is an act of violence which represses the 'productivity of language'. This violence is also associated with the New Criticism which, for Hawkes,

forms part of what Barthes dismisses as 'dishonest' criticism, based on the assumption that the work criticized exists in some objective concrete way *before* the critical act; that, however complex or ambiguous it may be, it can ultimately be reduced to a univocal 'content' beyond which it is improper to go.[17]

By contrast, Hawkes argues that the critical process should not be presented as the analysis of an objective text but a process of creativity in which the critic '*creates* the finished work by his reading of it, and does not remain simply an inert *consumer* of a "ready-made" product'.[18]

There are a number of problems with this position though. First, Hawkes implies that the absence of an objective text prior to the critical act means that all readings are equally valid: 'None of these readings is *wrong*, they all add to the work. So a work of literature ultimately consists of *everything* that has been said about it.'[19] But such a suggestion misrepresents his own position. Not only does he have no problem identifying a difference between 'realist' texts by writers such as Tolstoy and 'avant-garde' texts by writers such as James Joyce, but he would also maintain that any attempt to read the latter as a representational narrative would be inappropriate or wrong – if only because it violated the 'productivity of language'. Second, while he may be right that the significance of a text is related to the way in which it has been read, these readings may misrepresent the text and its conditions of production. In fact, the New Criticism itself is an example of this situation. Certainly its significance is related to the way in which contemporary critics have reacted against a certain interpretation of it, but it is still the case that this reaction by contemporary critics is based on a misrepresentation of the movement and the context within which it was produced. This problem also relates to the third and final one. The identification of a 'unity' or 'meaning' in a text does not reduce one to the status of a simple 'consumer'. The New Critics themselves were careful to stress that the 'unity' or 'meaning' of a text was a complex series of interrelations which required the reader to think through the issues, not accept or reject a specific conclusion. In fact, the New Critics' references to 'the heresy of paraphrase' – which are often seen as sealing the text off from its context – actually meant that the meaning of a text could never be resolved into a 'univocal content'; that it was an endlessly productive process.[20]

# 2    The historical context of the New Criticism

As has already been suggested, one of the problems with many of these theories is that they fail to locate the New Criticism historically, or else merely deduce its historical context from its theoretical positions. The little contextualization that is present is usually based on the work of John Fekete. In his book, *The Critical Twilight*, Fekete concentrates on the criticism of John Crowe Ransom, whom he identifies as the 'Philosopher General of the New Criticism', and as representative of the whole movement. Fekete does consider the New Criticism in relation to the Agrarian critique of industrial capitalism, but he argues that in the move from Agrarianism to the academy, the New Criticism was integrated into the 'dominant order' of American society:

> Where Agrarianism seeks to present itself as socially and economically programmatic for an aesthetic life as a totality to which art as such is to be subordinated, the New Critical perspective ... confines the broad scope of Agrarian ideology within the bounds of a literary criticism that champions art in safety from *within* the non-aesthetic life of the existing society. All possibilities of reshaping the exterior world are renounced to gain social sanction for the perfection of the interior world, the sensibility, through the strictly literary experience of life. We find, too, that the strong Agrarian critiques of industrialism are reduced to a critique of science, then to a critique of abused science, until, finally, peace is made altogether in the New Critical period, and the primacy of science is acknowledged. The New Criticism becomes widely known and influential as the defender of art by virtue of its view that art is necessary for truly human life and for knowing the world; but this is both knowing and living with the *established* reality through the contributions that the aesthetic sensibility can make. From the time of the Agrarian failure, the progression is an inexorable one toward the integration of critique into dominant rationality.[1]

There are two immediate problems with this position. First, while Fekete refers to a 'dominant order' and so suggests the existence of alternative orders, his argument is far too 'structural'. It is developed in very polarized terms, as if the choice between integration or opposition were between absolutes. 'Established reality' is never fixed and immutable. It is always composed of a variety of groups and alliances in struggle with one another.

11

There is no reason to argue that Ransom, Tate and Warren's movement into the academy could only represent submission or integration. After all, Fekete works within the academy, but does not appear to believe that he has been integrated into the 'dominant order'. In fact, Ransom, Tate and Warren's promotion of the New Criticism in the late 1930s and early 1940s was not a simple submission to the terms of the academy, but an active, tactical manoeuvre which aimed to challenge and redefine the politics of literary study within the academy. The second problem is Fekete's choice of Ransom as a representative of the movement as a whole. The New Criticism was always a diverse movement, and it developed in a variety of different ways after its establishment in the academy. In fact, while Ransom did come to 'champion art in safety from *within* the non-aesthetic life of the existing society'[2] after 1945, as Fekete claims, he did so in the period which *followed* the most significant battles over the New Criticism's establishment in the academy. Nor was the writing of this period his most influential. After 1945, he continued to teach and edit journals, and his earlier writings continued to be discussed and debated, but he wrote little criticism of any significance.

As a result, Fekete is right to argue that the 'New Criticism constitutes a substructure of modern critical theory',[3] but he fails to acknowledge the social basis of these theories; the political motivations behind their establishment in the academy; the different ways in which it developed in the 1940s and 1950s; and finally, the extent to which it established the terms of reference within which literary criticism still continues to be defined, even the forms of 'radical' criticism which Fekete defends. The latter problems all stem from the first though. For Fekete, despite its rejection of capitalist production, Agrarianism was an essentially bourgeois movement which did not reject capitalist forms of property. He fails to recognize that the Agrarian movement drew upon critiques of capitalist relations produced by the pre-capitalist social classes of the South. For example, they drew upon Southern paternalism which was defined by the specifically pre-capitalist relations of production associated with slave-labour. As Genovese has maintained, the Southern paternalist defence of slavery was not simply an ideological rationalization or nostalgic fantasy. On the contrary, it

signaled the maturation of the ruling class and its achievement of self-consciousness. Far from being mere apologetics or rationalization, it represented the formulation of a world view that authentically reflected the position, aspirations, and ethos of the slaveholders as a class.[4]

Genovese's argument is that through paternalism the planter class articulated a consciousness of its relation to the capitalist economic relations of the North.

Like Marx, the Southern planter class came to argue that capitalist relations organized *all human relations* through the cash-nexus. As a result, paternalism was a way of defining a series of organic relations between the members of society which were opposed to the acquisitive individualism associated with the capitalist market. This can be seen in the way in which Fitzhugh and others discussed the relationship between slavery and the family:

Fitzhugh linked slavery and the family in two ways: by suggesting that the majority even in free society was subject to a despotic power – that is, that it consisted of slaves in all except name – and by showing that despotic power, when conditioned by ties of affection and a sense of rational responsibility, need not be feared.[5]

Of course, the South has always been more deeply implicated in the capitalist world market than it has often cared to admit, but this does not make the Southern slave society a capitalist society. Whether or not the Southern slaveowning class was dependent upon the capitalist world market, the relations of production which defined it as a class were not capitalist, but pre-capitalist. This is not to imply that the phenomenon of Southern slavery pre-dates the development of capitalism. Rather it draws upon the Marxist analysis of capitalism in which capitalism is defined in terms of the relations of *production* and not *exchange*: as Genovese puts it, 'Capitalism is here defined as the mode of production characterized by wage labor and the separation of the labour force from the means of production – that is, as the mode of production in which labor power itself has become a commodity.'[6] The problem with defining the South as a capitalist society is that labour-power was *not* a commodity within the Southern slave system, nor could it be. Even Southern populism with its defence of individual property cannot simply be described as bourgeois. It was directly opposed to the forms of individualism associated with the wage relation of capitalist production. It may not have offered a convincing solution to capitalist production, but it was not easily compatible with it either. In fact, the Agrarians argued that farmers should attempt to achieve self-sufficiency as a way of achieving independence from the cash-nexus of capitalist relations.

The New Criticism was developed within this context. It was a cultural criticism of bourgeois society which complemented Ransom, Tate and Warren's economic criticisms. While these writers may not have been able to win support for their economic programmes, their cultural criticism became highly influential. The appeal of this cultural criticism was not that it failed to challenge capitalist relations or that it submitted to capitalist rationality, but that it argued for the need to reorganize aspects of society and culture. In his analysis of the dominance of the New Criticism, Fekete plays down the ideological struggles which took place, and many of the actual issues at stake. The New Criticism was not simply accepted as a movement that was culturally and politically unchallenging. The New Critics had to struggle against a series of different and opposed approaches to culture: those which supported a cultural market and the cash-nexus; Neo-Humanism; Marxism; and academic scholasticism. According to Fekete, the New Criticism merely filled a cultural vacuum left by the absence of adequate approaches to literature and culture on the left. He ignores the specific strengths of the New Criticism. Throughout the 1930s the New Critics had fought against alternative theories. They had identified their weaknesses and developed more sophisticated positions. Their struggle to reorganize the teaching of English within the academy was not a mere capitulation to capitalism. It was a politically motivated in- tervention which sought to establish a basis for their particular criticism of culture and society. It was defined in direct opposition to the dominant forms of culture.

Fekete's failure to acknowledge the distinctiveness of the New Criticism leads him to argue that it was a form of positivism or empiricism which may have been a reaction against capitalist relations, but ultimately reproduced the alienated structure of those relations. If the New Critics saw the social world of human activity as alienated and debased by capitalist relations, he argues, they did not try to change society. They merely sought refuge in aesthetic contemplation and appreciation. For Fekete, Ransom could not imagine an alternative to established reality, and merely countered the will to power of capitalist rationality with the concept of a desireless knowledge. He idealized nature, and converted it into an object of contemplation. This position is contrasted with the literary theory of Lukacs by Fekete. For Fekete, the New Critics' concept of imitation or mimesis did not act as a commentary upon social life, while Lukacs argued that genuine art involves a catharsis which results from the collision between everyday life and the possibilities suggested by the construction of the text. This collision forces the individual into an awareness of the limitations of everyday life, and so compels the individual to change that way of living. By contrast, Ransom is accused of seeing art as merely a basis for contemplation. It never requires action.

As has already been argued, the central problem with Fekete's argument is his use of the term 'integration'. Integration could imply an alliance between groups – even if one force is dominant in that alliance – but Fekete uses it to imply a process of absorption in which the dominant completely negates the specificity of that which is absorbed, but does not have to substantially change in order to accommodate it. For this reason, Fekete is unable to identify the specificity of the Agrarian movement and the New Criticism. He regards them as forms which were simply defined by the logic of capitalist relations and the commodity form. Such a position fails to recognize that even capitalist relations and the commodity form develop within historical conditions, and as historical forms. His analysis tends to ignore the historical specificity of these forms in favour of totalizing and abstract categories. He does not acknowledge, as Marx did, that one must constantly move between abstract categories and their concrete forms.[7] For example, a class does not develop strictly according to an abstract category. As Genovese puts it:

A ruling class does not grow up simply according to the tendencies inherent in its relationship to the means of production; it grows up in relationship to the specific class and classes it rules. The extent to which its inherent tendencies develop and the forms they take will depend on the nature of this confrontation as well as on the nature of confrontations with *other* classes outside its immediate sphere of activity.[8] [My emphasis]

It is therefore important to identify not only the different classes and class factions which make up any hegemonic grouping, but also their specific historical relationship to one another. These classes or class factions will not only affect the form of that hegemony, but one another's development.

The presence of the South, for example, has been highly important to the development of American society and culture. As Genovese stresses:

American conservatism has always displayed two contradictory tendencies: on the one hand, it has espoused the nineteenth-century liberalism of *laissez-faire*, as we were reminded by the decision of the Republican Party in 1964 to enter the lists to defend the honor of Dulcinea del Toboso; on the other hand, it has spoken for a return to an organic society, although as Allen Guttmann points out in *The Conservative Tradition in America*, this tendency is largely to be found in literary circles. Since it would be presumptuous for a Marxist to try to settle the family quarrels of those who rally to the conservative standard, I shall restrict myself to the observation that whatever right Goldwater, Buckley, and Hayek have or do not have to call themselves conservative, their theoretical position in general and their espousal of neoclassical economics in particular clearly separates them from anything important in Fitzhugh. The second group requires closer attention, especially since Southern literary conservativism, as formulated most sharply in *I'll Take My Stand*, has generally been of this kind.[9]

Genovese's reference to *I'll Take My Stand*[10] is significant given that it was produced by the same group of writers who would develop the New Criticism in the decade following its publication in 1930. This reference also clearly separates this group from the tradition of bourgeois liberalism. Certainly the New Critics' distance from bourgeois liberalism does not necessarily make them positive, but as Raymond Williams has shown, one should not reject a position simply because it is conservative. One might even find reasons 'to rejoice' over a specific conservative.[11] It is true that the New Critics' conservatism did have tendencies towards what Berman refers to as the 'neo-olympian perspective appropriated, distorted and magnified by the modern mandarins and would-be aristocrats of the twentieth-century right',[12] but Berman also stresses that this tendency is also present in contemporary critics of the left, such as Herbert Marcuse and Michel Foucault.[13] In fact, the Agrarian/New Critics often managed to avoid the worst excesses of the Frankfurt School and post-structuralism, while their very conservatism enabled them to develop an acute criticism of capitalist society and culture. Nor did this criticism confine them to the right: it could also develop into a radical, leftist criticism.

Gerald Graff's awareness of these issues makes his account of the New Criticism one of the most accurate analyses of this movement. He sets out by refuting the post-structuralist attacks on the supposed scientism of the New Criticism, and identifies the forms of impersonality and objectivity associated with the New Criticism with the anti-rationalist, Christian doctrine of Original Sin.[14] According to Graff, the New Critics adopted this position as a way of countering the abstractions of the capitalist will to power, which they associated with the cash-nexus and with scientific positivism. Graff's contention is that the New Critics *share a common concern* with the anti-rationalist modern critics who criticize them. He also stresses that the practice of close reading was not intended to ignore the context of literature, but to focus the student upon the signifying processes of literature. As a result, he argues that modern criticism grows out of the unresolved problems of the New Criticism; that the sense of criticism as a form of Nietzschean 'play' is the 'heresy of paraphrase' taken to its logical conclusion.[15] Despite these strengths, he fails to identify the *specific* social origins of the New Criticism, or explain why this anti-bourgeois, anti-liberal, anti-scientific movement should become dominant in a flourishing capitalist society such as post-war America.

Many of the writers associated with the New Criticism were Northern, liberal, or bourgeois, and even left-wing in some cases, but the central figures of the movement were Southerners. It was these Southerners – John Crowe Ransom, Allen Tate and Robert Penn Warren – who were responsible for drawing the diverse group of critics together. Their campaign to reorganize the teaching of English gave this group a sense of identity, and while this movement was held together by a shared sense of dissatisfaction with industrial capitalism and its culture, it was the Southerners who offered the intellectual and organizational coherence necessary to create a common sense of purpose. This is not to imply that there were no differences or disagreements within the movement – or even between the three Southerners themselves – but it was the intellectual project of these three Southerners which remained central. The fact that Ransom, Tate and Warren were all Southerners is of fundamental importance because, as both Richard Gray and Richard Godden have illustrated, it defined their specific interests and activities in a way which was highly distinctive.

Gray argues that the New Critical stress on the organic nature of the text was related to Southern paternalism. He argues that the New Critics drew upon the deep 'sense of evil, human fallibility and limitation'[16] which distinguished Southern culture, and was associated with the concept of Original Sin. Gray also relates this Southern 'structure of feeling' to the experience of slavery within the South, and identifies the similarities between Ransom, Tate and Warren on the one hand, and defenders of slavery such as Fitzhugh on the other. His argument is not that these writers were pro-slavery themselves, but that they drew upon a specifically Southern way of thinking which developed in reaction to capitalist forms of rationalization. By contrast, the Southern preoccupation with Original Sin, it is argued, acknowledged the complex historical and material conditions of human existence, and rejected abstract and ideal solutions which failed to take these conditions into account. This way of thinking led the South to value organic ways of thinking which sought to place contradictory elements in 'harmonious', 'balanced', or 'stable' relationships. For this reason, Gray does not accept that the New Criticism was simply integrated into the dominant rationality after the 1930s as Fekete and others claim. In fact, he states that Ransom, Tate and Warren 'never reneged on the impulse that made them try to interpret historical experience according to the Southern code'.[17] For Gray, the New Critical defence of organicism was a product of the Southern code, not a form of bourgeois humanism.

Richard Godden makes a similar case. He argues that the New Criticism was a part of a Southern reaction against capitalist production and market relations. For Godden, the New Critics' description of the text as a 'verbal icon' must be seen in relation to the textual strategies of a variety of Southern writers such as William Faulkner. These Southern writers, it is argued, were concerned with 'iconic' forms of representation because these offered an alternative to the modes of representation associated with commodity culture.[18] In this way, Godden relates this 'iconic' mode of representation to Southern society, but he also seems to imply that it was merely a nostalgic illusion. This implication is the result of Godden's use of Umberto Eco. Godden's aim is to illustrate that modes of representation are defined by class, but Eco simply argues that the apparent resemblance between the 'iconic' signifier and the referent is not natural but conventional; that even in iconic signs the relationship between signifier and signified is arbitrary.[19] The use of Eco obscures the main issue. The Southern preoccupation with 'iconic' representations was not arbitrary. It was contingent.[20] The 'iconic' mode of representation was the specific way of thinking of Southern culture; it was dependent upon specific social relations. It was an awareness of this situation that lead the New Critics to promote 'iconic' modes of representation. They recognized that it presented the object in a way that was directly opposed to the abstractions of capitalist rationalization. It did not seek to rationalize the object, but presented it as a complex entity.

As a result, while it is certainly true that the New Criticism was appropriated by bourgeois intellectuals in the 1940s and 1950s, this was not because it was a bourgeois form. In fact, the case is quite the reverse. As Pierre Bourdieu has pointed out, the position of bourgeois intellectuals is a difficult one. While still members of the dominant class, bourgeois intellectuals are described as the 'dominated' section of the dominant class. They are dependent upon the section of the bourgeoisie involved in the sphere of economic production. In this situation, the section of the bourgeoisie which works in the sphere of culture is forced to struggle with that section which works in the sphere of economic production in order to increase the value of their cultural activities in relation to economic activities. It is for this reason, it is argued, that the cultural section of the bourgeoisie not only tends to claim an autonomy for cultural activities to defend these activities from economic criteria, but also tends to adopt a political position which opposes the dominant economic and material interests of their own class. Hence the irony that bourgeois intellectuals often claim to be anti-bourgeois in their politics.[21]

While Bourdieu claims that this usually takes the form of left-wing politics, the situation of America in the 1940s and 1950s made it difficult for bourgeois intellectuals to adopt the stance of left-wing radicals. Not only had many become dissatisfied with the Communist Party, but left-wing politics was dangerously associated with support for the Soviet Union. As a result, many were attracted to the New Criticism. It offered them an anti-bourgeois ideology which had no taint of Soviet sympathies, and provided them with an image of an unalienated pre-capitalist culture of the past. In fact, even many overtly left-wing critics of the period chose to oppose capitalist America with the image of pre-capitalist or traditional societies, rather than socialist alternatives.[22] As a result, while the New Criticism was appropriated by sections of the bourgeoisie, not only was its anti-bourgeois politics the very basis of its appeal, but it was also appropriated by many on the left. In fact, it was used in a variety of different ways, and as a result, its appropriation for bourgeois ends was neither as inevitable, nor as total, as critics such as Fekete imply.

Cleanth Brooks is a particularly interesting figure in this context. His work in the late 1930s and 1940s can be seen as that of a transitional figure. Though he knew Ransom, Tate and Warren, and had worked with them throughout the 1930s, he had not been old enough to become involved in the Agrarian movement. He did write one essay, 'The Christianity of Modernism', which was published in the *American Review* alongside Agrarian pieces by the other three, but it was basically concerned with the religious ideas of literary modernism.[23] In fact, until the late 1930s and early 1940s, he did not play a major role in the activities of the New Critics. He did edit the *Southern Review* with Warren with whom he also collaborated on text-books such as *Understanding Poetry*, but he did not contribute a great deal to the development of their ideas. Rather he remained dependent on their influence. It is for this reason that he is not discussed in much detail within the rest of this book. His importance is mainly a result of his contribution to the New Criticism after the period and the struggles with which this book is primarily concerned. During the 1940s and 1950s, Brooks produced a series of books which developed and promoted the New Criticism and it is this work which made him such an important figure.[24] This period represented the maturation of his ideas and his move from a position of dependence on the others. In fact, as Thomas Daniel Young has suggested, from the 1940s onwards, the writing of Ransom and Brooks can be seen as a kind of dialogue or debate over the nature of literary activity.[25] Another feature which makes Brooks a transitional figure is the political nature of his New Critical writings. The influence of Ransom, Tate and Warren upon Brooks was mainly in the field of literary rather than social criticism. His New Critical writing does not share their sense of the political dimensions of literary activity or literary criticism. It does rely on much of Ransom, Tate and Warren's social criticism, but mainly as assumptions, rather than political positions to be championed.

Like the others, Brooks was not uninterested in the relationship between literature and society. For example, he argued that modern society was sick and that literature offered a diagnosis of its problems. Most particularly, society was said to have lost a sense of community. Individuals lacked any shared set of values through which they could relate to one another. Their primary relationship was a functional one defined by the division of labour. In this situation, it was argued, writers became alienated from society. The lack of any sense of community (or culture) forces them into a position of opposition with regard to the social order, and in many cases this alienation becomes their 'overt theme'.[26] For Brooks, literature offers an image of order and community, and so highlights the inadequacy of existing social forms. It was for this reason that he valued Southern literature and culture. The South, it was argued, had not been fully transformed by capitalist relations, and still had a real sense of community. As he put it: 'the Southern community is beginning to dissolve, [but] there is still enough left of it to constitute a real resource for ... writers'.[27] As a result, he was opposed to asocial formalism, and he even went as far as to claim that 'Nobody in his right mind, of course, is really interested in empty formality.'[28] If Brooks claimed that the writer should attain a position of distance from modern society, this was due to society's inadequacy. He did not suggest that writers should be unconcerned with social life. On the contrary, it was the duty of writers to oppose and criticize their societies, and to identify their faults. As a result, literature offered a form of knowledge, but one which was different from that provided by scientific positivism. It viewed the situation in its wholeness and achieved this through its linguistic features, particularly its use of metaphor. It did not try to impose abstract ideas upon the situation, but developed its understanding of the situation through its metaphors. This use of metaphor was not merely expressive of some statement or meaning, but the way in which literature understood its subject matter. Through an investigation of its metaphors, literature examined the complexity of the situation. For this reason, the meaning of the literary text was inseparable from its form. The use of metaphor *was* the literature, and could not be ignored. Hence his discussion of the 'heresy of paraphrase'. For Brooks, literature was a form of social criticism which highlights the alienation of modern society.

# 3    Before the New Criticism

It should be pointed out, however, that while these writers drew upon modes of thinking developed by the Southern planter class, none of them were members of this class, nor were they concerned with a defence of slavery. In fact, they began writing in the second and third decade of this century, and they began to organize their literary and critical activities as a group in 1922 through the publication of a poetry magazine, *The Fugitive*.[1] The significance of this date is worth stressing. It was the year which produced the two most immediate images of literary modernism – Joyce's *Ulysses* and the final form of Eliot's *The Waste Land*. In fact, Ransom, Tate and Warren began to publish *The Fugitive* in response to many of the developments of literary modernism. This period was also distinguished by other social and cultural changes, such as the development of corporate capitalism,[2] the rise of consumer culture,[3] changes in the position of women,[4] and the growth of scientific management.[5] In the South, these changes did have an impact, even though, after the abolition of slavery, the Southern planter class had managed to limit the development of capitalist relations of production by developing the sharecropping system.[6] The sharecropping system did not come to an end until the late 1930s and 1940s, but in the period following World War I, the system was breaking down and capitalist industry began to develop more rapidly within the South.[7] In fact, Nashville, the town where the fugitives came together, was the city which William Jennings Bryan referred to as 'the center of Modernism in the South'.[8]

It was Tate who kept the group acquainted with the various debates around literary modernism. He was particularly excited by Eliot's poetry, and in 1923, he clashed with Ransom over 'The Waste Land' in the *New York Post's Literary Review*.[9] During this period, however, Ransom was the clear leader of the group, and the articles which he wrote for *The Fugitive* anticipated many of the positions which he would develop as a New Critic. In fact, in 1924, he already maintained that poetic form involved a tension between a logical structure of meaning and a material form of sound patterns which opposed the dominance of rational logic.[10]

The concept of irony was also central to the New Criticism, and in 1925, he not only claimed that irony was the 'ultimate mode of great minds',[11] but also that it involved a tension between 'both creation and criticism, both poetry and science'.[12] It was in the summer and fall of 1926 that Ransom seems to have gone furthest in this direction though. During this period he was writing a book, *The Third Moment*.[13] The book was never published and the manuscript was destroyed, but Ransom did describe it in a letter to Tate. In this description, he commented on the three moments referred to in the title. While he emphasized that these moments were highly idealized, he defined the first two as: the moment of raw sense data in which the original experience is free of all intellectual content; and the moment of cognition. The second moment is, for Ransom, associated with science, and he maintains that its 'means are *abstractions*; and these, it must be insisted, are subtractions from the whole'.[14] It was the third moment, Ransom argued, in which these first two moments were reconciled. It imaginatively reconstructs the complexity of the original experience, but in ways that challenge the methods of science. This imaginative process is associated with poetry, dreams, daydreams, religion, and morals by Ransom, for whom 'Poetry is always the exhibit of Opposition and at the same time Reconciliation between Conceptual or Formal and Individual or Concrete.'[15]

It was the arguments which surrounded the Scopes Trial of 1925 which seem to have forced Ransom, Tate and Warren to clarify and develop their positions though. The Scopes Trial focused many debates about the South's relationship to modernity, and in response, Ransom, Tate and Warren began to define themselves in opposition to modern society. They claimed that the South offered the image of an alternative social order to that dominant in modern America. This new commitment is visible in their letters and it was within these communications that they began to identify themselves consciously as Southerners for the first time.[16] Ransom's defence of the South was directed against the forms of Southern modernization associated with the New South, and in April 1928, he published an article entitled 'The South – Old and New'. The South, it was claimed, had a distinctly different set of values from the rest of the nation, and as a result, the modernization of the South was neither desirable, nor certain. For Ransom, modern American society saw 'the volume of material production' as the principal means of evaluating a social order. It abstracted economic values from broader social and cultural values. It not only destroyed the complex relations between people, but also between humanity and nature. By contrast, Ransom argued that the Southern way of life 'did not value material production over all else' and so 'permitted the maximum activity of the intelligence'.[17]

Ransom, Tate and Warren also became interested in Southern history during the late 1920s. Both Tate and Warren wrote biographies of figures associated with Southern history, as well as reviewing historical accounts of the South and the Civil War period.[18] Ransom and Tate also published works on religion in which they criticized modern value systems. In Tate's article, 'The Fallacy of Humanism', he maintained that the problem with humanism was that it relied on the concept of reason which was drawn from naturalism and science, and that this resulted in a reification of values.[19] He also argued that a religion can only define values if it is able to acknowledge the limits of rationality and so represent the problem of 'evil'. This argument is similar to that of Ransom in his book, *God without Thunder*, where he used religion to counter science. In his account of Ransom, Louis Rubin maintains that this work was a rejection of the materialist analysis of culture,[20] but it argues that religion should not be an ideal construction, separate from other human activities. It should be involved in all activities in a way of life including social and economic activities.[21] The thesis of Ransom's book is that, unlike religion, science is not concerned with the concrete world, but with abstractions. It defines material objectives as ends in themselves, and is unable to acknowledge the various social and material limits to such objectives. Ransom also maintains that science does not see pleasure as a necessary element in the pursuit of material objectives. It is only seen as relevant to the intervals between these pursuits. Such a definition of pleasure, he argues, separates work from play, and defines play as an activity which is only concerned with the consumption of material objects. According to Ransom, this situation results in a loss of memory, and of the sense of 'evil'. People lose touch with the richness and complexity of their social and material contexts, and the extent to which those contexts remain intractable to their desires. By contrast, religion is a way of representing the experience of 'evil', and of establishing social and economic relations which counter the will to power of scientific rationality.

By 1929, the group began to feel that the existence of an active community of Southern intellectuals was vital if they were to develop a coherent and organized response to the New South. In planning to achieve this community, Ransom, Tate and Warren considered many different activities, and they eventually published a symposium on the South entitled *I'll Take My Stand*. This book was not regarded as an end in itself though, but as one element in a much larger struggle. These writers recognized that the South needed to develop forms of cultural production which would combat the dominance of Northern, capitalist culture, and they laid out a programme which called for the establishment of an academy of Southern intellectuals, and Southern organs of publication.

They were aware that culture was a material process, and though many of these proposals were never realized, some of them did affect the organization of the New Criticism.[22] The only major product of this period was *I'll Take My Stand*, but even this produced dissension amongst its contributors. Tate and Warren complained that the title was too focused on a defence of the South as a locality, rather than their critique of modern society.[23]

It was Ransom who wrote the statement of principles for the book in which he explained the Agrarian critique of industrial capitalism. It maintained that culture must be regarded as a material activity related to an economic base, and that a truly humanistic culture cannot develop from a purely natural impulse, but only in relation to a whole way of life. For Ransom, industrial capitalism had produced a degraded form of culture which could only be changed through a social and economic reorganization of society, and the establishment of social relations which were fundamentally different from those of industrial capitalism, social relations which he identified with the Agrarian society.[24]

Tate's contribution to the symposium, 'Notes of Southern Religion', was also significant, and developed his interests in religion and society. It argued that the ante-bellum South had failed to produce a religion which sufficiently distinguished its own values from those of the North, and that as a result, the South had been unable to challenge industrial capitalism effectively. Interestingly, Genovese agrees with Tate on this point, and he argues: 'That the South was Protestant rather than Roman Catholic proved to be unfortunate, as Fitzhugh appreciated in his day and perhaps only Allen Tate has appreciated in ours.'[25] For Tate, industrial capitalism is unable to develop a proper religion. It is associated with scientific positivism which, for Tate, is at best a 'half-religion'. In this argument, Tate uses the image of a horse, arguing that while religion is concerned with the 'whole horse' or the horse as 'icon', scientific positivism is only concerned with abstractions. It does not see the whole horse, but only its abstract value, only its 'horse-power'.[26] The South's failure, according to Tate, was that while its social relations challenged the materialist abstractions of industrial capitalism, its adherence to Protestantism rather than Catholicism cost it dear. It became 'a feudal society without a feudal religon'.[27] This situation prevented the South from achieving self-consciousness until it was too late. If the South had a religious way of life, it had no formalized expression of that way of life.[28] It lacked the religious structure necessary to identify its own strength, and challenge industrial capitalism.

In many ways, it is Warren's contribution to the symposium which is the most interesting of the three. He experienced great problems writing it, and the intellectual struggles which he went through in order to 'take his stand' are both visible and complex.[29] Warren's problem was that while the article was intended as a defence of segregation, it was also a serious attempt to discover a basis for racial equality. For Warren, racial equality could only be achieved if blacks had a vocation or a place which gave them economic independence within American society. His objection to industrial capitalism was that it denied the worker any independence from capital, and encouraged industrialists to play black and white workers off against one another in a competition for wages. For Warren, this situation not only weakened the bargaining position of both groups, it required the white to recognize that 'the fates of the "poor white" and the negro are linked in the same tether. The well being and adjustment of one depends on that of the other.'[30] Unless the white worker recognized his common interests with the black, the latter would continue to be used to undermine the white worker's position. The solution to this situation, Warren argued, could not be achieved by education alone, but only through a fundamental social and economic transformation. Only the Agrarian society would free black and white workers from a dependence upon capital, and give them a secure place in an American society which would be free of racial conflicts and exploitation.[31] This argument prefigured Warren's arguments *against* segregation later in his career. Unless the white worker is able to concede 'equal protection' to the black, Warren argues, he 'does not properly respect himself as a man'.[32] The article produced a row in the group though. By acknowledging that the black had been systematically exploited within American society in general, and the South in particular, Warren horrified others in the symposium, especially Donald Davidson.

This preoccupation with Agrarianism continued throughout the first half of the thirties when Ransom, Tate and Warren were developing the literary positions which would become known as the New Criticism. Indeed, in 1931, Ransom was preparing a book on Agrarian economics which was tentatively titled 'Capitalism and the Land'. Though this volume was never published, sections of it appeared in the *New Republic* and *Harper's*.[33] In 'The State and the Land' which appeared in the former, Ransom argued that the capitalist economy had a tendency towards over-capitalization which led to overproduction; and that this overproduction displaced large sections of the population from economic production. For Ransom, the solution to this situation was that this displaced population should be relocated on the land. He insisted, however, on a distinction between 'two land economies: a modern *capitalistic* or money economy, and a much older *agrarian* economy'.[34] The land did not offer a solution in itself. It could only provide the answer if pre-capitalist forms of agriculture were employed, forms which countered capitalist relations. According to

Ransom, farmers should not be concerned primarily with production for the market. This placed them in a position of economic dependence. They should be largely self-sufficient. This would also enable them to develop more pleasurable and creative forms of labour. Ransom's case was not only that 'the American commercial farmer is doomed',[35] but that commercial farming employed the same types of rationalization as industrial capitalism. The profit motive dominated broader social and cultural interests. It stressed the cause of efficiency over the potential enjoyments available in the agricultural way of life.[36] This critique of modernization and rationalization was extended in his essay, 'The Aesthetic of Regionalism', where Ransom opposed the dominance of modern economic activity within culture. For Ransom, economic activity should be seen as a means to an end, not the end in itself. To put it another way, economic activities should be related to the whole way of life. In a society which tempered the economic will to power with other values, economic activities could also become pleasurable, and even aesthetic.[37]

During this same period, Tate was concerned with the relation between forms of class rule on the one hand, and social and cultural forms on the other. In 1933, for example, he wrote to John Peale Bishop, claiming: 'The end in view is the destruction of the middle class capitalist hegemony.'[38] For Tate, monarchies and aristocracies had justified their power by defining responsibilities for themselves, but the middle class failed to 'pay a price for power'.[39] It had justified economic inequality, and identified itself with the cause of social equality during the period of the Civil War. In the process, it defined social equality as the access to 'material commodities'.[40] Against this definition of equality, Tate argued that equality must have a firmer economic basis. Individuals must both own and control their own means of production. According to Tate, the absence of such a firm economic basis meant that the majority of the population came to regard 'making a living' and a 'way of life' as 'quite different pursuits'.[41] They saw economic activity as something entirely separate from culture. This separation, it was argued, reduced tradition and culture to a collection of conventions and activities which were not fundamental to all activities, but mere objects of decoration. By contrast, Tate claimed that the truly Traditional society was based on the premise that the way of life (culture) and the ways of making a living (economics) must be one and the same.

The writings of Donald Davidson are particularly interesting in this context. He had worked with the others at Vanderbilt as a member of the Fugitive group, and he was instrumental in establishing the Agrarian movement. For example, he was one of the main forces in the organization of the symposium which became *I'll Take My Stand*. But unlike Ransom,

Tate and Warren, he did not make the transition to the New Criticism. At the beginning of his involvement in the Agrarian movement, he had shared the interests which motivated their defence of the South, but by the mid-1930s, his interests had diverged significantly from those of his three friends. While they began to play down their defence of the South in order to concentrate attention on the specific *way of life* which they championed, Davidson went in the opposite direction. He began to champion Southern causes irrespective of the way of life which they offered. As a result, it was not Ransom, Tate and Warren who abandoned their Agrarian ideals. They merely felt that their position had become over-identified with the South as a region, and their shift to the New Criticism was a way of refocusing attention on their criticisms of modern society. It aimed to distinguish their image of the aesthetic way of life from too great an association with the South. By contrast, Davidson became more and more involved in a sectional defence of the South, and the way of life which it offered became more and more irrelevant to him.

For example, in *I'll Take My Stand*, Davidson had criticized industrial capitalism and its effects on culture. He argued that industrialism not only converted art into a mere commodity, but also believed that material progress would create the best conditions for art by rationalizing its production and consumption. Davidson's objection to modern society was that it destroyed the aesthetic way of life. It alienated the aesthetic from society as a whole and made it into a mere spectacle. These problems are also related to the process by which capitalist relations distinguish between work and leisure. In modern society, it was argued, work was solely concerned with efficiency and lacks any aesthetic pleasures, while leisure was merely seen as the passive consumption of material goods. By contrast, the truly aesthetic way of life was argued to be one in which the aesthetic was not alienated from other activities, but involved in all aspects of life.[42] According to Davidson, the situation of modern society also presented great problems for the writer who became alienated and opposed to his social world. As he put it: 'The artist is no longer *with* society, as perhaps even Milton, last of the classicists, was. He is *against* or *away from* society, and the disturbed relation becomes his essential theme, always underlying his work, no matter whether he evades or accepts the treatment of the theme itself.'[43] As a result, Davidson's defence of the South was, at this stage of his career, a defence of the aesthetic way of life. He did acknowledge that the South had produced little great literature, but he argued that it had an aesthetic way of life which was rich in folk arts.

In contrast to these earlier positions, Davidson's writings in the mid-1930s did not defend the South as an image of the aesthetic way of life so much as oppose criticisms of the South as a region. For example, his essay in *Who Owns America* is primarily concerned with a defence of regionalism, but lacking any discussion of the aesthetic way of life, this defence is highly problematic. Davidson was careful to distinguish regionalism from sectionalism which he saw as anti-national, and he claimed that the former is 'not anti-national but the condition itself of nationalism in a country as large and as notably diverse in its geographical divisions as our country is'.[44] Regional diversity, it was argued, 'enriches national life'. It allows 'the interplay of points of view that ought to give flexibility and wisdom'.[45] Unfortunately, it is this very 'interplay' which became a problem for Davidson. He was concerned to challenge 'regional imperialism' or the domination of one region by another, but was unable to suggest any positive safeguard against this problem. Instead the proper conditions for regionalism were simply defined in negative terms as 'independence' or freedom from constraint, but this position limited the very interplay which was supposed to make regionalism valuable. Davidson ended up arguing against *any* criticism of the South as though it were a violation of regional integrity and autonomy.

This position resulted in a defensive retreat into regional isolationism. It was also related to a shift from 'Agrarianism' to 'Regionalism'. In fact, Davidson himself admitted that his regionalist position did not have its primary foundation in the positions of the Agrarians, but in the social sciences. As he claimed: 'The Southern theory of regionalism... took shape in two notable books, Rupert Vance's *Human Geography of the South* and Howard Odum's *Southern Regions.*'[46] This shift in position also involved a shift from the critique of capitalist economic relations to a defence of Southern race relations.[47]

It is for these reasons that Davidson was unable to make the move to the New Criticism and became isolated from his three friends. As a result, on 23 February 1940, he wrote to Tate and referred to the 'third revolution' in the interests of Ransom, Tate and Warren – namely, their involvement in the struggles over teaching of English in the academy. He had been a part of the two previous 'revolutions' – the Fugitive movement and the Agrarian movement – but in this third stage, he claimed: 'I am decidedly grieved by being isolated from my friends. I don't mean physical isolation, deplorable though it is. I mean that I find myself suddenly at a disagreeable intellectual distance, for reasons that I do not in the least understand.'[48] Tate had accused Davidson of being 'contemptuous of art'. He claimed that his friend Davidson no longer saw aesthetic activity as a challenge to modern society, but merely an expression of regional cultures. None the less, as Davidson recognized, this isolation dated back to the mid-1930s: 'it began before any of you left these parts'.[49]

# Conclusion

If Ransom, Tate and Warren did support a notion of individualism, it was not one defined by the economic relations of bourgeois society. Nor did it define the individual as natural or asocial. On the contrary, they argued that the market destroyed the possibility of genuine individualism. It limited the realm of individual choice and action by defining people as simply producers or consumers. Increasingly, the relations between people were simply economic exchanges. In contrast, they called for an alternative social form in which economic activity was seen as merely a means to an end, and was tempered by other social and cultural values. They referred to this alternative social form as the traditional society, and they did so for two main reasons. The term was not only meant to define this type of society in opposition to modern society, but also to stress that it had a stronger sense of the past. It did not promote some abstract theory of progress, but had come to terms with the 'burden of the past'. It had developed ways of living which took an account of the material and historical limitations upon human action.

Their literary criticism was also developed in terms of these social criticisms. Literary modernism, they claimed, was a response to this social situation. It was developed in a society where the rationalizing tendencies of industrial capitalism and bourgeois thought created a distinction between thought and feeling, abstract systems and empiricism. If they argued over the strengths and weaknesses of specific modernist writers, they agreed that the truly aesthetic text sought to reject such divisions. It neither denied intellect nor sensation, but always subjected ideas to the test of experience and vice versa. It created a collision between the two which questioned available social forms in a similar way to Fekete's reading of Lukacs. In this way, the aesthetic text was regarded as both critical and creative, but also as a form which established the necessity for social change. Cultural activity was a critical activity which highlighted the inadequacies of existing social activities.

In this way, aesthetic activity offered a form of knowledge, but a form which was different to the abstract forms of scientific positivism. The latter sought to dominate and rationalize the object, while the aesthetic activity was a creative process embodied in the linguistic forms of the text. It was for this reason that aesthetic texts were often identified as ironic in form. This term referred to both the critical attitude of the text, and its linguistic processes. Ideas were used, it was argued, but they were treated critically or with scepticism. This concentration upon the linguistic forms of the text was one of the New Criticism's major contributions. It clearly defined an object for literary study. It was they who established the language of the text as the proper focus of academic attention, rather than its content, the intention of the author, or the responses of individual readers. The language of the text became its literary features, the embodiment of its attitudes and values.

If these writers did abandon Agrarianism and concentrate their efforts on transforming the teaching of English in America, it was not, as Fekete suggests, due to an integration within the dominant order. Instead it was due to a change of tactics. By the mid-1930s, the political and cultural context of America was changing, and they were forced to face the fact that they could not get support for the 'restoration of the Agrarian society'. They were also attracted to the New Deal. They recognized that it failed to alter the fundamental problems of economic organization, but they believed that its policies could be influenced by criteria which were not purely economic; that the New Deal could be influenced by other social and cultural motives. Also, after 1935, the establishment of the popular front led to a growth in support for the Communist Party, and the New Deal administration began to move away from the forms of centralized organization in which Government and business collaborated in running the economy. The New Dealers became concerned to establish a sense of stability, community, and national consensus in the hope of challenging criticisms both from within America, and from outside – namely the potential threats from abroad.[1] In this changing situation, the Agrarians found their interests very much closer to the New Deal.

More significantly, the period around 1935 saw the development of a debate surrounding the function of literary education in American universities. Both the depression and the steady expansion of mass education over the first half of the twentieth century had led many inside and outside the universities to question the social relevance of many academic disciplines. In the case of literary study, the New Critics were able to offer a form of literary study which answered the apparently contradictory requirements of social relevance and intellectual discipline. For these writers, this intervention was not an abandonment of their attack on modern American society. Instead they saw it as a way of establishing a basis for their social and cultural criticisms within the activities of literary education. They published text-books which distributed their positions on literature and culture, and developed literary criticism or theory as a respected and independent activity within university departments of English. They helped establish the dominance of modernism as a literary form, and established a space for critical intellectual activities within the departments of English. In this way, they defined the very terms of reference for literary study which became a critical analysis of the linguistic forms of the text.

Once established within the academy, the New Criticism did not cease to be contentious, but continued to be the focus of struggle. It was not only attacked by some but also appropriated by others. If it was depoliticized by certain groups, it was also used by many on the radical left. Within this context, Ransom, Tate and Warren also continued to develop their theories, even though their positions began to diverge from one another. After 1945, Ransom did distance himself from the social and political positions of his earlier work, but not only was the work of this period of little influence or significance, it also followed a very different line of development from that of Tate and Warren. The literary criticism of the latter two writers was still connected to a critique of modern American society. Even so, these two developed in different ways from one another. While Tate continued to associate himself with the radical right and became involved in the anti-communist Congress of Cultural Freedom, Warren was frequently allied with the radical left in struggles such as those over desegregation, Civil Rights, and American withdrawal from Vietnam. In fact, while Warren came to be seen as a major 'Southern liberal', he was not complacent about American society. Instead he continued to present a radical criticism of economic, political and cultural life in America.

The next part examines the New Critical positions of Ransom, Tate and Warren as they developed in the 1930s in relation to the Agrarian challenge to industrial capitalism, while part three discusses the motives and tactics behind their transformation of the teaching of English in the American academy. Part four then moves on to consider the different ways in which Ransom, Tate and Warren developed as New Critics after the establishment of the New Criticism within the academy in the late 1930s and early 1940s. Finally, the conclusion discusses the ways in which the New Critics defined the terms of reference for contemporary criticism. This conclusion argues that contemporary criticism has not corrected the supposedly ahistorical theories of the New Criticism, but tends to be far more ahistorical. Contemporary criticism, it is claimed, is even more vehement in its attempt to limit literary study to an analysis of the linguistic forms of the text than were the New Critics.

*Part II*

# The formation of the New Criticism

## Introduction

The literary and cultural criticism produced by Ransom, Tate and Warren has a great deal in common. All three writers drew on Southern paternalism, but they each gave a different inflection to this mode of thinking. Each focused on different problems and developed different formulations. Of the three, Ransom was the most limited. He did claim that aesthetic activity was opposed to the scientific rationalism of industrial capitalism, and believed that the Agrarian society would redeem culture, but he did not conceptualize *intermediate* responses to industrial capitalism. He called for the end of industrial capitalism and the restoration of pre-capitalist relations without offering political strategies for achieving these objectives. He did become involved in the struggle to institutionalize the New Criticism within the academy, but eventually came to see no alternative to industrial capitalism. Aesthetic activity no longer called for an alternative way of life; it simply became the 'commemoration' of a desirable but unobtainable mode of existence.

By contrast, Tate concentrated on the situation of the writer within specific forms of social organization. He wanted to define a social function for the writer which would not limit the critical aspects of literature. To this end, he called for the creation of a profession of letters within America. Not surprisingly, Tate's position was more flexible than that of Ransom. It enabled him to develop interests and activities which were opposed to industrial capitalism, but could exist without the envisaged restoration of the traditional society.

It is Warren's career though which has endured longest and developed most significantly since his involvement with Agrarianism. Part of the reason for this may be that his involvement with the Agrarian movement was both more marginal and more critical than that of Ransom and Tate.

During the early 1930s, Warren concentrated on the relationship between the writer and politics, and challenged both those who saw literature as merely a type of propaganda, and those who saw it as an autonomous and asocial activity. His aim was to define a form of aesthetic activity which was social and critical, without reducing it to propaganda. This concern with social criticism was associated with another feature which distinguished Warren's writing from that of the other two: his interest in fiction and narrative.

## 4 John Crowe Ransom: the social relations of aesthetic activity

Despite the limitations of Ransom's literary theory, his contribution to the development of the New Criticism was considerable, and it can be divided into three stages. During the first stage, which covers the period up to approximately 1936, Ransom was writing the articles in which he clarified his New Critical positions, articles which he published in *The World's Body*.[1] The second stage covers the period from 1936–1941 when Ransom was involved in the arguments over the study of literature in the universities. Finally, in the period after 1941, he began to severely limit the range of his criticism. Consequently, Ransom's New Critical positions were not developed after his involvement in Agrarianism, but were clarified during his engagement in the movement. During this period, he was concerned with the relationship of literature to both traditional and modern societies, and he sought to distinguish the modes of cognition offered by literature from those associated with scientific positivism.

### Aesthetics and ways of living

Ransom's concentration on the formal aspects of aesthetic activity was not intended to isolate it from other social practices, but to examine the relationship between literary forms and specific types of social organization. The 'formal approach' to the process of literary production was not viewed as a mere matter of technique, rather it incorporated the 'point of view from which the poet approaches his object, and its prescription of style and tone'.[2] Nor was the poet's mode of approach defined as a question of individual choice or temperament. For Ransom, it develops from the given way of life available to the poet. Literary modernism, for example, was not characterized as a mere technical development, but as a specific attitude which was produced in relation to the loss of traditional ways of living: 'modernism is skepticism and disillusionment, and ends in despair. We come to such a degree of self-consciousness that we question our natural motives of action and our inherited patterns of behaviour.'[3] In the modern world, the writer is unable to identify a rational basis for action

35

and retreats into pessimistic introspection. By contrast, Ransom claimed that the Southern way of life offered the writer an alternative to modern society. The Southerner was under less pressure to dispense with the traditional way of life, even though many Southerners had not taken advantage of this situation.[4] The Charleston writers,[5] for example, had ignored the character of the South according to Ransom. They had concentrated on superficial details, rather than drawing upon the 'fixed basis of judgement, and ... conventional way of talking about things' which was available in the South, though all but lost in other regions.[6]

If Ransom criticized the Charleston writers for failing to draw upon this 'Southern character', he did not suggest that Southern writers should accept it uncritically. He did identify a relationship between specific forms of society and culture on the one hand, and specific modes of aesthetic activity on the other, but he did not see this relationship as one of direct reflection or expression. Instead, aesthetic forms, it was argued, are always produced out of an active and creative engagement with the values of their social and cultural context.[7] The distinctly Southern forms of literature were ones which concentrated on the local and particular, not the global and the abstract. This concentration on the local and particular was different from the Charleston writers' preoccupation with local colour though. It examined the Southern way of life through its concrete instances, rather than simply detailing its peculiarities of dialect, fashion, and so forth. As Ransom puts it: 'it is not the specifically Southern localism that matters but the fact of localism at all; that is, the reference of everything in the story to the genius loci, or spirit of the local background'.[8] It is this approach which Ransom refers to as the formal mode of literary activity. It is an investigation of traditional ways of life or what Ransom referred to as the 'formal society'. Consequently, while a concern with the local and particular is identified with the specifically Southern character, it is not unavailable to writers from other regions. Writers are always able to investigate their society and culture, and identify their strengths and weaknesses. In fact, for Ransom, it is their responsibility to do so. For example, among the many non-Southerners who have exemplified this approach, Ransom makes particular mention of Henry James.[9]

It is the preoccupation with the local and particular which, it is argued, places the formal writer at odds with modern society and culture. In the late 1920s, Ransom claimed that art and tradition are opposed to science and modernity and vice versa. The latter are concerned with the global and abstract while the former were distinguished by their concern with the local and particular. As he puts it: 'Art has always been devoted to the representation of the particularity which real things possess, and therefore it has always been a witness against the claims and interests of science.'[10]

For Ransom, the abstractions of science and modernity were products of industrial capitalism and the market economy. The modern world was concerned with the search for constants within nature, or forms of quantity rather than quality. It sought to impose abstract values upon objects in order to rationalize existence. By contrast, Ransom claimed, 'art, as a representation of nature, represents it in its dual capacity as composed in part of constants and contingents. If it were lacking in either feature, it would fail in realism.'[11] Aesthetic texts reject the abstractions of the modern world and act as 'just so many rebellions against science'.[12]

Art and science were distinguished by their different approaches to the world and this position was clarified by Ransom in 1933, when he discussed the difference between work and play. Work, it was argued, defines the object in economic terms; the object is valued for its utility. Play, on the other hand, is associated with the aesthetic. It values the object in its totality, rather than specific abstract features. It develops broader social and material relations to the object, and explores its complex and diverse features. Play does not reduce the object to a single, direct use, but acts as a restraint upon the rationalization and exploitation of the object. It counters purely economic interests with other interests. This position draws upon Southern paternalism, and its critique of capitalist relations. The Southern paternalists argued that the capitalist was only interested in the labour-power of the labourer, and that, as a result, capitalist production failed to establish social or cultural restraints on the exploitation of the labouring classes. By contrast, the plantation was claimed to have established relations which were not purely economic, but more broadly social and cultural. Its organization was not designed with the sole aim of maximizing the productivity of the slave. Whatever the injustices of the plantation system, it was different from the capitalist system of production in which the only relationship between the capitalist and the labourer was that organized through the cash-nexus.

Just as the Southern paternalists had seen the plantation as a check on the exploitation of labour, so Ransom argues that 'aesthetic forms are a technique of restraint, not of efficency'.[13] They 'contrast themselves with other and more common forms in the remarkable fact that they do not serve the principle of utility'.[14] This argument does not imply that the aesthetic should simply exist as a complement to other social activities. Mankind's humanity, it was argued, resided in its ability to move beyond the satisfaction of purely economic needs and develop other interests. The economic was merely a means to life. A fully human existence could only be attained when it was integrated with other activities and interests within an aestheticized way of living.[15] One point that is worth noting here is that the article within which this position was developed was published within six months of Ransom's essay, 'The Aesthetic of Regionalism'.[16] This latter article was one of his contributions to the Agrarian movement, and it called for a way of life in which the economic and the aesthetic were not seen as separate forms of activity, but were fully integrated. Within a truly Agrarian society, even economic activities would afford aesthetic pleasures.

If Ransom criticized the modern world for separating the economic from the aesthetic, he also associated this separation with issues of gender and sexuality. It is culture, he argued, which distinguishes the 'gentleman' from the 'caveman'. The former employs a code of manners through which he is able to relate to the object of his desire without simply consuming it. The use of such cultural codes counteracts the 'increasing condensation'[17] of desires through which individuals define their sexuality and its object. It prevents the frustration which can develop if the object becomes 'disproportionate... to the vast set of interests which it climaxes'.[18] This opposition is highly idealized, but it implies that the humanity of sexuality depends upon the ability of individuals to see their desires – and the object of those desires – in terms that are culturally meaningful. It requires them to develop a wide range of interests and relations with regard to the objects of their desires.[19] This position draws upon characteristically Southern definitions of masculinity. The paternalist patriarch sought to define his gender and sexuality in opposition to the figure of the Northern, materialist Yankee through the cult of chivalry, a cult which required the male to 'kneel down before the altar of femininity and familial benevolence'.[20]

This position did not depose the authority of the male, but rather it required that he rely upon a code of manners which regulated his relationship to women. He did not surrender authority but did claim to revere and respect feminine values. For this reason, while Ransom stressed that the rationality, aggression, and acquisitiveness associated with masculinity should be checked by an aesthetic sensibility, he continued to define masculinity in distinction to the unintellectualized sensibility which he associates with femininity. In Ransom's essay, 'The Poet as Woman', which appeared in 1937, he comments on the poet Edna St Vincent Millay, particularly the way in which she presents the relationship between her gender and her poetry. This emphasis on her own femininity is criticized by Ransom who claims that it results in a lack of intellectual quality. He writes that she 'is rarely and barely very intellectual, and I think everybody knows it'.[21] His objection is not to women poets in principle, nor does he privilege the masculine values of intellect and rationality. The distinctions which associate the masculine with the intellectual and the feminine with the non-intellectual are acknowledged to be social rather than natural. In fact, Ransom challenges the attempt to isolate the masculine from the feminine, and criticizes Millay for her association with the feminine at the expense of the masculine, not for her association with the feminine itself. The masculine values of intellect and rationality are important to Ransom, but only if they are fused with the feminine. In fact, it is argued that men can never deny the female qualities: 'man, at best, is an intellectual woman. Or, man distinguishes himself from woman by intellect, but it should well be feminized.'[22] It would be wrong to suggest that Ransom is egalitarian in his sexual politics, but it would also be inaccurate to claim that he simply privileges masculine values. His position develops from a profound discomfort with the distinctions between masculinity and femininity, intellectuality and sensibility, abstraction and experience. These distinctions conform to the very definitions of rationality which he challenged in most of his critical writing. If he criticized the modern world for privileging the abstract over the concrete, and the intellect over the sensibility, he could not support gender hierarchies which reproduced the selfsame distinctions.

There is a continuity here with Ransom's differentiation between 'pure' and 'impure' forms of literature. As has been shown, Ransom did not regard the aesthetic sensibility as a natural or inherent quality which existed in isolation from society. He opposed the idea that the aesthetic should just be a way of contemplating the world in isolation from other activities, and called for the aestheticization of the whole way of life. In much the same way, he argued that poetry should not be associated with either 'pure' or 'impure' forms, but should examine the relationship between the two. In the process, he differentiates poetic forms 'by virtue of subject matter, and subject matter may be differentiated with respect to its ontology'.[23] This procedure identifies three types of poetry: 'physical poetry' which is associated with the Imagists' concentration on 'things in their thingness';[24] 'platonic poetry' which presents abstract forms and ideas; and 'metaphysical poetry' which moves beyond these two forms and concerns itself with figurative language, particularly metaphor. The first two are distinguished by associating them with the image and the idea respectively. The image is identified with the act of perception which is 'pre-intellectual and independent of concepts'.[25] The idea, on the other hand, is identified as an abstract form. It is intellectual and conceptual, but is independent of specific concrete instances or experiences. However, Ransom is critical of these forms. They are presented as idealized and problematic. On the one hand, it is stressed that the image always pre-figures ideas, and is unable to make the 'thingness of things' meaningful in themselves. On the other, a poetry of ideas, it is argued, must always have a physical, imagistic element. It must have some reference to experience if it is to be valid: 'A discourse which employs only abstract ideas with no images would be a scientific document and not a poem at all, not even a Platonic poem.'[26]

In fact, Ransom goes further. He argues that a fully developed poetry would not just have to include both the image and the idea, but examine them in relationship to one another. It would involve a collision between image and idea in which the experience is invested with meaning, even while the poem challenges abstractions by subjecting them to experience.[27] In this way, poetry acts to challenge the dominance of abstractions, but it does not do so by rejecting ideas altogether. Such an attempt would result in a return to a state of pre-intellectual innocence. Instead, Ransom suggests that poetry should subject ideas to the test of experience, and so re-examine both elements. It should act to reconstruct knowledge and experience.[28] For Ransom, the aesthetic form is not one that privileges the abstract idea or the pre-intellectual perception, but one which involves an interaction and integration of these two elements.

This division between abstraction and experience is not seen as merely a formal problem, but one intrinsic to modern society as a whole. The dilemma for modern writers is that while their traditional function did not distinguish between ethics and aesthetics, or the public and the private, in the modern world, the two are isolated from one another and even come to oppose one another.[29] This position is clarified through a comparison between two forms of modern poetry in which the work of Wallace Stevens and Allen Tate are used as examples. The former is identified as 'pure' poetry, a practice which is not concerned with public or social issues. Its subject matter is described as 'trivial'. Tate's poetry, on the other hand, is identified as impure. Its subject matter is significant, public and social, but it tends towards 'obscurity'. By refusing to offer an abstract position, it finds it difficult to make moral or ethical commitments. Ransom is calling for a poetry in which the aesthetic and the ethical comprise a structural unity.[30] This structural unity cannot just be created by the individual poet though. It is emphasized that just as the division itself is a product of a specific social order, such a unity would also depend upon a specific social foundation, and one which is different to that of modern society.[31]

If the type of poetry which Ransom privileges is one which counters the opposition between purity and impurity, ideas and images, abstractions and experience, he argues that it achieved this end through its use of certain linguistic forms. While he acknowledges the importance of elements such as metre, it is the use of tropes or 'figures of speech' which are seen as central to this form of poetry. An interrogation of the trope is not only supposed to distinguish 'metaphysical poetry' from 'platonic' and 'physical' poetry, but also from the forms of scientific discourse. Tropes are claimed to threaten rational or abstract forms of discourse:

Figures of speech twist accidence away from the straight course, as if to intimate astonishing lapses of rationality beneath the smooth surfaces of discourse, inviting perceptual attention, and weakening the tyranny of science over the senses.[32]

Consequently, scientific discourse attempts to repress the trope, while metaphysical poetry is said to be distinguished by an abundance of tropes. Ransom pays particular attention to 'the conceit' which he links to metaphor. This device is said to focus upon its own linguistic processes in such a way that its meaning is not located in a reference to a semantic object. It exists in the tension between the conceptual and the perceptual.[33] It is language investigating itself. The character of this form of poetry and its linguistic processes is identified by Ransom as miraculous, rather than rational. Still he argues that it remains realistic. Its investigation of language not only identifies the limits of abstractions, but also the existence of particularity.[34] This linguistic form, it is argued, defines a specific relationship to objects and produces a specific type of knowledge, and it is these characteristics which validate it as an aesthetic form.

### Cognition and mimesis

The relationship between linguistic and cognitive forms is of critical significance to Ransom. It enables him to distinguish the knowledge provided by the aesthetic from that provided by science. Scientific positivism, he claims, ignores the process of cognition. It is merely concerned with the accumulation of information, and only values the utility and instrumentality of knowledge. Aesthetic activity, on the other hand, is seen as providing a different form of knowledge; one whose value is not defined by its utility. For example, in his critique of I. A. Richards, Ransom claims that Richards is a positivist and a behaviourist who is only interested in physical activities, and ignores 'spiritual happenings'. Richards is supposed to concentrate on neurology, rather than the activity of the human intelligence, and it is claimed that, as a consequence, he can only explain the utilitarian value of poetry, or its effects. He is unable to discuss its intrinsic value or 'the value of poetry to the mind that entertains it'.[35] For Ransom, Richards' positivism ignores the process of cognition peculiar to poetry. He simply identifies poetry as false in the positivistic sense – that is, it is not a genuine record of real events or certifiable facts – and as a result, he fails to acknowledge that poetry can offer an alternative form of knowledge. According to Ransom, Richards' concept of poetic value is limited to the claim that 'poetry has the charms to soothe the savage breast';[36] that it creates 'balance, poise and peace'. For Ransom, this position deprives poetry of its role as a critical investigation of society and culture.[37] It defines poetry as a form of 'hedonism', an asocial entertainment or a retreat from alienated activities. For Richards, poetry merely complements or enriches existing ways of living, and does not pose a critical challenge to them. In response, Ransom claims that while poetry is not concerned with the presentation of statements which refer to real events or certifiable facts, it does 'seek the truth' and 'obtain a cognition',[38] despite the fact that this cognition is different from the abstractions of scientific positivism. Poetry is defined as both critical and creative. It examines abstractions in relation to experience, and identifies both their strengths and their limitations.[39] In this way, it explores its social and cultural context. Ransom's critique of Richards' positivism did not seek to define the aesthetic as an asocial form – rather it sought to identify its specific social significance.

A similar concern is also evident in Ransom's essays on Aristotle. Here Ransom is careful to distinguish aesthetic mimesis from simple reflection, or from the imitation of objects or events. The term, it is stressed, was not originally meant to imply that the art work should be indistinguishable from the real.[40] Instead, Ransom argues that mimesis is a type of imitation which aims to represent the particularity of objects, and develop specific relationships to them.[41] In this way, the work of art provides a mode of cognition which is unavailable in the scientific positivism of modern society. None the less, Ransom insists that this imitation is not simply an escape from scientific or modern ways of living, nor even a compensation for them. It is for this reason that he is critical of Aristotle's theory of catharsis. For Ransom, this theory ignores the critical aspects of aesthetic activity. It defines the aesthetic as a distraction from, or a compensation for, the existing way of life. Aristotle's theory is based on the assumption that those interests, attitudes or emotions associated with the aesthetic are harmful to the effective running of social life. They have to be kept separate from social activities in general, and evacuated in harmless ways. According to Ransom, Aristotle sees aesthetic activity as one of these harmless means of evacuation.[42] Ransom's objection to this position is that it presents aesthetic mimesis as an essentially uncritical activity which simply exists to ensure the smooth running of society,[43] rather than a cultural activity which acts to highlight the poverty of specific ways of living. Ransom does describe poetry as a form which contemplates objects at a distance from action, but this position is not meant to imply that aesthetic contemplation is an asocial activity. On the contrary, it is suggested that poetic contemplation establishes a distance from the demands of scientific positivism in order to examine social forms, and so develop attitudes and values which call for their transformation.

For this reason, while Ransom claims that the literary text is an objective form, he does not imply that it exists as an entirely independent object which has no relation to its social and cultural context. Instead he suggests that the literary text should never be simply identified as the reflection or expression of its author or its context. Such a position would not only ignore the process of literary or aesthetic production, but also the social nature of linguistic forms. This position is also related to Ransom's claim that the aesthetic text examines objects at a distance from action. The processes of aesthetic production, it is argued, require writers to free themselves from the limits of their own egos. They do not simply express themselves, but work with a language which is public and social. As a result, writers must distance themselves from their own everyday personae. According to Ransom, this was the reason that Milton took on the persona of a Greek shepherd in *Lycidas*; he was attempting to dramatize himself through a correlative.[44] It was not that any 'sanctity or authority attached particularly to the discourse of a Greek shepherd'.[45] Instead this persona 'delivered [him] from being Milton the scrivener's son, the Master of Arts at Cambridge, the handsome and finicky young man, and that was the point'.[46] The distance between the writer's everyday persona and the one developed in the process of aesthetic production also enables a dialectic between writers and their culture. Freed from purely practical and everyday interests, writers can critically examine the forms available within their tradition. Writers investigate the attitudes, interests and values of their society and culture. They identify their strengths and weaknesses, and so extend and improve them.[47]

At this time, Ransom still believed that traditional ways of life were not entirely lost, and that they could be resurrected. The poet's role was regarded as that of a critical conservative. The poet should criticize and challenge the present through a comparison with an available past.[48] It was only when traditional forms became redundant or limiting that the poet became a revolutionary, and in the 1930s, Ransom did not believe that this was the situation. The process of aesthetic production was seen as being of immense significance, and always required a serious and concerted effort on the part of the poet. It was in this sense that he referred to poetry as a career. It is as rigorous and important an activity as any other.[49] For these reasons, attempts to read Miltonic verse as merely an expression of the poet's other interests and activities fails to acknowledge the specificity of poetic activity.[50] For Ransom, poetry was a form of social criticism, but it did not work according to the principles of scientific positivism or capitalist rationality. It was a process through which the society and culture are investigated and re-examined.

## Conclusion: the role of the critic

Consequently, Ransom did not define literary texts as autonomous or self-contained objects which were separated from, and unrelated to, other social activities. His critical positions were developed as part of an Agrarian critique of modernity, and they not only sought to illustrate that aesthetic forms were affected by their social and cultural context, but also that they were a response to that context. These positions were developed in reaction to other forms of criticism, particularly those practised by the Neo-Humanists and Stalinized Marxists. For example, the existing forms of Stalinized Marxism were attacked for their abstract and anti-traditional tendencies; not only did they exhibit the worst excesses of modernist rationalization, they also sought to reduce art to a form of propaganda. This approach was dismissed as inherently reductive and repressive. On the other hand, while Ransom acknowledged that Neo-Humanists such as Paul Elmer More and Norman Foerster were traditionalists, he regarded their critical approach as inadequate too. They were accused of being too abstract and devoid of any understanding of the specificity of aesthetic activity.[51] They failed to acknowledge that traditional aesthetic practices were inappropriate within modern society, and that admirable social and cultural criticisms do not of themselves make good literature.

In opposition to Stalinized Marxism and the Neo-Humanism, Ransom argued that the role of criticism was not simply to support or reject the social statements found in literary texts. The critic should assess the validity of the literary forms through which writers investigate their tradition, not their specific conclusions, nor the overt position which they might take.[52] This did not entail that aesthetic forms should avoid serious issues. To this extent he agreed with the Marxists and the Neo-Humanists that the substance of art should not be futile or superficial, and that it should involve an engagement with its society and culture. As a result, Ransom places a great deal of responsibility on critics. Their task is to establish the validity of literary values through an analysis of the linguistic forms used in their production. As such, they not only acted as critics of literature, but also of their society and culture.

# 5  Allen Tate: the social organization of literature

Tate's contribution to the development of the New Criticism is less easy to characterize than Ransom's, though in many ways it was at least as fundamental. These difficulties arise from the fact that his contribution was not restricted to the impact of his critical writings – it was also a result of his personal influence on Ransom, Warren and others. Tate did not see himself primarily as a critic – at least in the 1920s and 1930s. He was more concerned with his status as a poet. In fact, he maintained an uneasy relationship with the academy until the 1950s. He did spend periods as an academic, but mainly as a way of paying off debts. The uncertainty of this relationship with the academy is important to the development of Tate's ideas and activities. Much of his writing concerned the social and economic situation of the writer in the modern world. He examined the social organization of literary and cultural production. Like Ransom, this interest led him to contrast the traditional society with those forms associated with modernity, forms such as scientific positivism and the cash-nexus.

Tate's career was also similar to that of Ransom in another way. Its development can be divided into three stages, but with a strong line of continuity running through them – namely his claim that the modern writer lacked a social basis for aesthetic independence. It is the shifts in the strategies and tactics that he used to establish this basis which distinguishes these stages. In the period up to 1935, Tate was concerned with the decay of the traditional society, and his involvement in Agrarianism was a call for its reconstruction. Like Ransom, it was during this period that Tate developed his critical position, and wrote a substantial number of the essays which would later be seen as seminal examples of the New Criticism. His New Critical theories were not a retreat from his Agrarian critique of industrial capitalism, but were developed in conjunction with it. After 1935, he turned his attention to the universities. He had never had much confidence in the possibility of reconstructing the traditional society through the Agrarian movement, but he came to see the universities as a possible social basis for artistic independence. This independence did not imply the separation, isolation or distance of the writer from society. Instead it was identified as a precondition for a critical engagement with society, a precondition which also depended upon appropriate forms of social organization. Finally, after the establishment of the New Criticism within the academy, Tate returned to a concentration upon literature, but his essays from this period continued to display a hostility to modern society.

## Culture and order

Tate's first book, *Reactionary Essays on Poetry and Ideas*,[1] is often seen as an important collection of New Critical articles, but it was actually a selection of papers and reviews on both literature and society which he had written during the first stage of his career. For example, his essay on Emily Dickinson was originally published in 1928 when he was still trying to establish the movement which would become known as Agrarianism. It argues that the destruction of the traditional society was caused by the development of industrial capitalism, and that this destruction produced great problems for literature, culture and society. For Tate, it was the tradition available to Dickinson which enabled her to develop her unique form of poetry. It established an order of values in relation to which she could define and differentiate both herself and her poetry. Consequently, the term 'tradition' does not refer to a fixed, or static entity, nor even to the repetition of established forms. Instead it is defined as 'points of critical reference passed on to us from a preceding generation',[2] points of critical reference in relation to which individuals could position themselves and so define a unique identity. It was this sense of tradition which, Tate argues, was missing in his own age, and its decline is traced back to the introduction of mill industries into America in 1790. These industries, he suggests, removed the foundations for the traditionalism of the New England theocracy which he describes as 'the most interesting historically of all American ideas'. It integrated the whole of society, and gave 'a final, definite meaning to life, the life of the pious and impious, of learned and vulgar alike'.[3] However, with the rise of industry, the theocracy no longer had a basis in the whole way of life. It became separated from the economic activities of society. In this situation, culture came to be defined as a mere addition or complement to social and economic life. It was simply defined as a collection of fine objects or forms. As Tate puts it: 'New England became a museum.'[4] These changes, it is argued, destroyed the tragic vision of puritanism which was the distinguishing feature of the New England theocracy. Individuals no longer felt themselves to be ultimately connected to the whole way of life, but instead became isolated from their culture. The writings of Emerson are used as an instance of this transformation. For Tate, Emerson's philosophy removed the tragic aspects of puritan theology and converted humanity into the ideal.[5] Humanity was no longer seen as being limited by culture, nature, or even God. Instead it became capable of attaining perfection. Though Tate's interpretation of Emerson is debatable, he is trying to identify a more general tendency, a tendency to deny that humanity is limited by its past and present, or by its own materiality. For Tate, human beings could not attain perfection, whether as individuals or as a group. They must work to improve themselves through an investigation of their concrete situation, not by trying to attain some abstract image of the ideal. Consequently, Tate did not deny the social and material relations which constitute individual identity. On the contrary, he drew upon Southern paternalism and the concept of Original Sin in order to develop a critique of bourgeois individualism. He argued that the individual was not a free and autonomous being, but one always defined and limited by social, cultural and material relations.

A similar position was developed in relation to literature. He did claim, in relation to Dickinson, that one cannot trace 'the rich quality of her mind'[6] to any direct cause, such as the disappointment in love to which her biographers attribute it.[7] None the less, this did not mean that he saw literature as independent of its context. Instead his position was that literary forms are produced through a series of relations that are so complex that one cannot identify any specific 'cause'. For example, while Dickinson's poetry was defined in relation to the puritan theology of New England, it was not simply a reflection or expression of that tradition. It did not simply accept that theology, but treats its ideas critically as forms to be probed and explored.[8] For Tate, Dickinson's poetry must be understood as an active investigation of her society and culture, and its richness is founded upon 'a tension between abstraction and sensation in which the two elements may be, of course, distinguished logically, but not really'.[9] This approach is contrasted with the revolutionary approach which, Tate argued, seeks to overthrow tradition. Literature, it is claimed, seeks to recapture and reconstruct tradition. It 'does not dispense with tradition; it probes its deficiencies'.[10] The writer '*discerns* [the tradition's] real elements and thus establishes its value, by putting it to the test of experience'.[11] Far from denying the relationship between literature and society, Tate was concerned with the problems encountered by the writer as a result of the loss of traditional forms within modern society. As a solution to this situation, he called for the establishment of a profession of letters which would establish specific social relations between writers and their public.

## The profession of letters

For Tate, tradition is a form of code which defines the typical forms of behaviour in a society and culture. By probing its deficiencies, the writer provides a criticism of existing forms of activity, and works to reconstruct the code.[12] However, the effectiveness of this form of artistic engagement is dependent upon the social relations which exist between writers and their public. Tate seeks to illustrate his argument with reference to the situation in France where, it is claimed, great responsibility and authority was bestowed upon the profession of letters. This situation is contrasted with that of the United States where, Tate claims, the public 'sees the writer as a business man because it cannot see any other kind of man, and respects him according to his income'.[13] This problem is identified with specific forms of organization or *class rule*:

Under feudalism the artist was a member of an organic society. The writer's loss of professional standing, however, set in before the machine, by which I mean the machine age as we know it, appeared. It began with the rise of mercantile aristocracy in the eighteenth century. The total loss of professionalism in letters may be seen in our age – an age that remembers the extinction of aristocracy and witnesses the triumph of a more inimical plutocratic society.[14]

As a result, much of Tate's writing was a discussion of different forms of social organization, and the ways in which they affected the relationship between writers and their public. His main concern was with the impact of the cash-nexus, scientific positivism, and types of political collectivism such as Stalinized Marxism, but he also discussed both the advantages and problems encountered by Southern writers.

For Tate, the problem with the cash-nexus as a mode of social organization is that writers become separated from their public, and can only reach a public through the market. Sales become the primary mode of social exchange between writers and their readerships, and to reach a public, writers are forced to concentrate their efforts on the requirements of the market.[15] This situation is contrasted with the relationships which were established between writers and their public during periods in which they were defined as members of their patron's household. As a response to the market, Tate called for the creation of a separate class of writers: 'until the desperate men today who mean business can become an independent class, there will be no profession of letters anywhere in America'.[16]

The importance of the Agrarian movement, for Tate, did not necessarily reside in the fact that it might actually succeed in restoring the traditional society. Rather it enabled him to imagine the possibility of a society in which the writer was related to the whole way of life. Tate did acknowledge faults in the intellectual life of the South though. The ante-bellum South may have offered many of the conditions necessary for an effective profession of letters, but it was hampered by its political organization. This problem was claimed to have been partly the result of external pressures from an over-aggressive North, but he also claimed that

it was partly rooted in the kind of rule that the South had, which was aristocratic rule. All aristocracies are obsessed politically ... The best intellectual energy goes into politics and goes of necessity; aristocracy is class rule; and the class must fight for interest and power. Under the special conditions of the nineteenth century, the south had less excess of vitality for the disinterested arts of literature than it might have had ordinarily.[17]

Within this context, the South prevented the development of a profession of letters by denying literature its seriousness. Literature was simply seen as a polite diversion. Nor was the problem solved with the destruction of the ante-bellum South. Tate argued that even in his own period, Southern writers had failed to take advantage of their changed situation. They had yet to establish themselves as a class 'whose ethics consist in devotion to the craft'.[18] By concentrating on the craft of writing, Tate did not imply that literary activity is uninterested in its social context. In fact, his specific criticism of the situation of writers within modern society was that the craft of writing had failed to acquire a function with relation to society as a whole. Writers may have been freed from the restraints of plantation society, but they had also lost any sense of social or cultural purpose:

The industrialist knows little or nothing, neither imaginative literature nor political philosophy. If the modern writer, unlike the old South writer, is emancipated from the demands of social conformity, it is not because he is intelligently emancipated; it is rather that the decay of social standards has left him free, but nevertheless hanging in the air. The place of the old Southern writer was narrow, it hardly existed, but to the extent that it did exist, it was defined.[19]

Tate did not claim that the act of writing should be autonomous from society, and was in fact highly critical of any such position. He argued for intellectual independence, but only to the extent that the act of writing should not be dominated by economic or political interests and so denied its own specificity. Writers should engage with society through a critical investigation of that society. They should not be limited to the role of an apologist for particular economic or political positions. This independence also required a specific social and material base. At the very least, it required 'an independent machinery of publication'.[20] As Tate put it, the South 'can never constitute a Southern criticism so long as it must be trimmed and scattered in Northern magazines, or published in books that will be read as curiously as travel literature, by Northern people alone'.[21] If Southern writers were to constitute themselves as a group in contrast to the situation of Northern writers, they not only needed specific *means* of production, but also an alternative *mode* of production.

Whilst literature should not be regarded as an entirely autonomous activity, Tate still believed that it was important to distinguish it from other social activities such as politics. Different activities have different characteristics. They require specific modes of engagement and specific forms of social organization. For example, Tate was worried that modern society threatened to distract the writer from the specific forms of social engagement appropriate to them as writers by placing great pressures upon them to commit themselves in political terms. This situation did not allow writers the independence to investigate their society and culture critically, but demanded that they commit themselves to specific ideas or programmes. The problem is that, according to Tate, while literature requires intellectual independence if it is to exercise its critical function of investigating the given forms of social activity,[22] politics requires a commitment to certain ideas and principles. It can only entertain criticism to a limited degree and requires some degree of organized conformity. Tate's worry was that by committing themselves to political programmes, writers ran the risk of ignoring their critical function and of converting literature into propaganda. It is in this way that Tate distinguishes literature from politics as an activity.

For this reason, Tate was opposed to certain forms of politically motivated literary criticism. This position is clarified in a review of T. S. Eliot in which he challenges interpretations which he identifies as 'communistic', interpretations which are only directed at the political or philosophical foundations of Eliot's poetry. Tate's objection to these forms of criticism is that they reduce Eliot's poetry to an expression of his doctrine, and ignore its poetic 'quality' and form. These forms of criticism evaluate the poetry in terms that are described as entirely positivistic. They are merely concerned with assessing its accuracy, use or relevance according to the criteria laid down by specific political programmes. By contrast, Tate states that the 'doctrine has little to command interest of itself',[23] and that 'Mr. Eliot's critics are a little less able each year to see the poetry for Westminster Abbey; the wood is all trees'.[24] For Tate, it is the poetic 'quality' which is significant, and this 'quality' is defined in opposition to the claims of positivism.[25] No matter how admirable the doctrine might be, Tate argues, it does not in itself constitute good literature. To concentrate on the doctrine at the expense of other features 'witnesses the powerful modern desire to judge an art scientifically, practically, industrially; according to how it works. The poetry is viewed as a pragmatic result, and it has no use.'[26] It is the process of investigation which distinguishes literature for Tate, not the conclusions the writer may arrive at, and this process of investigation is one which is embodied in the linguistic forms of texts.

### Literature and form

In Tate's estimation, aesthetic evaluation should not be based upon the acceptance or rejection of a poet's beliefs. Instead it should be based on an analysis of the attitudes to the world which are developed through the linguistic forms of literary texts.[27] These attitudes are not defined as asocial, but they are distinguished from the writer's beliefs. While attitudes are specific relationships, beliefs are identified as positivistic forms. They are judgements of fact or practicality. They correspond to the form of a statement, and can only be evaluated by proof or falsification. As was the case with Ransom, Tate defined the aesthetic in opposition to scientific positivism, arguing that the latter was only interested in information, and thus lacked the capacity for critical judgements and was incapable of supporting a developed intellectual order.

This position did not prevent Tate from describing aesthetic attitudes as objective in character, but he was careful to stress that this form of objectivity was different from that associated with scientific positivism. It did not alienate the social and material world, but challenged the will to power of scientific objectivity. Tate's position drew upon Southern paternalism and Christian concepts of Original Sin. He maintained that the aesthetic acknowledges the complexities of the world and does not reduce it to a mere object of use. This type of objectivity was defined as a check on the alienated, abstract forms associated with scientific positivism, the cash-nexus, or political behaviour. It did not repress those aspects which did not correspond with the rationalization and control of the social and material world, but rather it emphasized and celebrated them. In this way, it was not only distinct from alienated, abstract forms, but actively opposed to them. It was not simply a retreat from society, but a call for social change.

This position is clarified in Tate's essay, 'Three Types of Poetry', in which he identifies three forms of poetic language: allegory; romantic irony: and the 'creative spirit'.[28] This essay was written in the same period as Ransom's consideration of physical, platonic and metaphysical poetry, and both essays were produced out of joint discussion and mutual influence. The first two types of poetry – allegory and romantic irony – are both defined as products of the 'practical will' of scientific positivism and industrial capitalism. In allegory, the literary form becomes a mere expression of a particular position, while romantic irony is the mirror image of the practical will. It sees no alternative to the dominance of the practical will within modern society, and can only counter this practical order by isolating the individual; the individual can only escape the alienated world by attempting to retreat into an asocial space. This asocial retreatism is the position usually associated with the New Criticism, but Tate is quite clearly critical of it. In fact, he defines his own position in direct opposition to it. He also associates these literary forms with specific historical moments. Allegory is claimed to be the dominant form both within his own period, and within the period which saw the origins of modern society and scientific positivism. Romantic irony, on the other hand, is identified as a reaction to the industrial revolution at the end of the eighteenth and the beginning of the nineteenth century.

These claims about allegory are not meant to apply to all of its manifestations. In the case of Dante, for example, Tate identifies two forms of allegory: the poetical and the religious. The distinction between these two was that while the first was seen as literally and figuratively true by Dante, the second was only seen as true in a figurative sense. It was this second type of allegory which was associated with the modern period. According to Tate, his own period could not accept the former, while the latter conforms to the structure of scientific positivism and propaganda.[29] It involves the dominance of abstractions in the construction of the text, and forces its materials in a single direction. These materials are merely used to express a specific position as in the case of propaganda.

The principal problem associated with romanticism, on the other hand, is that it is claimed to alienate literature from society. According to Tate, as the arts came to find themselves deprived of an involvement in the whole way of life and were alienated from the order of science, the romantic movement came to oppose all forms of order. They saw all forms of order as essentially the same as those of science, and so rejected them. They saw the only solution to the alienated world of scientific positivism and industrial capitalism as being the affirmation of the individual will in opposition to society and culture.[30] Not only does Tate criticize this position for failing to identify an alternative to industrial capitalism, he also criticizes it for reproducing the alienated structure of scientific positivism. The individual will becomes an abstraction which is isolated from the social and cultural context. In such a position, not only does it repress its own fallibility and limitations, but it also seeks to dominate the world and impose its own vision upon it.[31] Like the social relations of industrial capitalism, romanticism isolates writers from their tradition and from the way of life as a whole, the very forms with which Tate wanted to reconnect them.

In contrast to these previous forms, the 'creative spirit' is claimed to offer a series of values and relationships which are opposed to the will to power of scientific positivism and industrial capitalism. It does not simply retreat from society, but calls for the creation of an alternative social order. These positions draw upon the Agrarian critique of science and capitalism, and they are developed in a discussion of Edmund Wilson's *Axel's Castle*. In this essay, Wilson's position is identified as a form of economic determinism. It defines all art as an expression of, or an apology for, specific institutions or classes.[32] This position is not criticised for identifying relations between literature and society, but for failing to examine the complexity of these relations. It implies a mechanical model of causality. Consequently, Wilson is accused of ignoring the specificity of aesthetic activity, and of reducing all art to a form of propaganda. This concentration on determination and propaganda is also identified with a particularly modern problem. Wilson's position, it is argued, fails to acknowledge the limits of particular ideologies or programmes, or the breakdown of human control.[33] In contrast, it is a recognition of these limits which, Tate claims, shaped both the traditional society, and the 'genuine poetry of imagination'.[34] Literature does not simply present ideological positions. It establishes the limits of abstract programmes by examining abstractions in relation to experience.

According to Tate, this examination was embodied in the language of the text, and it was these linguistic processes which should be the object of critical attention. In this way, he argues that while the text was always produced in relation to its particular social and cultural context, one could distinguish the 'quality' of the text from its history. The text's 'quality' is identified with its specific linguistic forms, and while these were always a response to their historical situation, writers from different historical contexts could develop similar linguistic forms. For example, Baudelaire and Eliot are claimed to have similar literary qualities.[35] The qualities shared by Baudelaire and Eliot are identified by Tate as: 'irony, humility, introspection, reverence'.[36] While these qualities are distinguished from practical activities, they are not identified as a refuge from society, or even a compensation for its alienated activities. Instead they are seen as critical forms. It is suggested that they acknowledge the fact of human fallibility and the inevitable limits of all practical programmes. As a result, they define specific attitudes to the world which acknowledge those aspects repressed by practical programmes. In the process, they challenge purely practical interests and illustrate the need to develop a way of life in which the economic, political and aesthetic are fully integrated with one another.[37] They illustrate the need for a new aestheticized way of living in which human activities will not be alienating but fulfilling. As a result, it is not Eliot's doctrine which Tate claims to admire, but rather his religious attitude, an attitude which is embodied in his use of irony.

## Conclusion: the concentration of the critic

Like Ransom, Tate defined the role of the critic in opposition to the positions of the Neo-Humanists and existing forms of Stalinized Marxism which were, he suggested, characterized by a crude reductionism that failed to acknowledge the process of aesthetic production and merely judged texts as examples of social commentary. In response, Tate argued that the critic should concentrate on the use of language in aesthetic texts, and the way in which this language responded to its social and cultural contexts. He was concerned to warn against another form of reductionism though. It was stressed that all critical methods were limited. None could explain all aspects of the text, not even his own approach. It was only a way of dealing with certain aspects of the text. For example, in a discussion of Ezra Pound, he wrote that while he intended to analyse the symbolism of a poem, this symbolism was 'by no means the chief intention of the poet'.[38] It is not that he seeks to reject or invalidate this form of critical analysis, but rather that it should only be used if its limitations were acknowledged. In describing his own approach to Pound, he writes:

I am about to falsify the true simplicity of the cantos into a simplicity that is merely convenient and spurious. The reader must bear this in mind, and view the slender symbolism that I am going to read into the cantos as a critical shorthand, useful perhaps, but which when used must be dropped.[39]

Without this caution, it was warned, the symbolic method runs the danger of seeing the text allegorically. It threatens to force the materials of the text in a single direction and convert it into a type of propaganda. The purpose of criticism, Tate insisted, is not to explain the complexity of the poem in its entirety – an act which he regarded as ultimately impossible – but rather to establish the points of critical reference necessary to judge its literature, culture and society.

# 6    Robert Penn Warren: against propaganda and irresponsibility

Warren's work on literature up to the mid-1930s differs from that of Ransom and Tate in several ways, the most striking of which is his interest in narrative fiction. Also, while he was not very productive during this period, and while his work lacked the orderly clarification of ideas which distinguished that of Ransom and Tate, he was more flexible intellectually. He tackled areas with which the other two were less willing or less able to deal. This flexibility is partly due to the way in which Warren approached literary criticism. Ransom and Tate were more concerned with the philosophical study of literature in general and used specific writers as instances within more general patterns. Warren, on the other hand, tended to concentrate on the activity of writing as practised by specific writers or schools. His general theoretical positions evolved through a dialogue with specific texts.

Warren's concern with fiction also displayed a more overt interest in the representation of social life, or what might be termed 'realism'. The significance of this interest is that despite Ransom and Tate's interest in the relation of literature and society, and despite their critique of certain types of cultural organization, they were limited in their attempts to *challenge* modern society. Through his consideration of realism, Warren was able to define a far more flexible role for the writer. The writer was not limited to a call for the creation of an alternative society and culture, but could also engage in more localized and strategic struggles over social and cultural problems without ignoring the formal aspects of literary activity. Through a concentration on the relationship between realism and literary form, Warren was able to regard literature as a more active and strategic social force; to develop a literary criticism in which formal considerations were seen as forms of social engagement.

## The writer and society

Like Ransom and Tate, Warren's literary criticism was developed as part of his involvement in Agrarianism, and is founded upon a critique of modern society and its effect on literary forms. This is particularly clear in his essay on Ransom's poetry, 'John Crowe Ransom: A Study in Irony', in which he argues that the 'problem at the center of Ransom's work is specifically modern – at least we are accustomed to think so – but it implies some history'.[1] The essay discusses the 'effect of science on the poetic impulse',[2] but it argues that while the dominance of science had created the dissociation of sensibility, science itself cannot be abstracted from a more general context. If science is the most immediate cause, the 'problem is, finally, social'.[3] The dissociation of sensibility developed from the specific types of social organization associated with capitalism, and from the relationship which they established between writers and their public. Like Ransom and Tate, Warren argues that while the traditional society related all the elements within the whole way of life to one another, and so created a cultural structure which was 'religious' or 'mythic', modern society separates and isolates activities and so destroys these 'religious' or 'mythic' structures.[4] It results in a division between fact and value, and dissociates cultural and economic activities from one another. It also isolates the sensibility from various aspects of life, and so limits its development.

For Warren, this situation explains Ransom's involvement in the Agrarian movement. Modern society, it is argued, isolates writers from society and so frustrates them, forcing them to either extricate themselves from society, or else oppose it.[5] It was this latter option which was taken by Ransom and the Agrarians. As Warren stresses, the Agrarians did not oppose scientific or practical activities themselves, but rather their alienation from, and domination over, other activities and interests. These writers did not attempt to retreat from society into the sensibility, but called for the construction of an alternative society in which aesthetic and cultural values were applied to all activities in the way of life.[6] Ransom's poetry is not discussed as an autonomous or self-contained form, but is related to its social and cultural context. It is not treated as a mere reflection or expression of that context, but as a response to specific social and historical problems.

Warren also claims that modern literature is distinguished by a specific problem which was not shared by the literature of the past. Lacking a connection with the whole way of life, modern writers are claimed to have a problem finding and developing a theme. Writers of the past such as Hawthorne, Melville, Dickinson, and James, it is argued, had a specific culture to draw upon. This culture gave meaning and significance to individual behaviour, and did not treat it as merely a series of isolated and unrelated events. It placed it in a cultural context without reducing it to a passive expression of some more general process. This position, like those of Ransom and Tate, draws on Southern paternalism and its critique of industrial capitalism and bourgeois individualism. Warren argues that modern society alienates the individual from its social and cultural context, and represses the social and material conditions which constitute individual identity. By contrast, the strength of traditional societies, it is argued, was that they gave individuals a sense of their context.[7] These differences between modern and traditional societies are claimed to affect the ways in which writers approach their themes, and as a result, Warren makes a distinction between two different approaches. The first of these is identified as both the more traditional and the more desirable. It relates writers' activities, and even their own personalities, to their social situation. The writer of this type relates the personal to the supra-personal, or social.[8] The second approach is related to modern society and is defined as more abstract. It is not concerned with the social and cultural context, but concentrates on the writer's individual interests in isolation from their context. Social issues and themes are subordinated, or even opposed, to the writer's ultimate motive which is identified as the expression of their own personality. This second approach is criticized by Warren. Even though specific writers may have very great literary powers, he insists that the final outcome is ultimately unsatisfactory.[9] It is a product of the isolation from the traditional culture which is experienced by modern writers. It is a result of their inability to relate their individual selves, or their writing, to a context which would give them broader significance and meaning.

Not only does this situation encourage certain writers to retreat from society into a concentration on their own personalities, it is also claimed to encourage others to adopt an oppositional position in relation to modern society. This opposition is generally identified as positive, as in the case of Ransom, but it is also said to present certain problems. For example, writers might be encouraged to adopt a social or political programme as a way of obtaining a theme. They may try 'to reason [themself] into the appropriate position, to perform the ritual to evoke the wayward spirit'.[10] This tendency is identified with both the types of regional and proletarian literature which distinguished the 1930s. In discussing these literary movements, Warren makes some distinctions between them and examines some of their criticisms of one another. In the process, he develops some interesting positions. Not only is he more sympathetic to proletarian literature and Marxism than might be expected, but he is also quite critical of regional literature. Proletarian literature is criticized for being too concerned with the general over the particular. It is said to reduce individuals to merely instances of larger classes and processes. As a result, Warren prefers regionalism's concentration on the local and the individual, rather than the Marxist preoccupation with internationalism and class groupings. None the less, he agrees with the Marxist claim that most

examples of regional literature display bourgeois prejudices, class sentimentality, and even snobbery. However, it is the issue of property which
is really seen as distinguishing the two groups. According to Warren, the
proletarian writers could only conceive of property in its abstract or
capitalist form. They criticize property in general, while the regional
writers connected it

with [their] idea of the relation of man to place, for ownership gives a man a stake
in a place and helps to define his, for the regional writer, organic relation to
society.[11]

Modern forms of property are criticized for being abstracted and alienated
from both the individual and the whole way of life, but the solution to this
situation, Warren claims, is a reconstruction of traditional forms of
property, a reconstruction in which the individual and his livelihood would
no longer be alienated from the whole way of life. It is for this reason that
he opposes the collectivism proposed by the proletarian writers of his
period.

   Despite these criticisms, Warren is far more ambivalent towards
Marxism than might be expected. He is sympathetic to the way in which it
criticized the situation of culture within modern society – even though he
sees problems in the specific ways in which it related politics and literature,
problems which he also identifies with regional literature.[12] He particularly
commends the Marxists for their rejection of bourgeois individualism, and
for their criticism of the relationship between writers and their public
under capitalism. However, he warns that the danger inherent in both
proletarian and regional literature was that it attempted to solve the
dilemma of modern writers by giving them the right propaganda. The
difficulty of finding a theme, he argues, can not be solved simply through
the adoption of a specific political commitment. In such a case, the writer's

very sincerity, the very fact of the depth and mass of his concern, may not do more
than imperil his achievement unless his sensibility is so attuned and his critical
intelligence so developed that he can effect the true marriage of his convictions, his
ideas, that is, his theme, with the concrete projection in experience, that is, his
subject.[13]

One point that is worth noting here is that it is regional literature which is
used as an example of this problem, not proletarian literature. Whatever
the strengths of regional literature as a social and cultural programme, it is
criticized when applied to the process of literary production. In this
situation, it frees writers from the effort of investigating their themes and
encourages them to rely on a ready-made solution. It implies that no
intellectual effort is necessary because the answers are already available.
Warren also argues that regionalism in literature can become a mere

affectation, rather than a fully developed attitude. As he puts it, the 'danger in regionalism lies in the last syllable, in the *ism*. As a fad it is meaningless.'[14] This tendency is linked to a kind of 'get-rich-quick psychology' which is founded on the belief that one can produce literature simply though the illustration of an already formulated social or political position. The problem with this position is that it fails to explore the issues with any real rigour. For example, in the case of literary representations of the 'hick', it is argued that despite the problems with the previous generation's attacks on this character, a simple reversal of this approach is no solution. The present simply mirrors the problems of the past when it presents this figure uncritically.[15] As a mere affectation, neither position really bothers to understand the complexities of this character or its situation. They merely adopt a fashionable position, and fail to make the character socially or culturally meaningful.

True regionalism, for Warren, is not something one can self-consciously adopt or will into being. It should not be associated with quaintness or local colour for their own sake, nor engage in 'the literary exploitation of a race or society that has no cultural continuity with our own'.[16] A novel cannot attain true regionalism or quality on the basis of its characters' social positions, and it should not try to achieve a connection with 'the common people' through a phoney simple-mindedness. For Warren, the conscious adoption of specific features or strategies such as these does not of itself make good literature, nor even a socially meaningful examination of its subject. The process of literary production, and even the political investigation of social problems, requires a genuine involvement and engagement on the part of the writer. This engagement is not a retreat from social or political concerns. On the contrary, it demands that writers relate both their themes and their subject to the broader cultural context, rather than simply celebrating the local and specific:

Even literary regionalism is more than a literary matter, and is not even primarily a literary matter. If it is treated as a purely literary matter, it will promptly lose any meaning, for only in so far as literature springs from some reality in experience is it valuable to us. The regime for the regionalist who wanted to be a writer would have its public as well as its private aspect.[17]

Warren's objection to the adoption of literary formulae is not that social issues are unrelated to literature, but rather that such an adoption is an abdication of social responsibility. It allows writers to avoid a full investigation of their subject and theme, and to ignore their broad social and cultural implications. In this way it shared many of the problems associated with literature which saw itself as an asocial, autonomous activity or merely the expression of an individual sensibility.

## Meaning and form

In his discussion of historical and realistic literature, Warren opposes those forms which are merely concerned with the particulars of social life. It is argued that unless these details are examined in relation to the social and cultural processes which shape them, they are not made meaningful. For Warren, writers should not simply transcribe or record the details and appearances of social life, but should ask questions of these features which relate them to broader and more underlying processes.[18] It is these questions which

will be asked by the writer, unless he is merely indulging in romance of the blue and the grey or of the leatherstocking; and they will be asked by the historian if he is enough of the poet to have interest beyond his crude mechanism of particulars.[19]

This position is similar to Lukacs' distinction between naturalism and realism in which realism is distinguished from a mere transcription of social appearances.[20] For Lukacs, realism did not just focus on the surface details of social life; it identified the social and historical processes that created these appearances. Warren's position also shares Lukacs' interest in historical fiction, and he argues that it is a concentration on these processes which distinguishes·much of the Southern literature of his own period. The interest in tradition displayed by many Southern writers is seen as an attempt to examine all elements of the way of life in relation to one another. It did not concentrate merely on the details of the region as was the case with writers of regional literature, but related these details to their social and cultural context. It did not trivialize these details by treating them as quaint or ornamental features, but sought to identify their meaning and significance. These Southern writers examined the complex relations which constituted their materials. They felt

that they cannot judge a situation or society, abstractly conceived, by an abstract set of values ... They are, rather, concerned with comprehension, and realize that such comprehension, which is their ideal art, cannot be achieved without consideration of both time and place in a very special sense.[21]

As a result, Warren's defence of this Southern literature does not privilege the details of the South as a region, but claims that the South offered its writers an available tradition. It provided a particular way of thinking which enabled them to identify the relation between elements within the Southern way of life.

Consequently, while Warren does criticize certain historical novels, his criticisms do not result from an antagonism to literary forms which examine social and cultural processes. Instead he attacks those historical novels which merely concentrate on the details and glamour of specific periods – such as their costumes and manners – rather than the social and cultural relations which give them meaning. These forms of literature are also condemned for failing to relate the historical processes active within the past to the situation of the present.[22] They fail to make the past meaningful to the present, except as a fantasy realm in which to escape the alienation of modern society. For this reason, Warren's New Critical positions do not marginalize those forms of writing concerned with social and historical issues. Instead they are highly valued, and the task of the critic is to evaluate the literary forms which are used to this end. He is not critical of literary 'realism' but distinguishes 'realism' from a mere transcription of social and historical particulars.[23]

In fact, Warren is highly critical of those writers who strove for an asocial formalism. For example, Archibald MacLeish is accused of seeking to avoid ideas and external reference in his poetry. This position contradicts many of the positions ascribed to the New Criticism by its opponents. Warren did agree with MacLeish that the evaluation of poetry should be based on its formal features, rather than an acceptance or rejection of its statements about the social world, but he does not agree that literary activity should dissociate itself from the social world. MacLeish is attacked for making a false opposition in which literature was either a type of propaganda or an asocial and autonomous formal activity, an activity which had no interest in, or relation to, its social situation. This opposition, it is claimed, resulted in a poetry which was not only purged of ideas and social concerns, but also lacking in any meaning or significance. Nor are these problems seen as external to the poetry's formal features. It is claimed that they make the poetry formless and vague.[24] Without addressing a social subject of some sort, the poet is unable to give his poetry a coherent formal structure. According to Warren, poets such as MacLeish accept the same oppositions and alternatives as the propagandists. Both groups maintain that there are only two alternatives. Either writers adopt a propagandist approach to literature, or they abandon the use of ideas and avoid all forms of social engagement.[25] Warren does acknowledge that MacLeish's poetry has positive features in so far as it respects the specificity of poetry as a form and refuses to reduce it to propaganda, but for Warren, this does not compensate for its negative features – the asocial formalism which prevents it from developing a theme. Warren did insist that poetry should be evaluated on the basis of its formal features, but he challenged MacLeish's claim that 'a poem should not mean, but be'.

For Warren, literature should not impose abstract doctrines upon its material, or reject social responsibility and engagement. Rather it should develop specific critical attitudes through the linguistic forms of the text. A formal concentration could still involve a type of social engagement.[26] For example, he examines Ransom's use of irony in his poetry in order to identify its 'fundamental motive'. This use of irony is supposed to criticize the 'dissociation of sensibility' in the modern world by comparing the limitations of the writer's situation with its potential.[27] This use of irony is also distinguished from that of Eliot. Unlike Eliot who, it is claimed, contrasts modern society with traditional social forms, Ransom is claimed to have used irony to focus on the psychological states of his characters.[28] Consequently, Warren regards irony as a critical form through which writers examine their social and cultural contexts and identify their limitations. In this way, Warren claims, the concentration on literary form could avoid the problems associated with propaganda without retreating from society into an empty formalism.

## Conclusion

Unlike Ransom and Tate, Warren is not greatly preoccupied with defining the proper practice of criticism during the period, but he did stress that the evaluation of literature should be based on an analysis of the linguistic forms of the text. This did not prevent him from discussing writers' responses to their social situation, but he claimed that these responses should not involve the use of abstract programmes or formulae. It should be a critical investigation of issues which was developed though the language of the text. As a result, he did not define literature as an autonomous and self-contained form which was unrelated to its social and cultural context. In fact, he criticizes those that did. For Warren, even those literary forms associated with asocial formalism were a response to the specific problems of modern society. He not only claimed that literature was produced in relation to its social situation, but also that it should involve a critical investigation of that situation. It was in this way that Warren attempted to define literature as a form of social engagement.

# Conclusion: the analysis of a Southern poet

One way of considering the relationship between literary and social criticism in the writing of Ransom, Tate and Warren is to examine the essays on Sidney Lanier which they published during the first half of the 1930s. These essays examined the relationship between three aspects of Lanier's writing: his status as a Southerner who had lived through the Civil War and its aftermath; the social and political positions which he took in relation to these events and processes; and the form of poetry which he developed. In the process, each of them claimed that his poetry was poor, and that its lack of quality was related to his social and political positions, but they did not see this relationship as one of direct reflection or expression. Instead, these weaknesses were seen to be the result of a common problem. Lanier was unable to consider social and poetic forms with any degree of rigour. He relied on abstractions which he failed to examine. The result was a limited understanding of both literary and social forms.

Tate's essay, 'A Southern Romantic', was the first of the three to be published, and it considers Aubrey Starke's biography of Lanier.[1] In opposition to Starke's defence of Lanier, it claims that Lanier's reputation as a poet was not based on a critical evaluation of his poetry or ideas, but on his claim to historical significance.[2] Tate does not regard this historical significance as irrelevant, but he stresses that a critical assessment of Lanier's poetry was necessary if this significance was to be properly understood. In fact, he claims that such an assessment was necessary because Lanier 'helped make us what we are today'.[3] As a result, Tate analyses Lanier's poetic forms and particularly his images. For example, he examines the poem, 'Clover', in which an ox stands for the 'course-of-things', and clover-blossoms represent the human souls over which it tramples.[4] In opposition to Starke's claim that Lanier's poetry was similar to that of the metaphysical poets, this image is contrasted with the use of the 'conceit' in seventeenth-century poetry. Tate's claim is that while this image is meant to represent a relationship, it fails to clarify that relationship. It is a mechanical and abstract image in which the relationship between elements is stated or imposed, rather than explored or developed. It stood for, or represented, the whole situation or idea. By contrast, the meta-physical 'conceit' is claimed to be a self-conscious device which required constant examination and investigation. It did not represent the situation or idea in its totality, but established ways of considering them.[5] For these reasons, Lanier's image is not defined as an example of 'the conceit', but as a symbol. Even as a symbol it is claimed to be weak: 'it is private and arbitrary, not objective and conventional'.[6] For Tate, these problems were all related to Lanier's romanticism. This romanticism encouraged him to concentrate on his own sensibility in isolation from its social and cultural context. It encouraged him to spurn social and cultural conventions and to see poetry as a form which simply existed to 'express' his feelings and positions. He did not take account of the social nature of language and literature, and failed to develop his ideas in terms of these forms.

If Lanier's literary weaknesses are identified with a failure to grasp the formal aspects of literary activity, they are also related to a failure to understand romanticism's 'social counterpart, industrial capitalism'.[7] It is argued that, as with his romanticism, Lanier's political position was based on an abstraction. Just as he had failed to examine the image of the ox, he failed to examine the political relations which were involved in American national history and the Civil War's role within it.[8] He regarded these events as the destruction of 'chivalry' by 'trade', and this prevented him from either understanding the social developments which would result from the War, or conceiving of an alternative to these developments. He could only call for a humanitarian approach to Trade. For Tate, Lanier's

refusal to look for a fundamental alternative to the beliefs of the Reconstruction era, and his acceleration of those beliefs under the illusion that he was correcting them, are in the intellectual tradition of our time. He was a nineteenth century leader who helped make us what we are today.[9]

His poor social and political analysis was ultimately related to his lack of literary quality. Nor was his lack of literary quality merely a formal issue. They were both products of the same problem – his reliance on abstractions.

Warren's discussion of Lanier is also developed in relation to Starke's book, and it argues that Starke had 'nothing important to add to the body of common discussion'[10] though this is not the limit of his objections. He claims that Starke failed to acknowledge that there was something seriously wrong with both Lanier's poetry and his social criticism. It is also interesting to note that in this context Warren claims that Lanier 'was not realistic'.[11] Warren's argument is that Lanier's poetry failed both as a literary form and as a representation of the social world. Lanier is accused of failing to understand the literary and social processes with which he was engaged. For example, his attitudes towards commerce, industry and nationalism are criticized for not grasping their relationship to one another. The two former features were referred to as 'trade' by Lanier who claims that 'Trade dries up the springs of Love, that its ethics are those of war, that it does not permit the labourer to recline'.[12] For Warren, Lanier's weakness was that despite this position, he did not reject nationalism. He failed to see 'that the nationalism mystically embodied in the *Psalm of the West* was a nationalism of Trade'.[13] A similar problem is identified in Lanier's attitude towards science. He 'failed to perceive that the science he adored was the handmaid of the industrial system which he detested'.[14]

These problems are also identified with Lanier's poetic activities. He is criticized for reproducing the romantic isolation of the poet's sensibility from its social and cultural context. He is accused of converting the sensibility into an abstraction.[15] Like Tate, Warren also claims that Lanier does not develop his ideas through poetic forms, but only sees these forms as a vehicle through which to 'express' his abstract statements and positions.[16] Lanier's problems are seen as an illustration of the dangers of romanticism, and Warren maintains that a critical assessment of these features is of vital importance. It is necessary to clarify the problems of the past in order to understand the historical processes which have led to the present.[17]

These criticisms provoked a response from Starke who sought to defend Lanier by identifying him as a precursor of Agrarianism. It was these claims which Ransom addresses in his article on Lanier where he stresses that while he did not want to reject a potential Agrarian leader, Lanier was not qualified for such a position because his position was quite different to that of the Agrarians. For example, even while it is acknowledged that Lanier had a sense of piety with regard to the natural environment, Lanier's attitude towards nature is regarded as inadequate.[18] He failed to understand that humanity's relationship to nature was shaped within specific social and cultural relations; that it was not enough to revere nature in isolation from one's society, if one was also required to deny this reverential relationship in other social activities. For Ransom, the sensibility was not an innate form which existed independently of one's society and culture, but needed to be rooted in specific social and economic activities. When separated from the activities of everyday life, it ceased to be a meaningful or developed form, and became simply a diversion – a holiday from other activities or simply the consumption of a spectacle.[19] Consequently, Lanier's attitude towards nature is differentiated from that of the Agrarians. While he defended the appreciation of nature as a retreat from modern society, the Agrarians called for the creation of an alternative social and cultural order in which the love of nature would be involved in all aspects of life.

These intellectual problems are also related to his poetic form. For example, while Ransom criticized Lanier's lack of realism and his failure to understand the politics of his period, he did not just attack his positions but the form of his thought, or his ways of thinking. One instance of this can be seen in his defence of Warren:

I do not imagine [Warren] means by the word [realism] to criticise the representation of ugly modern warfare by a mediaeval tourney, as Mr. Starke seems to think. Poets may prefer the Ptolemaic sword to the Copernican rifle, without altering also the spirit of the occasion; but if they do that, they may be blamed for unrealism, to the extent that the occasion can no longer be identified.[20]

For this reason, Lanier's discussion of the Civil War is regarded as inappropriate by Ransom. It is accused of a pessimistic and defeatist attitude which simply portrays the South as sentimental and backward, and so fails to adequately represent either the participants or their struggle. It ignores their complexities and their specificity, and merely presents an abstract allegory of their relationship. As a result, Ransom challenges Starke's main argument – that Lanier was an Agrarian in the same sense as Ransom, Tate, and Warren. For Ransom, Lanier's social and cultural criticisms, however acute they may have been, were not primarily formal objections like those of the Agrarians.[21] He did not call for the end of industrialism, but merely argued that it should be more humane in its practice. He never argued that

the poor should never have entered the inward-opening door to earn a wage but should have remained on the outside hills and farmed them. He does not actually say it; and I believe that it does not occur to him, but that he is saying rather awkwardly that Trade, instead of tightening the door to keep them in for longer hours at smaller pay, should let them out early to go and picnic over the hills, or spend their leisure time in cultural pursuits, et cetera, et cetera.[22]

It is here that Ransom sees the most pronounced difference between Lanier and the Agrarians. Lanier wanted to enrich the system, while the Agrarians wanted to create an alternative one. These problems were also associated with his poetry. It is not criticized for considering his social and cultural context, but for the *way* in which it considers that context.

Consequently, all three maintained that poetic form was related to social criticism. In the case of Lanier, for example, it was his use of abstract ideas and images which resulted in the poor quality of his poetry and his social commentary. In response, Ransom, Tate and Warren claimed that writers should examine ideas and images critically. They should explore the complexities and limitations of these forms. Such an approach would not only produce a rich and developed literature, but also make it a valuable piece of social criticism. Their objections to Lanier were neither purely formal, nor purely political. They illustrate the close links between these writers' Agrarian and New Critical positions during the early 1930s, and that the literary positions associated with the latter were not developed during the period which followed the collapse of Agrarianism.

# Part III

# The establishment of the New Criticism

## Introduction

In the mid-1930s, Ransom, Tate and Warren went through two major transitions. First, they moved away from Agrarianism and became involved in the struggles over the teaching of English in the academy; and second, they broke their attachment to the South as a geographical region. Ransom and Tate in particular physically moved out of the South and took up posts at academic institutions elsewhere. Despite their former attachment to the region, it had failed to satisfy their professional desires. Other regions offered greater rewards both in terms of financial benefits and intellectual resources. This problem was hotly debated in 1937 when Ransom was made an offer by Kenyon College which Vanderbilt University refused to match. For Tate in particular, this incident indicated that unlike other regions the South was not willing to provide support for a profession of intellectuals. Tate himself was having financial problems throughout this period. He could not support himself financially as a poet in the South. Consequently, he was not only forced to rely on short periods of teaching at various universities and colleges, but also on Northern publishing houses for the publication of his poetry. The two transitions were therefore connected. Vanderbilt's refusal to match the Kenyon offer only focused a general sense of dissatisfaction with their defence of the South. They became aware that while they were prepared to support the South, the South seemed unwilling to support them.

The period was not one of despondency though. The Kenyon offer showed that other opportunities were opening up. For example, this period also saw the founding of the *Southern Review*, by C. W. Pipkin, Robert Penn Warren, and Cleanth Brooks. There was a great deal of hope invested in this periodical by the group. It was seen, especially by Tate, as the opportunity for which they had long been waiting. As Agrarians, they had argued that the foundation of a Southern intellectual community depended upon the establishment of a properly funded periodical. Of course, the journal could not create such a community on its own, but it could publish material and provide a forum for dialogue. In so doing, it could generate a sense of common interests and identity.

Ransom, Tate and Warren's main activities during this period concerned the teaching of English in America. The political and economic crises of the 1930s had brought the function of literary education into question. With the rise of mass education, the existing forms of literary scholarship seemed to have little to offer the new student population, while those who argued that literary study should have some social relevance had little to offer in terms of either literary theory or teaching practice. In this context, Ransom, Tate and Warren were uniquely placed to offer an alternative. Throughout the late 1920s and early 1930s, they had criticized the existing approaches to literature offered by literary scholarship, Neo-Humanism and Stalinized Marxism. This work laid the foundations for a new approach which was to become popular as other intellectuals became disillusioned with the other existing approaches. In fact, in the case of Stalinized Marxism, they had identified many of the problems that led to this disillusionment, problems which were highlighted by the Moscow Trials, the Popular Front, and the restrictions imposed upon intellectual activities by their adherence to the party.

More importantly, Ransom, Tate and Warren were not only able to offer a purpose and a justification for the teaching of English, but also a specific teaching practice which they presented and illustrated through a series of text-books. Their objection to alternative approaches was that they were forms of positivism which were unable to identify the specificity of literary activity. Academic scholasticism, for example, did not study literary texts as literature, but merely concentrated on biographies of authors and the hunt for literary sources. It not only failed to adopt a critical position towards culture and society, but it ignored the process of literary production. Neo-Humanism and Stalinized Marxism, on the other hand, did adopt a critical relationship to culture and society, but they were also accused of ignoring the specificity of literary activity. They were solely concerned with the content of literature. According to the New Critics, these two groups sought to identify the values or messages of texts, and evaluated texts according to those values or messages. By contrast, the New Critics defined the linguistic forms of the text as the appropriate object of literary study. They argued that it was the way in which texts *used* their sources which was important, not their sources or their positions.

This position did not lead to a form of asocial formalism though. In the period after 1935, Ransom, Tate and Warren did not abandon their criticisms of modern America as Fekete and others claim. Their attempt to reorganize the teaching of English was merely a change of tactics. They hoped to establish an institutional basis for the distribution of their social and cultural criticism. After 1935, they consciously tried to develop a community of intellectuals through the establishment of periodicals such as the *Southern Review* and the *Kenyon Review*. They also collected the essays which they had written over the first half of the 1930s in order to identify the coherence of their position. Finally they struggled to alter the teaching of English. They delivered papers at the meetings of the Modern Language Association, and in 1938, Brooks and Warren published *Understanding Poetry*, the first of a series of text-books which presented a teaching practice which would disseminate their critical positions. These text-books were probably the single most important activity of the period. It was through these books that New Critical theories and methods were made available to most teachers and students. Unfortunately, the very success of these books has made it difficult for many later critics to see that they were more than a series of mechanical practices; that they involved specific critical positions which were based on the arguments developed during the late 1920s and early 1930s.

By the early 1940s, the New Critics were engaged in a struggle not only with the scholastic approach to English, but also with philosophical movements, such as logical positivism as represented by the work of Charles W. Morris.[1] Indeed Morris' work on language became a central text *against* which they defined their positions on the forms of language in literature and their relation to society. These struggles led to a symposium which was published jointly by the *Southern Review* and the *Kenyon Review*. It argued that criticism should be a vital element in the study of literature, and that it should become an independent activity within departments of English; that it was necessary to study the constitutive forms of literary activity. The success of these various activities changed the American academy and laid the foundations for contemporary criticism.

# 7 The origins of academic involvement

## Introduction

In the period between 1935 and 1938, Ransom, Tate and Warren did not abandon social and cultural criticism. They did shift from Agrarianism to an involvement in the debates over the teaching of English, but the goal of the latter activity was only seen as an intermediate one. It was hoped that the transformation of the academy would enable the distribution of their social and cultural criticism, and so encourage further social and cultural changes. The shift was not one of political position, but merely a tactical manoeuvre. They had simply identified a more immediate and practical way of promoting their position. In fact, rather than abandoning political activity, Ransom, Tate and Warren moved from an independent critical activity which only involved the writing of articles and participation in the occasional debate, and became active in a number of different areas. They consolidated their ideas in books, established organs of publication, and organized and agitated for institutional change.

These changes in activity were the result of many factors. Some changes, like their involvement in the publication of periodicals, were merely due to the opening up of opportunities. They had argued the need for a periodical since the late 1920s, but had not had the resources to achieve it. Their involvement in arguments over the teaching of English was partly due to their long running conflicts with other types of criticism, particularly over the issue of literary modernism. It was also provoked by the debates developing at the time. More generally, they were aware that Agrarianism had distracted them from their primary interest in literature. They were after all primarily literary critics and writers, not economic and social scientists. Agrarianism had taken up their time, but gained little success. By concentrating on the teaching of English, the three critics could not only concentrate on their primary interest – literature – they could also offer a coherent position which had a greater chance of success.

**The establishment of the critical quarterlies**

None of the editors of the *Southern Review* commented within the journal on its aims as a publication, but its interests were not limited to literature.[1] It contained a wide variety of articles on politics, society and culture. It did have a Southern emphasis, but it also included contributions from writers from outside the region, writers such as Kenneth Burke who were not interested in Southern issues, but who *were* respected by the editors.[2] In fact, the position of the magazine is best summed up by Allen Tate in his article, 'The Function of the Critical Quarterly', which appeared in the journal in 1936. The article deals with many of the issues that had preoccupied him throughout the 1930s. For example, it discusses the role of the critical quarterly within modern society, a society which, it is claimed, isolates writers from their public. The lay reader, Tate argues, had not been intimidated by literature in the past, but in modern society fact and value had become divorced from one another. In this situation, writers were forced to tackle ever more complex problems in their writing. The result was a difficult form of writing which alienated lay readers. It created a situation in which the communion between the reader and the writer is 'lost to us'.[3] In this context, it is claimed, the critical quarterly should investigate contemporary values, even though this would tend to alienate lay readers.[4] It should differ from the weekly and monthly publications which are mainly concerned with news and information. It had the time to develop terms of reference, or standards of judgement, which would enable the readers to make sense of the vast amounts of information with which they were confronted in modern society.[5]

This argument places Tate in a tricky position. He stresses that the quarterly should develop a coherent set of values, while also arguing that it should permit intellectual independence. His position is related to the economics of the quarterly though. He recognized that few good quarterlies have 'enough readers to pay the "cost of production." The quarterly must be subsidized; it either runs on a subsidy or does not run.'[6] Consequently the weekly and the monthly could usually pay more for contributions. As a result, if it is to have any hope of receiving a high standard of material, the quarterly has to develop a relationship with its contributors which is not primarily financial. The editor has to become a sympathetic and encouraging publisher who gives his contributors intellectual independence. This need not lead to intellectual anarchy within the journal though. If properly handled, Tate believed, it could create the conditions for a community of writers and intellectuals. By allowing intellectual independence, the journal should attract a high standard of writers, and create the conditions within which they could develop a shared sense of purpose and interests. Certainly the editors must choose the line they want to pursue and the people best able to follow it, but they must also give them a free rein. They must also encourage the individual interests of their contributors and accept as many contributions from them as possible. In this way, the fates of the quarterly and the contributors are mutually dependent. They can only generate coherent terms of reference and standards of judgement if the quarterly is able to generate a community of writers and intellectuals. If Tate is concerned with the independence of the writer here, he still maintained that this independence was a precondition for a critical analysis of society and culture, not an abandonment of social concerns; and that proper independence could only be established within specific social and cultural contexts.

The other periodical with which these writers were involved was the *Kenyon Review* which started its run in 1939.[7] Plans for it had begun in 1937 at the time of Ransom's appointment to Kenyon College, and Ransom had originally wanted Tate to join him as co-editor. Unfortunately, he was unable to raise the money to employ his friend. Financial reasons also meant that the *Kenyon Review* was a much smaller publication than the *Southern Review*. It was more narrowly focused on literary and philosophical criticism – though it did include some social and political articles, and some creative writing – and it lacked the Southern emphasis of the *Southern Review*.

The decision to leave the South and move to Kenyon College was a pivotal one for Ransom as an individual and for the group as a whole, and a public argument erupted over the manner in which the Southern institution, Vanderbilt College, which was Ransom's employer, refused to match the Kenyon offer.[8] The furore was largely organized by Tate who regarded it as a disgrace that the South would not provide the resources to make the region attractive to its own intellectuals. Ransom was not attracted to the Kenyon offer for purely financial reasons though. As Ransom wrote to Mims, the head of English at Vanderbilt University, on 8 June:

The difference between the Vanderbilt offer which I will receive and the Kenyon offer is...twofold; first, in the amount of salary; second, in the superior opportunity to work for myself.[9]

Not only was Ransom's work load smaller at Kenyon, allowing him more time to pursue his own writing, he had also been offered the chance to edit the *Kenyon Review*. This latter opportunity was deeply appealing to him. He saw it as a chance to challenge the standards of literary evaluation, and so counter the cultural values of modern society. Shortly after his letter to Mims was written, Ransom moved to Kenyon and began work on his book, *The World's Body*.[10]

## The clarification of theory

For Ransom and Tate, the importance of these quarterlies was that they would develop standards of judgement for both society and culture, but they also employed other tactics. In the mid-1930s, for example, they began to collect their social and cultural essays together with the aim of clarifying their theoretical positions. The result was two books: *Reactionary Essays on Poetry and Ideas* by Allen Tate which was published in 1936, and *The World's Body* by John Crowe Ransom which was published in 1938.

*Reactionary Essays* brought together many of the articles and reviews which Tate had written since the 1920s, and it offered a critique of modern society and a defence of literary modernism. In the preface, Tate clarifies the positions shared by the pieces, while offering a critique of the literary theory present in his own period. Contemporary criticism, he argued, should examine the problems faced by poets and by poetry in particular historical periods, and so provide terms of reference necessary for literary comprehension. It should not impose an abstract set of standards upon literature, but assess literature in relation to its social and cultural context. For Tate, poetic forms are related to their context, and modern criticism should not expect modern poets to write like the poets of the past. To put it another way, the 'duty of the modern critic [is] to notice the implication of the impossible, if only to warn the reader of modern verse, who is exasperated, that poets cannot write now like poets in 1579, or 1890'.[11] The problem was, he argued, that the criticism of his own period had failed to acknowledge the formal features of aesthetic activity, and it expected literature to conform to ahistorical and abstract concepts of form or content. It either dismissed modern poetry for not using the forms of the past, or for not conforming to its own abstract explanations of society. By contrast, Tate argued that while literature must always consider social experience, it should not be evaluated according to the programmes or positions it offers.[12] In fact, he saw poetry as a form which put abstract positions and programmes to the test of experience. It investigated values and identified their limits. It was in this sense that poetry was defined as 'ironic' in form. Poets were obliged to use abstract ideas, but they treated them 'ironically', acknowledging their limitations.[13] Tate's objection to the criticism of his own period was that its failure to identify the specificity of literary activity made it unable to understand the reasons modern poets developed certain forms within the context of modern society. It failed to see that modern society created problems for modern literature, problems which required new forms of writing.

Ransom's book, *The World's Body*, is often used by Fekete and others as evidence that Ransom lost interest in the relationship between literature and society after the mid-1930s, but like Tate's *Reactionary Essays*, it is mainly a collection of essays written and published during the early 1930s. The preface to the book also seeks to clarify the theoretical positions of the articles which are described as 'preparations for criticism, for the understanding and definition of the poetic effects'.[14] Poetry, it is argued, is an advance beyond science. It does not oppose science by seeking purity and innocence. It does not seek refuge from society and social activities in 'a private world where such injustice cannot be, and enjoys it as men enjoy their dream'.[15] Instead it confronts the forms of social life, and illustrates the limitations of social forms in a manner that calls for the construction of alternative ways of living. Most specifically, it recalls the richness and complexity of the world which is suppressed and forgotten by the scientific abstractions of the modern world.[16]

It is at this point that Ransom is often accused of retreating from social and political criticism. He argues that 'true poetry has no great interest in improving or idealizing the world, which does well enough. It only wants to realize the world, to see it better.'[17] Fekete, for example, takes this passage to mean that literature merely converts nature into an object of contemplation, and does not illustrate the need for social change. Such a reading takes the passage out of context though. In fact, for Ransom, the terms 'improvement' and 'idealisation' are associated with the abstractions of scientific positivism and its concepts of 'progress'. The aim of poetry is to overcome such abstractions; to acknowledge the richness and complexity of existence repressed by modern society; and so highlight the limitations of existing social forms. It seeks to remind the reader of the paradoxes and contradictions which scientific rationalism must forget, and so illustrates the need for social change. In this way, the interests of science and literature are opposed to one another according to Ransom. Unfortunately, while he still calls for a social order which would temper economic interests with aesthetic ones, he was beginning to see the conflict between economic and aesthetic motives as an eternal and irreconcilable contradiction within human existence, not the product of a specific social form.[18] None the less, the role of literary criticism was still to explain and evaluate literary forms as they developed and changed in relation to different social conditions.

### Criticism and the academy

These attempts to consolidate their theoretical positions were part of a new stage of activities for Ransom, Tate and Warren. They became involved in the struggles over the teaching of English, recognizing that the academy could offer a productive way of developing and distributing their social and cultural criticism. The shift to this stage was an important one for the three critics. Certainly they had worked as university teachers before, but the academy had not been the organizational basis of their critical activities, nor their primary audience. Instead they had relied on intellectual journals such as *New Republic, American Review, Sewannee Review,* and the *Virginia Quarterly Review,* and various independent intellectuals inside and outside the academy. Their alliances and their audiences were composed of small groups of intellectuals, and a largely unorganized reading public. The problem with this situation (as they had pointed out again and again throughout the 1920s and 1930s) was that it made an effective and coherent distribution of their ideas virtually impossible. This was one reason why they had failed to create an organized movement as Agrarians. The attraction of the academy was that it seemed to offer an alternative to this situation. It had a ready-made organizational basis and an almost captive audience. If the university departments of English could be persuaded to accept their critical theories as the basis for literary education and study, Ransom, Tate and Warren believed that it would establish a firm foundation for the development and dissemination of their positions.

For this reason, in 1936 papers were given at the meeting of the Modern Language Association by Tate, and by Brooks and Warren. These papers were on the analysis of modern poetry and they rehearsed many of the critical positions which these critics had developed during the late 1920s and early 1930s. For example, Tate's paper, 'Modern Poets and Conventions', was a defence of modern forms of poetry which tried to explain how these poems could be considered to be traditional. The poetry of T. S. Eliot, it was pointed out, is very different from the poetry which Eliot praises in his critical writings, and Tate asks what would make a traditionalist such as Eliot use the literary forms associated with modern poetry.[19] In answer, Tate stresses that literary forms are always historically specific – that they are always produced in relation to specific social and cultural contexts – and that the literary forms of the past are not applicable to the problems posed by modern society.[20] Traditionalism is not, for Tate, a repetition of past conventions which become redundant when used out of context. Modern literature is traditional, he argues, because it entails a critical and ironic attitude which highlights the limitations of contemporary social forms by comparing these with the forms of the past.[21] This argument not only sought to convince the teachers of English that modern poetry was valid as a form, but also that the New Criticism offered the best methods for understanding literature and its relation to society.

Brooks and Warren's contribution, 'The Reading of Modern Poetry', is also significant. Like Tate's paper, it is a clarification of their critical methods. In fact, it explains the theoretical positions which were to underpin their text-book, *Understanding Poetry*. It argues that while modern poetry had been criticized by a number of different groups, there was little agreement between these groups. These groups not only disagreed about the actual faults of modern poetry, but also about the forms which were appropriate to poetry.[22] In fact, there was not even any clear agreement over what it was that constituted poetry as a form. This lack of agreement was worrying to Brooks and Warren who argued that it constituted the central problem in any theoretical discussion of poetry. Unless one is able to identify the specificity of poetry, they argue, there is no way of evaluating poetry *as* poetry. This attempt to identify the specificity of poetic activity leads them to define certain aspects as external to the poem or poetry in general. For example, while they acknowledge that the poem's context and sources are inextricably related to the process of literary production, they stress that these aspects are not poetic in themselves. These aspects may be essential to an understanding of a poem, but they are not that which makes the poem poetic. Brooks and Warren also distinguish the 'proper reading' (or critical interpretation) of a poem from 'the types of misreading that derive from stock responses and the reader's personal history'.[23] In this case, they suggest that as the poem is always a form of communication – a process which includes both the moments of production and consumption – it cannot ever be reduced to a matter of individual response. Instead it is necessary to concentrate on the linguistic processes in relation to which these individual responses are formed. It was these distinctions which Wimsatt and Beardsley refer to as 'the Intentional Fallacy' and 'the Affective Fallacy', but it should be clear that they were not intended to disconnect the poem from its conditions of production or consumption, but to focus criticism upon the specificity of literary activity; to identify the textual processes in relation to which literary production and consumption were defined. Only then, it is argued, could one study poetry without reducing poetic forms to a mere expression of their context, or to a matter of purely individual response. In fact, for Brooks and Warren, such forms of reductionism were both types of positivism. They created a division between production and consumption, the abstract and the concrete, the social and the individual, fact and value. By contrast, Brooks and Warren want to challenge and overcome such theoretical oppositions and they 'summarize these two general types of misreading by saying that the first involves the substitution of an *a priori* informational frame of reference for the poetic reading, and the second involves the substitution of an *a priori* emotional frame of reference'.[24]

In response to these approaches, Brooks and Warren argue that the poem should be seen as an 'organic' whole. It was more than the sum of its parts and could not be reduced to its elements. The poem was a specific process of production which used its elements, but placed them in a series of complex relationships, relationships which forced one to see these elements in new ways.[25] It was the productivity of these relationships which was distinctly poetic, not the elements themselves. As Brooks and Warren state: 'the poetic effect is always dependent upon relationships'.[26] They also illustrate the strength of this position through a discussion of literary modernism. The obscurity and difficulty of Eliot's poetry, they argue, was not a mere affectation, but must be understood in relation to the context of modern society. The culture of the modern world, it is claimed, is confused and incoherent, and modern poets have to struggle harder than their predecessors and adopt new poetic forms if they are to make sense of their context.[27] This position clearly considers literary activity in relation to its social context, even if it refused to reduce literature to a mere expression of that context. It recognizes that literature is a specific process of production which does not only reflect, but also interprets its context.

In autumn 1937, Ransom also addressed the role and practice of criticism in an article, 'Criticism, Inc.', which he included in *The World's Body*. This essay clarifies many of the motives behind the New Critics' attempt to transform the teaching of English. Criticism, it argues, had never had a proper organizational basis. It had largely been practised by amateurs, and this situation had meant that it had never been adequately defined as an activity. According to Ransom, this failure had to be rectified. Modern society, he argues, brought about a loss of standards which made an organized practice of criticism essential. If criticism could organize and define itself, it could not only protect itself from this loss of standards, but also provide a challenge to the society which produced them. The task of organizing criticism, it is argued, was best performed by one of three groups – the artist, the philosopher, and the university professor of literature – and Ransom assesses the potential of each. The artist, he argues, was mainly intuitive as a critic, while the philosopher was too concerned with general questions, rather than literary ones. Consequently, he states that

it is from the professors of literature, in this country the professors of English for the most part, that I should hope eventually for the erection of intelligent standards of criticism. It is their business.[28]

Unfortunately, he argues that this group had generally avoided criticism. Instead, they had concentrated on the accumulation of historical and biographical information.[29]

As a result, Ransom does not regard reading and criticism as natural or unproblematic activities. On the contrary, he recognizes that specific forms of reading are produced in specific social contexts. As a result, he believed that it was necessary to promote specific types of reading and criticism as a challenge to those which were dominant within modern society, and the departments of English were the best site from which to promote them. The types of reading and criticism which he sought to promote were quite specific. In fact, he makes a distinction between appreciation and criticism. The first, he claims, is largely private and intuitive, while the second is public and objective. It studies the forms of literary activity, rather than simply deriving pleasure from those activities. Criticism is also distinguished from paraphrase, history, the linguistic identification of allusions and uncommon words, moral or ethical evaluation, or 'Any other special studies which deal with some abstract or prose content taken out of the work.'[30] For Ransom, criticism is a specific mode of inquiry, and must organize itself as such. For this reason, he is opposed to the claim of Austin Warren that criticism could be taught within the day-to-day activities of the departments of English. Criticism needed to clarify and define itself first. It should not be subordinated to other activities, but concentrate its energies on its specific task: the examination of that which constitutes literature. To this end, Ransom distinguishes poetry from prose, claiming that the poetic device is 'trying to represent that [which] cannot be represented by prose'.[31] Here poetry is associated with the literary, and prose with non-literary forms such as scientific discourse. Certainly Ransom recognized the existence of literary forms of prose, but he suggests that while scientific discourse is primarily concerned with the information and abstract categories which compose the content of the text, literary discourse 'celebrates the object which is real, individual, and qualitatively infinite'.[32] Literary discourse is distinguished from scientific discourse by its concern with the materiality of language. The elements which distinguish it are 'for the laws of prose logic, its superfluity; and I think I would say even its irrelevance'.[33] Literary discourse concentrates on its linguistic forms: its materiality and its figurative aspects. These forms, which Ransom refers to as the poet's 'irrelevance, or tissues', are said to work by 'elaborating or individualizing the universal, the core-object; likewise all [its] material detail'.[34] This position not only draws upon the critique of scientific rationality which Ransom had developed during the Agrarian movement, but it also anticipates many subsequent theories developed by himself, Tate and Warren.

## Conclusion

In 'Criticism, Inc.', Ransom also makes reference to an article by R. S. Crane which indicates that he was aware of the struggles being waged over the teaching of English.[35] Then, in January 1938, he wrote a letter to Tate in which he commented on the meeting of the Modern Language Association in Chicago, from which he had just returned: 'The professors are in an awful dither, trying to reform themselves and there's a big stroke possible for a small group that knows what it wants in giving them ideas and definition and showing the way.'[36] This recognition is of central importance. It illustrates that Ransom saw the possibility of a tactical manoeuvre by which the group could offer their own critical positions as a solution to this confusion. He was uncertain, however, whether they should organize as a tactical minority, or seek to define the dominant forms of critical activity. None the less, he suggested that they should organize a tactical intervention in these debates for the following year: 'Shall we be independent Chinese war lords, or shall we come in and run the government? Another question of strategy. There's so much congenial revolutionary spirit in the MLA that there's really something there to capitalize.'[37] By 1937, then, the group had come to regard the departments of English as the best location for the development and distribution of their social and cultural criticism. Their involvement in the academy was not an abandonment of the interests which motivated them as Agrarians. Instead they saw this manoeuvre as a way of promoting these interests, and establishing support for social change.

# 8 Understanding literature: textbooks and the distribution of the New Criticism

## Introduction

In 1938, *Understanding Poetry* was published. Written by Brooks and Warren, it was the first of a series of text-books which trained students in the New Critical approach to literary study. The importance of these books was immense. They did more than merely defend a particular theoretical approach. They presented a clear pedagogical practice. For this reason, these text-books probably did more to establish the New Criticism within the departments of English than any other activity. *Understanding Poetry*, for example, was designed to clarify the poetic features of poetry for the student. In the process, it challenged alternative approaches and associated these with positivism or idealism. 'Literary communication', it was argued, was not primarily concerned with the transmission of information, nor with the presentation of pure emotion, beauty or truth. It was an organic form which was not distinguished by the presence of any specific feature or quality, but by the complex relationships between its elements.

This position did not isolate the literary text from its context. On the contrary, it stressed that not only were specific literary forms produced in relation to specific social contexts, but also that literature should be engaged with significant social issues. They simply objected to alternative approaches which saw literary texts as transparent or expressive forms. For Brooks and Warren, literature was not just a product of its context, but also a productive activity which responded to that context in a critical manner. This productive activity also meant that it should not be evaluated on the basis of any statements or propositions which it might offer. Literary value resided in the way in which a text re-examined its materials, the way in which it related its materials to one another in new and complex ways. The literary process of production, it was argued, investigated social forms in relation to their complex social and material contexts. It acknowledged the paradoxes and contradictions which modern society sought to repress. In this way, it illustrated the limitations of existing social forms and identified the need for social change. Significantly, this position

81

itself was not so much stated as illustrated. Brooks and Warren presented their case to the student and teachers by developing it through a series of concrete studies and analyses.

## The nature of the organic text

Brooks and Warren published several text-books on the study of literature, but the two which had the greatest impact were *Understanding Poetry* (1938), and *Understanding Fiction* (1943). The purpose of each book was to identify the constitutive forms of their specific object of study, though they also address more general questions. Both books, for example, distinguish the object of literary study from other forms of communicative activity. This attempt to define the specificity of literature does not isolate it from its social and cultural context though. In the case of poetry, for example, Brooks and Warren stress that 'poetry is not a thing separate from ordinary life and that the matters with which poetry deals are matters with which the ordinary person is concerned'.[1] Literature, it is argued, offers knowledge of the world. It is distinguished from other forms of discourse by its form, not its subject matter. If literature was different in form from other types of discourse throughout history, it always acquired different forms within specific historical contexts. Brooks and Warren acknowledged – even emphasized – that literary forms changed and developed; that the forms which were appropriate to one society were not necessarily appropriate to another. If literature was a specific form of activity, it was also one which was defined within social and historical contexts.[2]

In the attempt to identify the specificity of literary activity, it is pointed out that not all forms of communication are primarily concerned with the transmission of information. Some, for example, are largely meant to affirm interpersonal relations:

we may do well to ask how much of the discourse of an average man in any given day is primarily concerned with information for the sake of information. After he has transacted his business, obeyed road signs, ordered and eaten his dinner, and read the stock-market reports, he might be surprised to reflect on the number of nonpractical functions speech had fulfilled for him that day. He had told the office boy a joke; he had commented on the weather to the traffic officer, who could observe the weather as well as he; he had told an old friend that he was glad to see him again; he had chatted with his wife on some subject on which there was already full knowledge and agreement.[3]

Even in the kinds of discourse which are primarily concerned with the transmission of information, it is argued, other considerations are always present. While one may transmit information in good faith, the meaning of that information is always linked to its context within specific human interests. Knowledge, it is argued, is always tied to human interests. For example, Brooks and Warren use the example of a car driver who asks for information about the quality of a road from two different road users:

Both the man on the haywagon and the man in the second automobile think that they are telling the truth. Both intend to be helpful and to give exact information. And both feel that they know the road. But each man's language reflects his own experience with the road. For the man on the hay wagon the road *was* tolerably good, but for the second motorist, anxious to make time on his trip, the road was devilishly bad.[4]

For Brooks and Warren, even scientific discourse cannot limit itself to pure information. It must include literary forms. It is always bound to make evaluations and interpretations. It can never be purely factual.

None the less, they do contrast the forms of scientific discourse and literary discourse. Scientific discourse, it is argued, must limit the context of specific objects and events and repress both the linguistic connotations and the reference of its terms, while literary discourse is preoccupied with the non-informational aspects of language and the contexts upon which specific objects and events depend. The analysis of literary discourse, they insist, should not be concerned simply to identify a message within the text, but with the linguistic processes through which issues were examined. It was not that Brooks and Warren see social issues as irrelevant to literature. On the contrary, they stress that literature should deal with important issues. They merely state that the importance of an issue was not itself a measure of a text's literary value. In this way, forms of literary analysis which defined literary texts as merely expressive forms are attacked for failing to acknowledge the materiality of texts as linguistic processes. For this reason, Brooks and Warren also claim that the literary text does not simply express the feelings of a writer in the same way as a burst of tears might express sadness or pain, nor could it recapture or express an experience in the same way as it was experienced. Literary activity, it is argued, is always a productive activity. It is obliged by its very nature to examine its materials. It does not simply express some message, feeling or experience, but must always involve an interpretation. Theories which defined literature and art as the 'pure realization' of beauty, or truth, are also challenged. For Brooks and Warren, literature could not be limited to beauty or truth. To examine the conditions of human existence, it should acknowledge the ugly as well as the beautiful, and it could not rely on abstract notions of truth. In conclusion, they claim that literary value does not reside in any one feature, material or subject matter, but in the linguistic processes of literary production. It was only through these processes that the features, materials and subject matter are examined. For this reason, they maintain that it is these processes which should be the object of literary study.

This position leads them to claim that the literary text is organic in form. Their contention is that the relationship between meaning and form is not a mechanical one. The form is not an object which contains a fixed meaning, but a process that produces it. The literary form is organic in so far as its elements were all interrelated, and its meaning was not merely an abstractable content.[5] Hence their objection to the 'heresy of paraphrase'. Given their claim that the poem was an integrated whole in which form and content could not be separated, they also insist that its meaning could not be reduced to a paraphrase. This approach also means that there can be no ideal form. One could not judge literary works on the basis of whether they compared or failed to compare to some abstract standard of literary form. Each poem must struggle to achieve its own unity through its use of various elements such as narrative, description, tone, imagery, and sound patterns. This struggle for unity is not merely a technical process though. It is an attempt to examine a specific issue. For Brooks and Warren, literature must have a meaning and significance though they also stressed that it was not the specific conclusion reached upon any specific issue which was of importance, but the quality of the process through which the issue was examined. Good literature, it was claimed, did not offer easy solutions, but acknowledged the difficulties of moral decisions and actions. It is in this sense that they claim that literature is ironic in character. It acknowledges that there are no absolute certainties. It rejects abstract solutions. Instead it examines the paradoxes and contradictions of specific issues or situations. As they put it, 'certainty can only come in terms of the [literary] process, and must be *earned*, as it were, through the process'.[6] In this way they do not reject attempts to resolve specific issues or problems. They merely argue that any resolution must be justified through an engagement with paradoxes and contradictions, not their repression. The appeal of the term 'irony' is that it covers both the form and the content of literature. It describes both the technical devices and the attitude which they establish:

They wanted a term which would accommodate reference to details of style, definition of character, symbolic force of action, and the like, as well as to the ordering of ideas and attitudes involved in the works. And the ordinary distinction between irony as a device and irony as a mode seemed to make possible the use of the term in this connection without too much wantonness.[7]

This position is clearly connected to these writers' Agrarian positions. It defines literature in opposition to the abstractions of capitalist relations. Literature, it is claimed, rejects abstract solutions by highlighting the paradoxes and contradictions of the material and cultural contexts of human action. In both the Agrarian and New Critical periods, aesthetic activity was seen by these writers as a critical activity in which writers take an ironic attitude to their society and culture, and so identify both their strengths and their limitations. Unlike the cash-nexus and scientific positivism, the ironic attitude of aesthetic activity acknowledges the limits of the capitalist will to power, and calls for the construction of an alternative way of life.

As a result, literature is never a purely personal activity for Brooks and Warren. The act of writing is always a social and cultural one. Writers always work with a language which is not solely their own. It is made up of structures, meanings and values from which the author can never escape, but must confront in the act of writing. For example, they point out that one such structure is that of an implied addressee in any text. However personal a text may be, the authors must always address themselves to a hypothetical other.[8] As a result, the use of language, particularly in literary activity, is always a social and cultural activity. For this reason, they are concerned to clarify the importance of history to the understanding of a literary text. While they stress that literary activity is always an engagement with the social and cultural values of its historical period, they distinguish between the text and its historical context. This did not result in an ahistorical and asocial formalism. On the contrary while the historical context was indispensable to the understanding of a literary text for Brooks and Warren, they also claimed that the literary process of production meant that the text could never be reduced to that context.[9] They do acknowledge that it is difficult to identify any precise point at which the process of literary production begins and the context ends, but this does not trouble them greatly. In fact they argue that the 'important thing is to see some line of connection between the experience and the poem which in its finished form interprets the experience'.[10] For Brooks and Warren, just as there is no ideal form, so there is no ideal process of literary production. All writers differ in their practice of writing. Some take a great deal of time in preparation and rewriting, while some seem to compose almost spontaneously. Even the apparently spontaneous text is, they claim, the product of a process of production though. There is no radical division between the conscious and the unconscious aspects of the productive process, and the spontaneous text may be the product of a long series of unconscious processes. This does not mean that the spontaneous act of literary production is independent of conscious thought. For Brooks and Warren, there is a continuous interplay between conscious and un-conscious processes. The spontaneous text is no more free of conscious control than the carefully prepared text is free of unconscious elements.

These problems are also related to the problem of defining poetic intention and meaning. As has been seen, Brooks and Warren reject the claims that literature was merely an expression of a statement. Instead they defined it as an exploration of 'the possibility of imagination and language'.[11] Moreover, their claim that the literary text was an organic form meant that, like de Man, they argued that literary meaning and intention could not be isolated from the process of production itself. As they put it, the poet cannot 'envisage the poem as the architect can envision the house', and until 'the poem is actually written down to the last word, the poet cannot be sure exactly what it will mean'.[12] The total meaning of the text is not reducible to the initial ideas or plans which motivated the activity of writing, but may even contradict those original ideas and plans.

### The New Critical pedagogy

As a result, Brooks and Warren's text-books seek to focus the student on the process of literary production. The teacher, they argue, should not try to show that individual literary texts can be enjoyable, but instead train the student to understand the formal aspects of literary texts, or 'literariness'. To this end, the books include comparisons between different texts as well as individual analyses. Their aim was not only to encourage students to understand how individual texts work, but also to clarify the process of literary evaluation. Through the practice of intensive or close reading, it is hoped that students will begin to distinguish between different texts, not on the basis of their subject matter alone, but also on the basis of their formal features. It was for this reason that Brooks and Warren promoted the practice of intensive or close reading, not because they were only interested in the analysis of individual texts. Quite the reverse; they saw it as the only way to train students to understand the linguistic processes which defined literary production in general.

It is generally agreed that these books revolutionized the teaching of English in America, but it is also important to recognize quite how they did this. Previously, the study of literature had been primarily concerned with philological questions or with historical source hunting. As Gerald Graff claims, '"literary studies" was established before it began to tackle literature as its subject'.[13] In philological scholarship, literature was used as documentary evidence in the study of etymology and grammar. Even those who opposed the philological approach did not associate literary study with the analysis of literary language. They regarded literature 'as a moral and spiritual force and as a repository of "general ideas" which could be applied directly to the conduct of life and the improvement of national culture'.[14] For Brooks and Warren, both these approaches failed to identify the specificity of literature as an object of study. In response, Brooks and Warren's method sought to train students to identify the constitutive features of literature, or 'literariness'.

The nature of this revolution in the teaching of English can also be clarified through an examination of the text-books and teaching guides which were being used prior to 1938. Such a study does present certain problems, but even these problems can be informative. The first problem is that the sheer number of publications make it difficult to assess which works, if any, represent the most typical or common types of educational practice, a problem which is further complicated by the fact that many of these titles are not readily available for study.[15] Of those which are available, one is primarily concerned with composition,[16] while others see the study of literature as a way of training the student in composition skills.[17] Those that concentrate on literature itself fall into two groups: those which are primarily theoretical introductions to the study of literature, and those which are primarily anthologies. There is little attempt to combine these two approaches, as Brooks and Warren did, except to the extent that the former use examples to illustrate their points, and the latter set tasks for the student to perform. Even in this latter case, these tasks only test the students' understanding of technique and information. They are only concerned with the students' general linguistic competence, not their understanding of the 'literariness' of literature. In fact, none of these books is primarily concerned with this form of understanding. Even Macpherson, who does address the structural and formal aspects of literary texts, does so in a way which is basically technical in approach.[18] His work is an example of the approach which sees literary form as merely an object in which the meaning is contained, or through which that meaning is expressed. All these examples suggest that the study of literature is related to humanistic concerns, but they fail to clarify this relation except in so far as they claim that 'reading maketh a full man'.[19] These problems should present no surprise though. The reason for the impact of the New Critical text-books was that they appeared at a time when there was no coherent practice for the teaching of literature *as literature*. Their strength was that they addressed this absence, and presented a series of pedagogical activities which could be used both inside and outside the classroom. More than any other New Critical activity, these text-books were responsible for redefining the object of literary study. They directed attention to the linguistic forms of the text, and defined the terms of reference within which literary studies largely continues to operate.

The teaching of literature, according to Brooks and Warren, should not simply accept the students' interests but develop them. It should clarify the relation between literary and human interests. Certainly students may have particular interests – they may have a preference for adventure stories over other types of literature – but they will still make distinctions between individual examples of the genre, distinctions which will be based on a wider set of interests than those concerned with adventure alone. The task of literary education was to get the student to examine this wider set of interests, and this will lead the student to tackle questions of form and its relation to subject matter.[20] Brooks and Warren do acknowledge that students may regard the effect of this training as a loss initially – it may seem to limit their areas of enjoyment by making them critical of writing which they had previously liked – but, according to Brooks and Warren, it is actually a widening of their interest and involvement in literature. It will show that they can find aspects to value in other types of literature.[21] None the less, critical training was not simply seen as a way of increasing the students' appreciation of literature. It was also seen in broader social and political terms. Through the study of literary form, students would be made aware of the paradoxes and contradictions repressed by capitalist rationality. They would be forced to investigate the values of their society and culture, and as a result, the study of literature would lead the student to 'an appreciation of the more broadly human values'.[22]

### Conclusion

These books were highly successful in distributing the positions of the New Critics, and in providing a clear pedagogical practice for the development of the student's critical faculties. However, they were only seen as the first stage in the education of the student. They were only meant to identify the object of literary study. Having identified the 'literariness' of literature, it was hoped that the student would read more widely, and begin to engage with the various problems raised by literary texts. The process of intensive or close reading was not an attempt to seal the text off from its context, but an introduction to the reading of literature *as* literature. The student was not supposed to abandon this approach altogether at later stages, but it was not an end in itself. It was supposed to direct students to an awareness of the paradoxes and contradictions of social and cultural activity, and hence to a critical engagement with their society and culture.

For this reason, Brooks and Warren did not see the organic text as a fixed, self-contained object. They explicitly stated that it was not a fixed object, but a series of interrelations, and that the meaning of the text could not be separated from these interrelations. It was not a statement or a paraphrasable content, but a process of production which took account of the paradoxes and contradictions repressed by capitalist rationality. As a result, the books were not an abdication of social and political involvement, but a critique of modern society and culture, a critique which not only sought to convince through argument, but also through a specific pedagogical practice. It was hoped that through their approach to the study of literature, students would develop specific cultural values which were opposed to the values of capitalist relations.

# 9 The form of criticism

## Introduction

By the late 1930s, Ransom, Tate and Warren were deeply involved in the struggle to establish their approach to literary study within the academy. In the process, their approach came to be known simply as 'criticism' in contrast to other approaches such as philology or historical source hunting. Yet the essays from this period are often used as evidence that they lost an interest in the relationship between literature and society. As a result, it is necessary to re-examine the theoretical struggles within which they were engaged in order to illustrate both the political nature of their intervention within the academy, and their continued interest in the relationship between literature and society. During the late 1930s, as had been the case in earlier periods, these writers challenged the claims of positivism which they associated with capitalist relations, but their particular targets became the theories of the logical positivists and the scholastic methods employed by most of the professors of English. None the less, they were careful to point out that these two approaches were only symptoms of a larger problem – the positivism of modern society. As before, their arguments had two main themes. First, they claimed that the form of literary discourse was different from the form of scientific discourse; that its language was different and it offered a different type of knowledge. Second, they argued that the object of literary study should be the linguistic forms of literary discourse, not merely the accumulation of historical information.

Ransom tried to clarify these positions in the late 1930s and early 1940s in articles such as 'Shakespeare at Sonnets', but he seems to have been particularly excited by the work of Charles W. Morris. Morris' work, he believed, enabled him to develop a critique of the logical positivists' theories of language and art. On 29 March 1939, for example, he wrote a letter to Tate in which he mentioned *The Encyclopedia of Unified Science*:[1]

The Morris one is really brilliant; he makes Richards look mighty small; his definition of designatum and denotatum would have special bearing on your topic, and in fact it's my feeling that now, with these definitive treatments of semantical and logical problems, the science boys have delivered themselves into our hands.[2] For Ransom, this was an opportunity to justify his claim that literary activity was not concerned with the transmission of positive information, but with an exploration of the figurative aspects of language, an exploration which identified the limits of rational discourse and action and required the reconstruction of an alternative way of living to that of modern society. Similar arguments were also developed by Tate during this period, and in 1938, he published two essays in which it was claimed that poetic form was not primarily concerned with the denotative or referential functions of language, but with language's figurative aspects. For Tate, it was through an investigation of these figurative aspects and their limits that literature was able to offer a form of knowledge which was different from that offered by scientific discourse.

By 1940, Tate found himself working at Princeton, and at odds with the scholastic approach to literature practised by many of the professors of English there. Consequently, in April of that year, he delivered a paper at the English Club which sparked a debate on the future and value of scholastic approaches. In response to these debates, the autumn editions of the *Southern Review* and the *Kenyon Review* jointly published a symposium on the topic, entitled 'Literature and the Professors'. This symposium attempted to define the object of literary study and the specific modes of activity appropriate to the teaching of English. It included a wide variety of writers and critics, but it was Ransom, Tate and Warren whose concerns drew the group together and gave it a coherent focus.

### Positivism, language and art

In 1939, Ransom began to develop his critique of positivism through an engagement with the work of C. W. Morris and the Chicago school of logical positivism. He sought to distinguish the forms of aesthetic and scientific discourse from one another according to their linguistic features and the objects of knowledge which were constructed by these features. He did not adopt 'a science of the text' or begin to mirror the forms of scientific positivism as Fekete and others have suggested, but as in earlier periods of his career, he continued to define his own position, and that of aesthetic activity, in opposition to the claims of positivism. His engagement with Morris began in the spring 1939 and the winter 1940 editions of the *Kenyon Review*, and it was continued by Tate in his article 'Literature as Knowledge', and by Ransom in his book, *The New Criticism*. For Ransom, art and science can be distinguished according to their very different objects of knowledge. The language of art is not concerned with the imitation of an object or its value, but with the figurative aspects of language, or the trope. Its exploration of these figures identifies the limits of rational structures. This position bears strong similarities to the deconstructive critique of language. In fact, like deconstruction, Ransom's position associates representation with the will to power of rationalism, as can be seen in his discussion of James Joyce, a discussion which has strong parallels with the positions of Paul de Man in his book, *Allegories of Reading*.[3] Of course, this should be no surprise given that during this period Ransom was working to define the terms of reference for literary study in the academy, terms of reference which defined the preconditions for forms of post-structuralist criticism such as deconstruction.

In the first of the two pieces in the *Kenyon Review*, Ransom attacks Morris for associating art with science. In opposition, Ransom claims that the pure sciences and art are governed by different rules, and cannot be linked together.[4] This leads him to consider the way in which other writers and critics had discussed the relationship between the two. Hegel, for example, is said to have seen art as a '*decorative* or "sensuous" version of science',[5] while Richards is supposed to have seen it as an 'emotional version'. By contrast, the logical positivist concentration on the relationship between forms of language and forms of knowledge is said to have created the opportunity to identify the difference between art and science in formal terms.[6] For Ransom, scientific discourse represses the figurative aspects of language in its preoccupation with the referencing of positive or empirical data. Aesthetic discourse, by contrast, is seen as concentrating on these figurative aspects of language. It examines the materiality and productivity of language in order to identify the possibilities and limits of rational discourse. In so doing, it produces an object of knowledge which is different to that of science, an object of knowledge which is not defined by an abstract meaning or use but one which acknowledges the paradoxes and contradictions of human activity. It is in this sense that Ransom refers to the aesthetic object of knowledge as 'a singular and individual object'.[7] It is not that he defines it as a self-contained form which exists independent of its context. Instead he sees it as a concrete and complex object which cannot be reduced to a single abstract meaning or use. Aesthetic discourse offers knowledge, but not through reference to some external object or process. It is a linguistic form which offers knowledge of its own processes.

Ransom's position is clarified in his critique of Morris's theory of aesthetics, and particularly Morris' definition of the art-work as icon. According to Ransom, Morris' position links art with science because it is still concerned with the practical possibilities of objects. Ransom concedes that Morris claims that the icon does not denote an object, but he objects that, for Morris, it still denotes 'the *value* of an object'.[8] Morris defines the object as an object of use. In response, Ransom does not dispense with the view of the art-work as icon, but argues that it has three levels of meaning. The first is concerned with the particularity of the object prior to its reduction to an object of use. This object is referred to as 'the sentimental object', and for Ransom, 'our affection is an attachment to its whole objective character'.[9] The second level is that at which this object is related to rational structures which define its value in terms of use and practicality.[10] The third and final level of the art-work is the level which is specific to art. It is the level at which the previous two are related or placed in tension. As Ransom puts it: 'The work of art symbolizes the reduction of the material world by the power of structure; or symbolizes the power of the material world to receive a rational structure and still maintain its particularity.'[11] This argument dates back to 1926 when Ransom was working on his book, *The Third Moment*. It defines aesthetic discourse as a form which dramatizes the tension between the image and the idea, experience and abstraction, and pure and impure forms. It claims that aesthetic discourse identifies the limits of rational structures and action.

In his discussion of James Joyce's *Finnegans Wake*, for example, Ransom maintains that Joyce is constantly interrupting or deconstructing language in order to question the structures of modern society. According to Ransom, discussions of Joyce fall into two main groups. On the one hand, some critics see the novel's stylistic features as a mere irritation without any relation to the content of the work. On the other hand, while some recognize that the stylistic features imply a thorough-going attack on modern society, they have too great an investment in modern society to accept the implications of this attack.[12] By contrast, Ransom sees the novel as a major work specifically because of the way in which its stylistic features undermine the ideals of progress and rationality by examining paradoxes and contradictions which these ideals need to repress.[13] In this way, Joyce becomes an exemplary case for Ransom who is able to show that the critical aspects of the novel are not presented as propositions, but through the use of language. Joyce's use of puns and the fluidity of his language constantly divert the referential aspects of language, and reveal the complex contradictory linguistic processes which rational discourse attempts to suppress. Like de Man, Ransom develops this position through a discussion of the pun and its relation to Euclidian geometry:

In Euclid, or for that matter in non-Euclidean geometry, it is said: let $a$ be this, and let $b$ be that; the terms remain fixed in their meanings throughout the problem. But $a$ has a homophone somewhere, or at least $b$ has, and puns are possible since there are terms of like sound to these terms, and by these tricks Joyce is equal to providing enough distraction to drown the original operation.[14]

This use of stylistic 'irrelevance' as a means of undermining the referential and rational aspects of language is not something which Ransom sees as unique to Joyce's writing though. For Ransom, Joyce's writing is merely an overt example of the features which define aesthetic discourse in general.

For example, a similar position is developed in Ransom's article, 'Shakespeare at Sonnets', in which he is critical of Shakespeare's poetry. For Ransom, the weakness of the sonnets is that they do not develop an 'objective' form, but rely on impressionism and subjectivism. For Ransom, language is not a medium of individual expression, but a social form; and poets should not use it to try to express their own impressions or subjective states. Instead, they should examine its form. They should develop and pursue its figures to their limits. Approaches to literature which see it as an expressive form merely act to ignore or repress its figurative processes. In this way, he distinguishes between subjective and objective forms of poetry, but he does not mean objective in a scientific sense. The objective form of poetry is defined as a poetry of knowledge, but its form of knowledge is directly opposed to the knowledge available in scientific discourse. Objective poetry is objective because it recognizes the suprapersonal nature of language; and while it gives knowledge, it does so through an investigation of its own status as language, not through reference to some external object.[15]

### Origins and forms

In the late 1930s and early 1940s, Tate continued to develop his literary theory in opposition to the positivism of alternative approaches. Most particularly, he argued that the object of literary analysis should be the formal features of texts, not their 'origins'. The essays in which this position is developed are often used as evidence that Tate was not interested in the relationship between literature and society, and that he saw texts as fixed, self-contained objects. In fact, the positions developed in these essays have a strong line of continuity with the social and cultural criticism which Tate had developed in the early 1930s. Rather than attempting to detach the text from its social context, he merely sought to define the relationship between text and context in order to identify the proper object of critical attention. He opposed forms of literary study which ignored the linguistic forms of the text and defined literature as a merely expressive form. He did not argue that the 'origins' of the work were unimportant, but that a literary text could not be *explained* by its 'origins': that it is a productive process which could not be simply reduced to its materials. In fact, like Ransom, he defined literary discourse in opposition to scientific discourse. Literary discourse, he argued, focused on the figurative features of language which rational discourse attempts to suppress, and in so doing, it identifies the limits of rationality itself. As a result, Tate's work of the period was part of the process by which the New Critics transformed the teaching of English. They defined the linguistic forms of the text as the proper object for literary study, and so laid the foundations for later developments such as post-structuralism. Consequently, it is hardly surprising that Tate defined the appropriate object of critical attention in ways that are very similar to many of the post-structuralist critics who are so eager to distance themselves from the New Criticism.

In fact, while Tate's disinterest in the 'origins' of a literary text is usually read as a disinterest in social and political issues, it was actually directed at both psychological discussions which concentrated on the personality of the author, and historical scholarship which was merely concerned with the accumulation of information about the materials of the text. For Tate, both approaches failed to take account of the process of literary production, and focused on details which did not even necessarily have any discernible relation to the text itself. They were not concerned with literary activity, but with other issues which may or may not have any significant relation to the text itself. Tate explores these problems in his essay, 'Narcissus as Narcissus'. The essay discusses his own poem, 'Ode to the Confederate Dead', but he argues that he is concerned with the poem's 'structure', not its quality or its 'origins': 'what I happen to know about the poem I shall discuss is limited. I remember merely my intention in writing it; I do not know whether the poem is good; I do not know its obscure origins.'[16] This passage is interesting because it distinguishes the poet's 'intention' from the poem's 'origins'. In so doing, it illustrates that the New Critics were not opposed to a discussion of aesthetic intentions so long as they were identified with the structure of the text, not as a mere external content which the text simply existed to express.

None the less, this passage is often read as a declaration of disinterest in the relationship between literature and society, but such a reading is inappropriate. It is actually directed against psychological accounts of poetic creation, particularly Freudianism, and it argues that the focus of critical attention should not be the poet's personality in so far as it exists as an object which is external to the text, but rather the way in which the poet's personality is realized in the linguistic forms of the text. As Tate is well aware, the process of literary production may well contradict whatever conscious or unconscious intentions the poet might have had prior to the process of literary production. For Tate, it is important to study literature as a process of production which transforms its materials, rather than to reduce the text to a transparent expression of its context. Another reason Tate questions the usefulness of forms of literary study which focus on the 'origins' of a work is that such knowledge cannot help poets to create poetry, given that the elements which might have been involved in the creation of one poem cannot be recreated for the production of another. The poet can only be helped through a focus on the linguistic forms of the text.[17] None the less, he is careful to distinguish his own arguments from a simple art-for-art's-sake position. He does not argue that literature has no relation to social and cultural issues, but merely that it cannot be valued according to the practical criteria of scientific positivism.[18] It does provide knowledge, but not through reference. It provides knowledge through experience. For example, he claims that his own poem is not *about* narcissism, but that the structure of the text gives readers knowledge by allowing them to see the workings of narcissism in the language of the poem.[19]

This position is developed further in his second essay, 'Tension in Poetry'. It makes a distinction between poetic language and a form of language which Tate refers to as 'mass language'. According to Tate, 'mass language' is associated with scientific positivism, and its users see poetry solely as a form of communication, a form which only exists to transmit a referential content. By contrast, Tate argues that poetry is opposed to 'mass language' and scientific positivism. Using the example of metaphysical poetry, he states that poetic language emphasizes the figurative features of language. Rather than primarily working to transmit a referential content, it pursues the logic of its figures. This position has much in common with various forms of post-structuralist criticism, particularly deconstruction, and Tate even goes so far as to claim that endless ambiguity and contradiction are endemic in these linguistic figures.[20] Poetry should not only entail the logical extension of the figure for Tate, but also its 'intension', or its connotations. He is critical of poetry 'which contradicts our ordinary human insights in so far as it fails to use and direct the rich connotations with which language has been informed by experience'.[21] This poetry is associated with the 'fallacy of denotation or reference'. It represses linguistic figures and connotations, or the points at which rational forms of meaning begin to break down. It is for this reason that he introduces the term 'tension' which is

derived from lopping the prefixes off the logical terms *ex*tension and *in*tension, which for all the use I mean to put them to may be taken as the same as denotation and connotation. What I am saying, of course, is that the best poetry's meaning is its 'tension,' the full body of all the extension and intension that we can find in it.[22]

For Tate, literature was distinguished by its linguistic forms, and it was these forms which he saw as the appropriate object of literary study.

This position was reiterated in his article, 'Miss Emily and the Bibliographer', which was published in 1940. It directed its attack at the scholastic forms of literary study, and took issue with many of the debates over the role of criticism in the academy. It is often read as an attack on those who study literature in relation to its historical context, but in fact Tate is quite clear that he is not claiming that there is no relation between literature and history. On the contrary, he criticizes a form of criticism which he refers to as 'the historical method', a form of criticism which is identified as an extension of scientific positivism. It fails to take account of the process of literary production. Rather than studying the relation of text and context, it simply regards the accumulation of historical information as an end in itself.[23] In fact, this approach is criticized specifically because it defines literature as a 'dead body' of facts, or a series of fixed, self-contained texts. It sees literature, culture and society as merely collections of objects, not active processes.

For example, Tate criticizes departments of English for their lack of interest in modern literature. Literary scholars, it is claimed, felt that there was no need to document the historical situation of modern literature, and argued that the works of modern literature had not yet had time to acquire fixed reputations. In response, Tate stresses that no reputations are ever fixed, and that the attempt to attain detachment from the past abstracts the literary text from any meaningful relation to the present. It converts it into a 'dead body' of facts, rather than seeing it as having any meaningful relationship to the culture and society of the present.[24] In this way, Tate's position is similar to that of Harold Bloom. Bloom criticizes the New Critics for seeing the text as an object whose meaning is fixed, rather than an object whose meaning is always produced through a dynamic relationship between the past and the present.[25] However, while Bloom converts this process into a lineage of strong and weak poets, and suppresses the specificity of the text in the process of reading or misreading, Tate writes: 'the literature of the past can be kept alive only by seeing it as the literature of the present. Or perhaps we ought to say that the literature of the past lives in the literature of the present and nowhere else; that it is all present literature.'[26] For Tate, the literary forms of the past must always be related to the present in order to define their meaning, but these forms still maintain a specificity within this process.

### Literature and the professors

Tate also delivered a speech in April 1940, in which he made similar criticisms of scholastic approaches to literary study. The impact of Tate's speech was dramatic. It started a heated and widespread debate over the role of both criticism and literary scholarship. In response, the *Kenyon Review* and the *Southern Review* decided to collaborate in order to publish 'Literature and the Professors', a symposium on the subject. This symposium was seen as only one part of a larger offensive on the academic institutions, and on 19 April, Ransom wrote to Tate with suggestions to this end:

About two weeks ago I wrote Cleanth proposing that they and we run two parallel and hot-stuff symposiums at the same moment, next fall, calling attention each to the other's symposium, and get it into TIME's notice; then circularize the whole membership of the MLA with the matter, with an idea not only to circulation of the periodicals but to some uproar at the next christmas meeting of the scholars in Boston; the rift has been steadily widening in that body.[27]

Despite his militant tone, Ransom had reservations. He was worried by the fact that the tone and approach of Tate's speech had received a great deal of criticism. As a result, he stressed that the offensive would have to be serious and persuasive, rather than a series of complaints and satirical remarks. None the less, he defended Tate for the passion of his former attacks, and seemed to be quite impressed and stirred by them. As he wrote to Mizener on 26 April: 'I feel sure that the young reporter got Tate's tone wrong... Otherwise I am forced to think that Allen is more excited over this issue than he has ever been in his mature literary life.'[28]

Ransom also responded to these debates in a piece entitled 'Mr. Tate and the Professors' which appeared in the summer edition of the *Kenyon Review*. It discusses a publication by Tate which was published in the *Princeton Alumni Weekly* of 8 March. Tate's article contrasts his own teaching practices with those which dominated the departments of English. Tate, who was teaching in the creative writing programme at Princeton, condemns the departments of English for their lack of interest in criticism. His argument is that creative writing instructors could not teach students how to write, but that they could give them the standards of judgement necessary for writing by teaching them to read critically. For this reason, he argues, the teaching of criticism should be the mainstay of the creative writing programme. In response, Ransom points out that it is not the task of the departments of English to instruct students in creative writing, but he does argue that they must address themselves to 'the structure of their works of art'.[29] The symposium which appeared in the two reviews was therefore intended to explain the importance of critical activity, and to highlight the problems of historical scholarship. To this end, the *Southern Review* claimed that

The lag between modern criticism and the current methods of teaching literature in most colleges and universities has from time to time occasioned comment. But such moments, though often acute and valuable, have rarely been systematic. In the light of this situation, the editors of *The Kenyon Review* and *The Southern Review* have felt that a useful service might be rendered by providing a forum for an extended discussion of the question.[30]

This symposium includes articles by Cleanth Brooks, Arthur Mizener, Sidney Cox, Hade Saunders, Lionel Trilling, Harry Levin, Wright Thomas, Joe Hornell, Allen Tate and John Crowe Ransom, but the following discussion will concentrate on the arguments by the latter two.[31]

Ransom's article was entitled 'Strategy for English Studies', and it argues that the usefulness of historical scholarship was coming to an end; that the departments of English had succeeded in accumulating vast amounts of information, but that they needed criticism in order to use and make sense of this information. It is also claimed that the professors had done such a fine job of covering the available materials that they had nearly exhausted them. They needed to develop new activities in order to prevent themselves from becoming redundant.[32] However, while these arguments are directed to the professors of literature, Ransom directs most of the article to their graduate students who, he claims, were most aware of the need for change. The problem faced by graduate students, it is argued, was that in the search for new areas of study, they were forced to concentrate on ever more minute and incidental projects.[33] It is also argued that given the information available to the student in hand-books, the relationship between students and their professors was becoming redundant. The student was no longer dependent on the professor for information, and a new relationship had to be established between them. Despite this situation, Ransom is not pessimistic about the future of literary education. In fact, he states that 'the future of the professorship of literature is immense'. He believes that 'the revolution will presently occur', and the scholastic modes of literary study will be replaced by 'the speculative or critical ones'.[34] The future of literary education, it is claimed, lies in criticism, an area which had previously been neglected. According to Ransom, the discussion of criticism had been limited to the history of criticism, an area of study which had remained documentary in nature and had failed to assess or develop the critical ideas of the past.[35] For Ransom, the task of criticism was to assess both literary activity and literary study in order to develop cultural standards which would challenge the incoherence and confusion of modern society. For this reason, the absence of criticism resulted in a failure to define ethical and aesthetic values in relation to literary material.[36] In this way, Ransom suggests that the absence of criticism was not just a matter of academic interest. A redefinition of the terms of literary study within the academy would also create the conditions for dramatic social and cultural changes.

If in this way Ransom claims that criticism had an important social role,

Tate defines this role in far more dramatic terms. His essay for the symposium, 'The Present Function of Criticism', claims that the society of modern capitalist America is a 'mass society', and he identifies it as totalitarian in nature. In this way, modern America, it is argued, has much in common with the fascist regimes of Germany and Italy. The growth of totalitarianism is also directly associated with the extinction of critical thought and with positivistic philosophies which overestimate the importance of instrumental action. Discussing the role of intellectuals, for example, Tate argues that this 'suppression of the critical spirit' means that the 'tradition of free ideas is as dead in the United States as it is in Germany'.[37] In this way, Tate's critique of totalitarianism is merely an extension of his critique of scientific positivism and industrial capitalism. They are all claimed to alienate specific activities from the whole way of life and elevate them into ends in themselves. For Tate, the scholastic approach to literature is merely a symptom of this situation. It is a mode of study which is distinguished by the absence of critical thought and a fetishization of information. In fact, Tate argues that the problem with education in general, and literary education in particular, is that educationalists had come to identify their own interests with those of modern society. They had come to regard their role as simply being to initiate the population into the activities required by bourgeois, consumerist society.[38] According to Tate, this situation is essentially the same as dictatorship. It does not encourage individuals to think for themselves, but trains them to identify with an abstract figure of the mass, or common man. As a result, individuals learn to defer to totalitarian abstractions such as 'the People' or 'the Party', and to abandon the struggles of critical thinking.

In this way, the scholastic approach to literature is seen as complicit with the totalitarianism of bourgeois society and culture:

These attitudes of scholarship are the attitudes of the *haute bourgeoisie* that support it in the great universities; it is now commonplace to observe that the uncreative money culture of modern times tolerates the historical routine of the scholars. The routine is 'safe', and it shares with the predatory social process at large a naturalistic basis. And this naturalism easily bridges the thin gap between the teachers' college and the graduate school, between the sociologist and the literary source-hunter, between the comptometrist of literary 'reactions' and the enumerator of influences.[39]

In response, it is argued, the universities need to develop forms of critical thought as a way of challenging the hegemony of the bourgeoisie. They need to develop alternative forms of study that seek to understand society and culture. In relation to literature, for example, Tate opposes the concentration on information and source hunting, and argues for a focus on the linguistic processes of literary activity. By failing to discuss literature in formal terms, he argues, critics also failed to consider the ways in which literary texts produce a form of knowledge which is critical of its social and cultural context. For this reason, the distinction between historical and formalist approaches to literature is attacked by Tate, who rejects both the view that literature is a transparent expression of its historical context, and the claim that it is an entirely autonomous form:

This essay has been written from a point of view which does not admit the validity of the rival claims of formalism and history, of art-for-art's-sake and society. Literature is the complete knowledge of man's experience, and by knowledge I mean that unique and formed intelligence of the world of which man alone is capable.[40]

As a result, his objection to these two positions is that they both fail to see literary activity as a process of production which critically examines its social and cultural context.

# Part IV

# The development of the New Criticism

# Introduction

By the early 1940s, the New Critics had established their critical positions within the academy, and in the period which followed, they revised and extended these positions in response to social and cultural developments. During this period, the work of Ransom, Tate and Warren began to diverge as they developed different potentials within their criticism. They continued to have much in common and remained friends, but their interests and their activities took different directions. In Ransom's case, he began to combat the politicization of artistic and critical activities during the war years, and he came to regard the restoration of the traditional society as an impossibility. As a result, while he continued to develop his defence of aesthetic activity in opposition to scientific positivism, he also began to isolate the literary text from other social activities and so limited its critical aspects. He came to accept the very position which he had formerly criticized; that literature was merely a refuge from, or compensation for, the alienated activities of modern society. During this same period, Tate did not dramatically alter his position, but he did become involved in the forms of anti-communism prevalent among intellectuals in the 1950s. This involvement was a part of his attack on the totalitarianism of modern society, but his association with organizations such as the Congress of Cultural Freedom forced him to flatter modern American society in opposition to communist societies. He was forced to play down both his objection to modern America and his previous insistence that it was as much an example of totalitarianism as other countries.

In contrast, it was Warren who made the most interesting contribution in the post-war period. He developed a form of liberalism which was critical both of American social, economic and cultural relations, and of the forms of individualism associated with them. During this period, he became engaged through his writings in the struggles for desegregation, Civil Rights, and the withdrawal of the United States from Vietnam while avoiding the dangers he had associated with propaganda. This writing worked by combining documentary prose with types of autobiographical and confessional self-examination. It examined the social and political forces which structured the relationship between the self and others. This led him to argue that art was an engagement with the problems of moral self-definition, and that this engagement required writers to investigate the social and political relations within which the self was defined. This is particularly important given the attack on the concept of self in contemporary theory. Warren maintained that the self is vital to the development of moral and political engagement, exactly because it was not autonomous or natural. The transformation of the social and cultural relations required an examination and transformation of the self. Warren also adopted an expanded definition of democracy which required social, cultural and economic change in order to prevent the exclusion of various groups from an active participation within American society.

As these cases illustrate, the New Criticism did not inevitably result in asocial formalism. In fact, it was only Ransom who moved in this direction and only as he limited aspects of his previous criticism. If the New Criticism did have a tendency to develop in this direction, it also had other tendencies which were illustrated by the work of Tate and Warren. Their work during this period shows a continued interest in the relationship between literature and society and a hostility to capitalist relations and the forms of individualism associated with it.

# 10 John Crowe Ransom: the isolation of aesthetic activity

## Introduction

After 1941, Ransom's academic career was well established, and he continued to develop his defence of literary activity in opposition to the claims of scientific positivism. However, America's entry into World War II seriously affected this position. During the war, great demands were made of artistic and intellectual activities, both of which became intimately involved in the defence of 'free culture'. Intellectuals became directly involved in the war effort, and began to identify American society with the cause of 'cultural freedom'. Rather than acting as critics of their society, many intellectuals came to its defence either as actual combatants, or as its ideologues. The war also affected intellectual activity in other ways. It redirected financial resources so that universities and journals were forced to reconsider both their budgets and their activities. During this period, Ransom continued to define literature in opposition to scientific positivism and political action, but he also opposed its co-option to the war effort. Unfortunately, he began to isolate it from society. He found himself unable to oppose the war effort, and consequently, he found it harder and harder to justify his opposition to American society. After the war, he became resigned to the impossibility of restoring an aesthetic way of life, and as a result, his critical writings came to define literature as merely a parasitic or complementary activity which questioned the dominance of rationality, but which did not call for the creation of an alternative way of life. Finally, in 1945, Ransom announced that he no longer believed in either the possibility or the desirability of an Agrarian restoration. The aesthetic way of life became merely a necessary image. It was unobtainable in reality. It was at this moment that he was not only at his most apolitical, but also closest to later theories such as deconstruction. Furthermore, this position was not the high point of his theoretical development, but an intellectual dead end. He did continue to publish and to edit after 1945, but his output was small and far less interesting than his previous work. In fact, after *The New Criticism*, which was published in 1941, Ransom published no more books, with the exception of *Beating the Bushes*, a collection of essays, most of which come from the period 1941–1945.[1]

### The New Criticism and the war effort

*The New Criticism*, which Ransom published in 1941, was an attempt to consolidate his own theoretical position; to clarify and reorganize the terms of critical activity; and to demonstrate that a new type of critical writing had been developing during the first half of the twentieth century. Its position is fundamentally the same as that which Ransom developed during the 1930s, when he associated the aesthetic life with the Agrarian society, and opposed the aims of literary activity to the instrumentalism of scientific positivism and social modernism. In the book, Ransom claims that the newness of this type of criticism made it seem eclectic, and that it was necessary to explain the concerns which motivated it. He also aims to correct some of the theoretical errors of this criticism.[2] In the process, two main problems are identified. The first of these is described as 'the idea of using the psychological affective vocabulary in the hope of making literary judgements',[3] while the second is claimed to be 'plain moralism'.[4] The work of three exemplary figures – I. A. Richards, T. S. Eliot, and Yvor Winters – is considered before Ransom goes on to develop his own position in a chapter entitled, 'Wanted: An Ontological Critic'. Ransom's argument is that while these three critics had made significant contributions to the understanding of literature, a critic was needed who would attempt to define poetry in terms of its ontological interests as a discourse, rather than in terms of its morality or its psychological affects. It is these ontological interests, he claims, which distinguish literary and scientific forms of discourse. The claim is that while poetic discourse has a logical or rational structure, it also 'imports and carries along a great deal of irrelevant or foreign matter which is clearly not structural but even obstructive'.[5] This leads Ransom to propose the distinction between the structure and the texture. He argues that 'it is an *order* of content, rather than a *kind* of content, that distinguishes texture from structure, and poetry from prose'.[6] For Ransom, the texture is not simply an added component; rather it affects the structure and creates a wholly new form of discourse in which the language is not simply a vehicle for the structure, but continually emphasizes its own materiality. Poetry does not simply present abstract statements, but particularizes those statements. It forces them to adopt denser configurations and more complex associations.

For Ransom, while scientific discourse depends upon its reference to a specifically defined object, and while this reference must remain limited and constant, poetic discourse is 'iconic' by which he means that it is concerned with the particular which 'is indefinable; that is it exceeds definition'.[7] These iconic features, he maintains, imperil its logical aspects as a discourse, and require these logical aspects to particularize themselves.[8] It is this emphasis on particularity, it is argued, which makes the work of art a fuller representation of the world than science.[9] It is the direct consequence of the collision between the structure and the texture of discourse, or the form and the meaning of texts. The claim is that in aesthetic discourse, language is neither a vehicle for the structure or meaning, nor a decorative addition to the structure. Instead the texture is in constant tension with the structure: 'The composition of a poem is an operation in which the argument fights to displace the meter, and the meter fights to displace the argument.'[10] At this stage, Ransom still used the term organic to describe this relationship – he argues that 'the meter-meaning process is the organic act of poetry, and involves all its important characters'[11] – but he was careful to emphasize that this is a complex process of interrelation, rather than the simple unity of form and content.

The tension between these two elements, he claimed, has an effect on both elements. The structure is forced to adopt indeterminate meanings in order to accommodate the texture, and the texture is forced to adopt indeterminate sound patterns in order to accommodate the structure. For this reason, the poem is defined as a complex of determinate and indeterminate structures, and determinate and indeterminate textures. By emphasizing the texture of the poem or the materiality of its language, aesthetic discourse, it is argued, creates a wholly new form of discourse, which is clearly distinguished from the discourse of scientific positivism. It creates a discourse in which the texture is forced to particularize itself or rather develop features which do not exist simply to promote the dominant structure of meaning. None the less, aesthetic discourse is not distinguished by the texture alone. It develops from the ways in which these elements affect the composition of the work.[12]

Many of these concerns were intensified by America's entry into World War II. Intellectuals began to feel social and political pressures to involve themselves in the conflict, and Ransom attempted to resist these pressures just as he had resisted other pressures to involve art in political and social struggles. As in the 1930s, his argument was that the arts were not primarily instrumental in form, and that they embodied relations and attitudes to the world which opposed the domination of instrumental values in modern society. The attempt to convert art into an instrument of propaganda was claimed to be a denial of its very form. Art was not justified by its instrumental use, but the extent to which it critically examined its social and cultural context. In spring 1941, he restated this position in response to the emergence of *Decision*, a monthly review concerned with the defence of 'free culture'. He considered it right that the contributors should be militant in their defence of free culture 'following the experience of its defeat in continental Europe', and that they should 'wish to emphasize their credentials as citizens for a moment at the expense of their own practice of the arts',[13] but he identified a contradiction within their position. This contradiction was that their defence of 'free culture' was at odds with the call for artistic and intellectual activities to become involved in the war effort. He also added the rather weak claim that a 'free culture' was not a prerequisite for the aesthetic activity, even though it was desirable; that because writing was not a simple reflection of its context, it was still possible to develop aesthetic activities in hostile conditions.[14] This position was a fundamental assumption of his earlier writing, but in this situation, it registers a growing resignation in Ransom's criticism. He was coming to believe that literature would have to make do without the reconstruction of the aesthetic way of life.

The war also began to affect intellectual activities in more fundamental ways. At Kenyon it led to problems with the curriculum; with the teaching of English; and with the funding of the *Kenyon Review*. Ransom described these events in dramatic terms, in a letter to Tate written on 28 January 1942:

We've had a lot of turmoil here – as doubtless at Princeton, most at Princeton of all places as we hear in these parts – over speed-up curriculum. The liberal education is imperilled, though here at least we've tried to save it. Conferences, committees, faculty meetings, have made life pretty terrible.[15]

Ransom also commented on the *Kenyon Review*, the funding of which was threatened, as was that of the *Southern Review*, and he planned to merge the two journals in an attempt to save them. This project failed (though he did save the *Kenyon Review*), and in its spring edition, he made some editorial comments on the demise of the *Southern Review*, and on the position of the writer in the time of war. Ransom argued that art and artists should not be diverted from their specific tasks by the demands of the war; but even so he still implied that this task was not divorced from public activity in general. He claimed that 'writers as a group have more public conscience than other professional groups, not less'.[16] However, Ransom was becoming unable to define the function of the writer's social conscience, and this definition is left as an open question in his Kenyon piece, 'Artists, Soldiers, and Positivists', where he tries to defend art from the demands of the war effort. In this piece, Ransom argues that it is positivist to demand that art be effective in the pursuit of social purposes, and that while these purposes are particularly urgent in time of war, no society will ever be free of urgent problems. It will always be necessary to counter the question: 'what is the public service which art renders, that it should hope for reputation and favour?'[17] In response, Ransom claims this service is not related to its effectiveness, but to the attitude which it establishes. His problem is that he was unwilling or unable to criticize the war effort itself, and found himself defending modern American society. As a result, he found it difficult to argue that literature criticized the values of modern society, and required the establishment of an alternative way of life. This failure prevented him from defining the service rendered by art, except in abstract or formal terms, and he was forced to alienate literary activity from social and cultural engagement except in the most abstract terms. It was, therefore, only in his continued opposition to the positivists that he was able to defend art as a form of discourse.

**Positivism and art**

As ever, Ransom's fundamental objection to the positivists was that they failed to identify the specificity of poetic and artistic discourse. Positivism, he claimed, regarded all discourse as essentially the same as scientific discourse. It regarded all activity as concerned with instrumentalism, or with effective action. It could not account for the materiality of poetic language. This position is developed in several articles which Ransom published in the 1940s where he states that the positivists either defined the materiality of poetic language as a decorative addition to its structure or meaning, or as a form which was functional, or expressive of that structure. This latter point led Ransom to criticize certain tendencies within the New Criticism itself, particularly organic theories of poetry. Despite his own use of the term 'organic' in previous articles, he insists that this way of referring to the relationship between the various elements of poetic discourse was essentially positivistic since by claiming that form and content constitutes a unity, it defines the texture as functional, or a mere expression of the structure. For this reason, Ransom began to reject concepts such as Hegel's 'Concrete Universal', which he had used to describe the work of art earlier in his career. He now maintained that the structure and the texture could never be fully integrated, and that it was the tension between them which constituted aesthetic discourse, not their unity. For Ransom, the texture constantly acted to disintegrate the rational structure with particularity, so questioning the purposive forms of human activity. This argument places Ransom very close to the deconstructive position, in which the language of the text continually deconstructs its meaning, but in Ransom's case, it develops out of a retreat from social and political engagement, not a moment of critical activism.

Although Ransom continued to oppose art to science in his critique of positivism, this period also saw a qualification of his position. On 23 May 1941, he wrote to Tate:

> I am forced to regard poetic theory as science, though a new science, because about a new or 'different' kind of discourse. That's why I don't want taboos or restrictions, philosophical censorship, against the analytic work. If that is positivism, I guess I'm a member of the tribe.[18]

This quote has been used to prove that the New Criticism was a form of scientific positivism, but the position which it takes is not one common to the movement as a whole, but one unique to Ransom. Even so he still emphasized that the nature of its object made this form of science different from others. He also disagreed with the positivists that science is the only form of discourse, and stressed that 'so far as the absurd emphasis on scientific discourse as the only discourse goes, I'm far from being [a positivist]. And I hope I didn't give them much comfort; I didn't mean to.'[19] For Ransom, the positivists regard all human activity as being concerned with the domination of nature, or with instrumental control, and while he did agree that these are important aspects of human activity necessary for the material reproduction of the human species, he insisted that the purpose of some activities was not to dominate or control the world, but to revere it instead.[20] Through these non-instrumental activities, 'the human creature assumes suddenly a new humility; it figures in religion as a sense of awe, in art as a sense of beauty, and in sentimental life as an uncritical affection'.[21]

This argument is similar to the position which Ransom had earlier developed in relation to Agrarianism. It claims that such humility involves a contemplative or reflexive element which gives rise to a 'new humanity', or a humanity which involves more than the biological needs. He also claims that by associating the good and the true with effective action, the positivists could not comprehend the features which distinguish aesthetic activities from other activities. The positivists, it is argued, ignore the beautiful which has no effective or instrumental use, and question whether art is separate from other human activities or directly connected with them. For Ransom, the framing of this question creates a false dilemma. It presents a false opposition which acts to establish the positivists' own position that art is fundamentally the same as other forms of activities, and that 'aesthetic theory which had a separatist tendency was irresponsible and anti-social'.[22] By contrast, Ransom seeks to illustrate the specificity of aesthetic activity by opposing two fallacies which he connects with positivism: 'the reductive fallacy' and 'the genetic fallacy'. This definition of aesthetic specificity is similar to that of contemporary theory. It suggests that while aesthetic activity is related to other activities, it is not an expression of them. It may be produced in relation to its social and cultural context, but that context does not provide an explanation of it.

This position also returns Ransom to his distinction between the structure and the texture. For Ransom, claims that the texture produces an 'effect' ignore the materiality of language in poetic discourse. These claims, it is argued, are often another way of defining the texture as a mere expression of the meaning or structure, rather than a force which interrupts the abstractions of the text and distracts the discourse from the straight-forward communication of the structure.[23] While the positivists do not want language to act as a distraction to the meaning or structure, it is, for Ransom, this distraction which distinguishes poetry as a specific form of discourse. The same criticism is also said to apply to theories which do not see the texture as an expression of the structure, but as a decorative addition to it. This position is referred to as a form of hedonism. It sees aesthetic discourse as a mere indulgence of the senses without any other role or purpose, nor any relationship to the rest of social life. Once again this position defines the texture as a mere complement to the structure, rather than as a serious challenge to it. It is his opposition to these positions which leads Ransom to oppose the concept of the Concrete Universal – which he himself had borrowed from Hegel in the past – and to criticize other New Critics such as Warren. For Ransom, both the Concrete Universal, and many New Critics, were concerned with the unity between the structure and the texture, rather than acknowledging their radical difference. Ransom maintains that this emphasis on unity involves the domination of the abstract over the particular.[24] In fact, in this period, Ransom was growing dissatisfied with aspects of the New Criticism.

### Conclusion: art and the human economy

In Ransom's essay, 'Art and the Human Economy', he discusses the re-lationship between art and economic activity. He still distinguishes art from economic activity, and claims that it was not based on instrumentalism, but it is here that Ransom finally repudiates Agrarianism. The aesthetic life, he suggests, is lost forever and art could only mourn its passing. This repudiation of the Agrarian movement was related to a change in his aesthetic theories, a change that seriously limited their critical potential. Previously Ransom had insisted that art criticized modern society, and identified the need for an alternative way of living, but in 'Art and the Human Economy', he came to defend the capitalist division of labour in which art was alienated from other activities. Art came to be seen as merely a complement to, or at best a respite from, the emphasis on effective action within modern society.

This tendency was already present during the early 1940s, and it was responsible for Ransom's difficulty in defining the service rendered by art. He still claimed that this service was not related to instrumentalism, but he also insisted that art was not a purely passive activity. It had to have a purpose. It was for this reason that he criticized one writer for failing to acknowledge 'what a liability aesthetic experience means to the achievement of science'.[25] His problem was that having repudiated the possibility of achieving an aesthetic way of life, literature lost its critical function. Ransom could no longer convincingly demonstrate that art was a liability to science and society. By 1945, Ransom still maintained that the economy of society involved instrumentalism and the domination of nature, and that these forms ignored the richness and complexity of human and natural existence, but he now stressed that this lost richness could no longer be recaptured, except within the limits of the aesthetic text. This position was developed in relation to the aesthetic theories of T. W. Adorno and W. P. Southard whose topics were claimed to be similar: 'The unhappy condition that has risen under the modern economy, and the question of whether religion and art can do anything about it.'[26]

Ransom was very sympathetic to Adorno's aesthetic theory, despite the fact that he maintained that 'Mr. Adorno is evidently for collectivism in politics.'[27] For example, Adorno was commended for not relating art to the demands of the practical life, and for defining it as an activity with its own specificity. For Adorno, it was claimed, art concentrates on the mysteriousness of humanity and nature. It acknowledges that their relations are too complex for scientific analysis. Ransom's case was that, for Adorno, the practical life seeks to dominate nature and to convert it into objects of utility, and that this situation prevents humanity from experiencing their complexity. He also commented upon Adorno's claim that the division of labour limits the range of an individual's activities. Adorno, it was claimed, criticizes the specialization of tasks in which the labour of individuals becomes a mere component in a process of production over which they have no overall control or involvement. In this situation, their labour is unfulfilling and dependent. It is reduced to a single repetitive function and they lose any real relationship to the object of their labour. Ransom agreed with Adorno that this situation limits the relation of individuals both to their world and to other individuals. It makes them appear as limited beings, devoid of the complexities which make them mysterious. None the less, he could no longer accept Adorno's conclusions with regard to literature and art. According to Ransom, Adorno regards the work of art as an attempt to recapture the complexity of human existence repressed by modern society, and that, as a result, art involves an implicit critique of modern society.[28] Ransom was sympathetic to this position, but he no longer argued that art involves the imperative for change.

By 1945, Ransom saw art as only an imaginative return to innocence, rather than one which involves an imperative for change, and this position was clarified in his argument with W. P. Southard. According to Ransom, Southard maintained that the introduction of specialized labour gave rise to a form of decadence, and that art involves a form of repentance in which 'we go back into our original innocence, but vicariously or symbolically, not really'.[29] Like Adorno, Southard maintained that art affirms the need for social change, and calls for the restoration of the Agrarian society. It is this final position with which Ransom took issue:

without consenting to a division of labor, and hence modern society, we should have not only no effective science, invention, and scholarship, but nothing to speak of in art, e.g., *reviews* and contributions to *reviews*, fine poems and their exegesis ... The pure though always divided knowledges, and the physical gadgets and commodities, constitute our science, and are the guilty fruits; but the former are triumphs of muscular intellect, and the latter at best are clean and wholly at our service. The arts are the expiations, but they are beautiful. Together they comprise the detail of human history. They seem worth the vile welter through which homeless spirits must wade between times, with sensibilities subject to ravage as they are. On these terms the generic human economy can operate, and they are the only terms practicable now.[30]

Ransom had come to accept the division of labour and the alienation of aesthetic experience which results from it. Consequently, he no longer defined aesthetic activity as a form which was critical of modern society and called for the creation of an alternative social order. Instead, he claimed that it was a privileged form within that society. It preserved the sense of natural piety which was lacking in other social activities. It 'commemorates' the loss of the aesthetic life which was now dead and impossible to recreate except within the limits of the aesthetic work.[31] This position severely limits the critical role of aesthetic activity. Art becomes a mere complement to modern society, but does not require its transformation. It allows a retreat from alienated activities, but offers no alternative to them. However, this position was not the highpoint of Ransom's intellectual development, but an intellectual dead end. None of Ransom's following work matches that of preceding periods either in scope or in influence.

# 11 Allen Tate: the man of letters and the cold war

## Introduction

Whereas American capitalism had seemed a virtually moribund system prior to 1941, the Second World War sponsored a period of economic growth and prosperity which created a widespread optimism about the American capitalist system. This situation led many American intellectuals who had previously opposed this system to identify with it. This identification was also influenced by another effect of the war: the development of America as a world power. With the end of the war, America had given up isolationism and had come to define itself as a world leader, but at the same time, it began to perceive the Soviet Union, and the spread of communism in Eastern Europe and Eastern Asia, as a potential threat to that position.[1] In this context, many intellectuals became involved in anti-communist activities, such as involvement in the Congress of Cultural Freedom. Many came to identify American society itself with the cause of 'free culture'.[2] This situation limited the appeal of Tate's objections to modern society, and it was mainly his critique of communism which was influential during this period. None the less, while he became involved with the Congress of Cultural Freedom, his position was fundamentally different to that dominant among American intellectuals. He could not bring himself to identify with the American system itself, as Ransom had done by 1945, and this made his position in relation to the Congress highly problematic. Tate's politics was still defiantly reactionary, but for precisely this reason, he refused to abandon his critique of modern society and capitalism, and his claim that literature was a critical activity. His problem was that involvement in the Congress of Cultural Freedom required him to contradict his own position. It forced him to pay lip-service to the values and institutions of modern American society.

### History, literature and the image of man

Throughout the 1930s, Tate had been preoccupied with the idea of history which he associated with his theory of art. He claimed that both history

114

and art presented an 'image of man', an image in which humanity was shown to be inextricably related to its past. These forms were valued by Tate who contrasted them with modern views of humanity which emphasized human progress and self-transformation, and ignored its historical and material limits. Human beings, Tate argued, were products of their history. It defined their terms of reference, both enabling and limiting the course of human development. This emphasis on history was opposed to the 'historical method' which was claimed to have discounted concrete human situations in favour of an abstract conception of the historical process. In this sense, the terms History and Tradition were virtually synonymous for Tate, and he associated them with the Old South. During the late 1920s and early 1930s, while Tate was still engaged in the Agrarian movement, this association led him to attempt historical biographies of three Southern figures: Stonewall Jackson, Jefferson Davis, and Robert E. Lee.[3] These histories were attempts to assess the strengths and weaknesses of Southern culture, and the effect of the Civil War on the development of modern society. They produced problems for Tate and he was ultimately unable to complete his biography of Lee. In response to these problems, Tate turned to the writing of fiction, and he eventually produced two short stories and an historical novel, *The Fathers*.

This fiction was vitally important to Tate and to the development of his interests. In 1936 and 1937, he even suspended his poetic and critical writing to concentrate his efforts on *The Fathers*; these years were also those in which he made his transition from the Agrarian movement to the campaign for the New Criticism. *The Fathers* concerns the crisis of a family during the Civil War period, and it deals with the conflict between the way of life of the Old South, and the way of life of the capitalistic North. In the novel, these two ways of life are represented by two fathers, Major Buchan, an Old South landowner, and George Posey, a Northern merchant. Posey is also Major Buchan's son-in-law. In the book, the history of the Civil War period is related to a conflict between the historical imagination of the South and the lack of historical understanding in the North. The culture of the Old South is presented as one that was organized around rituals, games, and formal manners, all of which are seen as ways of dealing with 'the abyss': the chaos which underpins social reality and into which American society plunged as a result of the Civil War.[4] In contrast to Major Buchan who represents the culture of the South, George Posey represents the culture of the North. He fails to live by the game. Rather than existing in a state of balance over 'the abyss', the narrator claims that he always imagined Posey riding over a precipice into 'the abyss'.[5] The South's ability to acknowledge and deal with 'the abyss' is also related to what Tate refers to as the 'imagination'. While Major Buchan is able to develop ways of living which acknowledge the complexities and paradoxes of existence, Posey lacks 'imagination'. As the narrator puts it: 'I suppose he did lack imagination; he had rather a quality of mind that runs things down in a bee-line logic, that was misunderstood.'[6] For Tate, Posey is a positivist who reduces existence to abstractions, and is unable to acknowledge the limits of human comprehension and control.

Throughout the novel, Posey is shown to be unable to cope with the materiality of human and natural existence as represented by death and sexuality. He is a man who cannot face those aspects of existence which are beyond human control, aspects which Tate refers to as Original Sin or Evil. It was these aspects that limit humanity and prevented it from attaining the ideal, but which the Southern way of life had been able to represent and so deal with. This position can be most clearly seen in a long, but central, passage in which the narrator writes:

I have already said that I went upstairs to wait for it to get dark. Why I wanted the dark no one could remember after all this time. There are days when we consciously guide the flow of being towards the night, and our suspense is a kind of listening, as if the absence of light, when it comes, will be audible just because sight and touch are frustrated. Of course this is what we all know. But how many of us know that there are times when we passionately desire to hear the night? And I think we do hear it: we hear it because our senses, not being mechanisms, actually perform the miracles of imagination that they themselves create: from our senses come the metaphors through which we know the world, and in turn our senses get knowledge of the world by means of figures of their own making. Nobody today, fifty years after these incidents, can hear the night; nobody wishes to hear it. To hear the night, and to crave its coming, one must have deep inside one's secret being a vast metaphor controlling the rest: a belief in the innate evil of man's nature, and the need to face that evil, of which the symbol is darkness, of which again the living image is man alone. Now that men cannot be alone, they cannot bear the dark, and they see themselves as innately good but betrayed by circumstances that render them pathetic. Perhaps some of the people in this story are to be pitied, but I cannot pity them; none of them was innately good. They were all, I think, capable of great good, but that is not the same as *being* good.[7]

For Tate, it is the image of humanity burdened with Original Sin that distinguished the Southern way of life from that of the North. It required the Southerner to acknowledge that his being is defined by forces beyond his ultimate control. Modern society, on the other hand, is supposed to lack such an image. It simply sees the human and natural world as a series of objects which are available for rational and logical control. In the novel, Tate does acknowledge a weakness in the South though, and this is represented by Major Buchan's loyalty to the Union. Major Buchan is unable to see that the Union is incapable of sustaining his society. Tate's case here is essentially the same as his position in *I'll Take My Stand*, where he argued that the South's real failure was intellectual rather than military. It failed to develop a religious structure which could define and defend its distinctive, pre-capitalist economic and social order.[8] It is for this reason that, as Rubin has pointed out, there is a third father in the novel. This figure is the Roman Catholic priest who enters the novel. He represents the religious structure which, Tate argued, the South lacked, but which Tate himself eventually adopted.[9]

The Old South had much in common with art and history for Tate. Like the Old South, these latter forms present an 'image of man' which acknowledges that the human being is composed of both rational and irrational elements. This image offers a critique of modern society. It emphasizes those elements which the modern world seeks to repress. It is for this reason that Tate criticizes positivist aesthetics. He argues that positivism is solely concerned with instrumental control; that it can only see truth and morality within these terms; and that, as a consequence, it is unable to acknowledge the limits to its control. For this reason, it is unable to comprehend the significance of poetry's irrational elements. In 1941, for example, Tate developed a critique of Morris' theory of aesthetics in which he considers the relationship between science and literature. In contrast to Matthew Arnold who, it is argued, saw these two as separate from one another, Tate asks: 'Are not subject and language one?'[10] For Tate, Arnold's failure to see language as more than a vehicle for the idea defined language as external to literature. This position is likened to that of the positivists. It associates literature with statements and meanings, rather than its linguistic and formal features. Even positivists such as Morris who define the language of poetry as more than a mere vehicle for its meaning are unable to explain the development of values within poetry or the relationship of these values to reality. Positivists such as Morris, it is claimed, define these values as irresponsible feelings. They cannot identify a use from these values, and as a result, separate them from concepts of truth or intellect.

In contrast, Tate argues that reality or the 'actual world' must be seen as more than a collection of objects or facts if one is to understand the relationship of aesthetic values to reality. Theory must recognize the presence of human experience and of subjectivity as objective aspects of the actual world. Tate's argument is that aesthetic values are produced by the imaginative power to produce meaning by relating aspects of the actual world to one another. For Tate, the actual world refers to the subjective field of human experience, but he argues that this field 'sufficiently reflects or gathers in or contains all that we ever know of any other world or worlds that appear to lie beyond it'.[11] His position is similar to that of post-structuralists such as Derrida who claim that there is nothing outside the text. Like the post-structuralists, Tate's position is also defined in reaction to positivism and empiricism. He argues that positivism maintains that 'physicalism' is the sole legitimate field of discourse and defines all imaginative and subjective forms of discourse as lacking in content. In response, he argues that the empiricism of the positivists makes them incapable of understanding how we can know about the world in anything but mechanistic terms,[12] and dramatically limits the field of knowledge. By contrast, Tate uses the figure of the hovering fly in Dostoevsky's *The Idiot* to discuss the process through which the imagination creates knowledge of the actual world which is unavailable to positivism.[13] For Tate, this form of knowledge cannot be produced through mere observation, but only through the imaginative figuration of the actual world.[14] The presence of the hovering fly at the death bed of Natasya, it is claimed, emphasizes the privation of life through the presence of its own life. It also comments on the human order of life through a comparison with its own 'wholly different order of life'.[15] The presence of the fly creates an imaginative act of figuration through which the actual world can be known. It is Tate's claim that it is only through this kind of imaginative activity that we can come to know and understand the meaning of human experience. Without it, human experience is random, individual, and meaningless.[16] Tate also insists that this form of knowledge is a challenge to the domination of human experience by the demands of the practical life. Humans may be social beings before they are religious beings, but once they have achieved social being, they acquire a religious being which can never be sustained by the alienated activities of modern society. Literature, it is argued, not only addresses those aspects of humanity which are not primarily preoccupied with practical objectives, but also challenges the dominance of rationality and instrumentality by emphasizing these aspects. In opposition to mere empirical knowledge of existence, it creates a form of knowledge in which both the rational and irrational aspects of human existence are imaged and imagined.

### The man of letters in the modern world

These interests persisted throughout the 1950s, during which Tate not only continued to examine the relationship between modern society and the activities of the 'man of letters', but also became involved with the Congress of Cultural Freedom. Under the auspices of this organization, he delivered two lectures, 'To Whom is the Poet Responsible?' and 'The Man of Letters in the Modern World', in which, as before, he defined aesthetic activity as a form of social criticism which represented humanity as being composed of both rational and irrational elements. For

Tate, the critical aspect of the text was that this depiction of the dual aspect of the human being challenged the dominance of rationality in modern society. This position is similar to post-structuralist critiques of rationality which emphasize the limits and repressions involved in modernity and rationalism.

In 'The Man of Letters in the Modern World', for example, Tate maintains that the development of the alienation of modern society was linked with the philosophy of Descartes. Descartes' distinction between thought on the one hand, and nature on the other, is accused of dividing humanity against itself. It separates human thought from the materiality of human nature, and encourages the former to dominate the latter. Tate does not imply that Descartes is solely responsible for this situation, or that man would not have been in conflict with himself without this specific division. He simply claims that Descartes defined the terms of the modern division. For Tate, this division involves a secularization of human activity and of nature, which are rationalized and organized as mechanisms or machines. It also creates a situation in which the only moral terms are associated with the effectiveness of these mechanistic activities. In this situation, human beings are placed in conflict with themselves. Their activities are dominated by rationality which not only denies both the life of the senses and the basis of human interaction,[17] but also dehumanizes humanity in the process. It represses their sensual and interactive aspects, and orders human beings as though they were mere things.

For Tate, this situation also results in the emergence of the 'power-state', a form which he comes to see as representative of modern society's destructive tendencies. The practice of politics in modern society, he argues, is purely concerned with efficiency. It no longer works for human happiness but operates as a system of power. It orders and oppresses its subjects. It becomes a totalitarian force. While Tate argues that in such a situation writers must withdraw from an involvement in the 'power-state' and combat its debased language of control, he does not mean that they should cease to be concerned with the social world. Quite the contrary: he maintains that it is the writers'

> duty to render the image of man as he is in his time, which, without the man of letters, would not be otherwise known. What modern literature has taught us is not merely that the man of letters has not participated fully in the action of society; it has taught us that nobody else has either. It is a fearful lesson.[18]

This duty is not only critical, it is also a challenge to modern society. For Tate, the knowledge available in art distinguishes humanity from the machine, and cannot be wholly or permanently repressed. It is not concerned with rational control or mastery, but acknowledges the irrational aspects of existence which escape human control. By providing this knowledge, art not only acknowledges those features repressed by modern society, but also highlights the crimes and limits of that society. He does acknowledge that many modern writers have often given in to negativity and pessimism, but he stresses that this is not their fault. Instead he describes it as 'the inevitable creations of a secularized society, the society of means without ends, in which nobody participates with the full substance of his humanity'.[19]

In considering the relationship between modern society and literary activity, Tate also made a distinction between communication and communion. According to Tate, modern society involves greater amounts of communication, or exchanges of information, than previous societies, but he argues that this communication lacks the element of communion without which it is incomplete. In contrast to the exchange of information, communion is defined as a sense of interconnection with others which involves an awareness of both the rational and irrational aspects of human existence. For this reason, he opposes theories which define literary activity as a form of communication, and claims that literature is distinguished by a sense of communion. It does not simply convey information about the world, but reveals the lack of communion in modern society. It illustrates that modern society is repressive and undemocratic, and that it represses or enslaves aspects of human existence.[20] Writers are not seen as unrelated to society, but are claimed to be responsible for the defence of democracy, and fulfill this responsibility by acknowledging the aspects of humanity which are repressed by the 'power-state'.

This position was developed in Tate's essay 'To Whom is the Poet Responsible?', where Tate asks the question: for what is the poet responsible? According to Tate, Van Wyck Brooks and Archibald MacLeish had maintained that the writer 'was saddled with the total responsibility for the moral, political, and social well-being', and they had blamed this figure for a series of social and cultural crises which beset modern society.[21] This position is opposed by Tate who maintains that it over-emphasizes the importance of writers. They were not the only group which had failed to defend democratic values. In fact, he claims that the scientists and social scientists were more at fault. They had repudiated social responsibility through their commitment to both positivism and the principle of free inquiry, both of which refused to acknowledge the social implications of knowledge. They considered the investigation of human nature as less important than the philosophy of science, and rejected the philosophy of being. Tate also associates scientific rationality with the rise of the power-state, and argues that both repress the complexities of human existence and impose abstract solutions upon society. For this reason, he regards the concept of reason as essentially undemocratic. For Tate, democracy does not repress aspects of human existence with abstractions, but must involve concrete men and women in the attempt to define goals and identify choices.[22] He argues that intellectuals had been undemocratic in their reliance on reason. They had imposed abstractions upon the world which prevented the full involvement of the population within society.

For this reason, Tate claims that writers' first responsibility was to their own sense of knowledge and judgement. This did not disconnect them from social criticism. He not only asserts that society is their first point of reference, but maintains that their sense of knowledge and judgement require them to develop criteria of justice with which to assess contemporary social reality. If Tate claims that writers must distance themselves from the demands of society, it is only so that they can judge the extent to which society does justice to human nature. This is the sense in which he claims that writers are not responsible to society, but to the specificity of literary activity.[23] It is their responsibility to define a critical stance in relation to society, and to develop forms of language which are opposed to the debased language of technique and control. By offering an alternative language, literature presents an image of a more fulfilling way of living which is not dominated by rationality. If Tate saw the state as representative of the destructive tendencies of modern society, he saw literature and culture as opposed to the state: 'The state is the mere operation of society, but culture is the way society lives, the material medium through which men receive the one lost truth which must be perpetually recovered: the truth of what Jacques Maritain calls the "supra-temporal destiny" of man.'[24]

This position was clearly developed from Tate's earlier criticism. He continued to discuss literature in relation to its social and cultural context, and to oppose modern American society. For this reason, his involvement in the Congress of Cultural Freedom placed him in a contradictory situation. Previously, he had identified the problems of modern American society by contrasting it with traditional societies such as the South, but in his involvement in the Congress of Cultural Freedom, he had to identify the problems of the Soviet Union by contrasting them with those of modern America. The problem was that while Tate was an anti-communist, his anti-communism was only one aspect of his attack on *all* modern societies including contemporary American. As a result, his attempt to distinguish between America and the Soviet Union, and to identify America with the cause of 'free culture', was highly problematic.[25] Yet it was a necessary part of his involvement in the Congress of Cultural Freedom which was largely constituted to convince Europe that neutrality was futile and that it must accept American leadership in the struggle against communism. It was, therefore, inevitable that Tate's involvement would require him to pay lip-service to American society. Not only did this position contradict his hostility to modern America, it also contradicted the distance which he argued that writers should adopt in relation to their society. As a result, his own case became a prime example of a writer who was caught up in the politics of the 'power-state', and acted as an apologist or even an ideologue for that state. For these reasons, his position is not only ideological and propagandist, but contradictory and unconvincing.

### Conclusion

It is inaccurate to claim that Tate's literary criticism became a type of asocial formalism after his involvement in the Agrarian movement. He continued to define literary activity in relation to society, and maintained that modernist literature involved a critical process which was challenging to modern society. In fact, he saw the formal analysis of literature as a necessity specifically for this reason. In order to judge the social and cultural significance of literary activity, he argued, it was necessary to identify the ways in which the linguistic forms of the literature were a critical response to the debased forms of language associated with instrumentalism and control. In a discussion of the relationship between literature and history, he clarified this position. He argued that while the New Criticism had been identified as indifferent, or even hostile, to the use of history in the analysis of the text, 'in neither Empson nor Cleanth Brooks is history left out; it ceases to appear methodologically; it no longer devours the literary text; it survives as contributory knowledge'.[26] The historical situation of literature was of major importance to the New Critics, but the New Criticism did not reduce literature to an expression of its history. Instead, it analysed the active way in which literature responds to its historical situation. In fact, Tate continued to be highly critical of all methodological and systematic forms of criticism, even in the New Criticism, and he refused to see criticism as a science. He maintained that criticism had no substance of its own, and that it was defined purely by its relationship to literature. His concern was that criticism should not impose fixed or abstract standards upon literary activity and thereby limit the discussion of literature to one feature or set of features. As Tate put it, 'There can be no end to the permutations of the critical relation to literature.'[27] No one aspect of the text could be identified as its essence, and no critical method could discuss the text in its totality.

These positions can be identified in two essays published by Tate in 1951, on Dante and Poe. He argues that while unity and coherence are central criteria in the process of literary evaluation, it is impossible to comprehend the whole structure of a literary work at any one moment. In the case of Dante, for example, Tate concentrates on one figure, or line of imagery, and comments on its relationship to other aspects of the text. For Tate, Dante's work is a product of 'the symbolic imagination', a form which predates the scientific rationality of modern society. This 'symbolic imagination' is based upon the belief that the intellect is incapable of attaining any direct knowledge of essences. As a result, Tate claims, Dante's allegories are different from modern forms of allegory. They do not suppress the richness of experience with an abstraction. Instead they involve an intensification of experience in which abstract essences are represented through a process of 'reflection'. These essences are embodied in concrete images. For Tate, Dante's thought predates the division between intellect and experience which emerges with modern society, and as a result, these essences are presented as forms to be experienced not facts to be transmitted.[28]

In contrast, Poe's work is claimed to be a product of 'the angelic imagination'. Tate argues that Poe did not fully understand the issues with which he was engaged, and that he can be seen as a transitional figure whose problems as a writer were both the result of, and a response to, 'the disintegration of the modern personality' (or the division between the rational and irrational aspects of humanity created by modern society). According to Tate, Poe's writing presents a nightmare world in which the senses are alienated from the pure intellect by the quest for essential knowledge, but return to suffocate the intellect which has dominated and denied them. Despite Poe's reaction to modernity, Tate suggests that he only partially understood the problems which resulted from the separation of sense from intellect, and reproduced many of its problems.[29] Poe's opposition to modern society tended to mirror its problems. Consequently, Poe ends up in an apocalyptic position, a position which represents the search for unity as one which leads to annihilation.

However abstract Tate's historical model, his discussions of both Poe and Dante do not isolate their literature from their social and historical contexts. Instead they consider these literary forms in relation to the development of modern society, and the division between sense and intellect which it creates.

# 12 Robert Penn Warren: literature and social engagement

## Introduction

During the late 1940s and early 1950s, Warren developed a type of liberalism in his social and cultural criticism, but this liberalism was not an uncritical assessment of American society, or a form of asocial formalism. It drew directly upon his Agrarian positions of the late 1920s and 1930s. The term 'liberalism' is a complex one which covers many different and diverse positions. This is particularly so in the South where, as Comer Vann Woodward has pointed out, the term has been used to describe both the New South school of Henry Grady, and the positions of Warren and Woodward himself – despite the fact that these latter positions were directly opposed to those of the former.[1] In the South, the term 'liberalism' has been used to describe *both* an uncritical and optimistic promotion of industrial progress, which called for a reconciliation between classes and races under an anti-populist, white rule; and the critical, populist, and anti-racist positions developed by writers such as Woodward and Warren. The term 'liberalism' was further complicated by the rise of post-war liberalism in the 1940s and 1950s. This was a complex movement which embodied many diverse and contradictory elements, but it has often been accused of an uncritical and over-optimistic assessment of the American economy and society, and of the possibilities of reconciliation and consensus within them. This may be true as a general criticism, but it is important to note that post-war liberalism incorporated many elements to which these criticisms do not apply. The case of Warren is an example. He not only countered the complacency present in much American liberalism, but presented literature as a critical engagement with its social context.

A frequent criticism of liberalism is that presented by Raymond Williams who argues: 'Liberalism is ... a doctrine of certain necessary kinds of freedom but also, and essentially, a doctrine of possessive individualism.'[2] Yet, the significance of Warren's 'liberalism' is precisely that it challenged both bourgeois individualism, and abstract determinism. For Warren, both these positions result in a lack of real social and political engagement. They either see the individual as an autonomous being which is independent of its context, or as a mere expression of a more general process. By contrast, Warren saw the individual self as a being which was defined through its relations with others, but it was not a mere passive product. The self was defined in a dynamic process which required it to face dilemmas and choices. Human existence was a condition fraught with ironies and dualities in which action tended to escape human control. For Warren, this position did not lead to a philosophy of resignation or inaction. It was this very situation, it was argued, that required the individual to struggle to define itself as a morally responsible being. For Warren, the complexities of social life could not be resolved by simple adherence to an abstract set of values, but only through active moral struggles. Individuals not only had to develop concepts of justice, they also had to investigate their society in order to find strategies which would realize those concepts. For this reason, Warren's criticisms of mass organizations were not an example of the elitist reaction against democracy of the type which Raymond Williams discusses in *Culture and Society*.[3] Instead he reacted against the totalitarian tendencies of these organizations, tendencies which repressed the moral struggles of individuals and groups. Such positions were also a feature of Warren's critical writings and literature.

During the 1950s, Warren's positions were challenged and tested by major changes in American society. Consequently, there was a major development in Warren's writing. During the war, the government had reformed the race policies of various sections of the armed forces, and with the development of the post-war economy, there was a large migration of black workers from the South into the rest of the country. These developments led to a major reorientation of race relations in both the North and the South. Then, in 1954, the Supreme Court declared that segregation was unconstitutional, a decision which focused a wide variety of debates over the relationships between blacks and whites within both the South, and American society as a whole. In this situation, Warren claimed that the movement against segregation was one instance of the larger struggle to develop the concept of justice. His case was twofold: first, he argued that the black struggle was a positive instance of the struggle to extend the concept of justice; and second, that it also necessitated the involvement of the white community in this process. It needed the white community to redefine its sense of identity. For Warren, justice required individuals and groups to *enable* others to be actively involved within society. People should not be excluded from aspects of social life, but able to play an active role within that society. In this way, Warren's position sought to avoid the pitfalls of totalitarianism, liberal paternalism, and bourgeois individualism.[4]

### Literature and history

Warren's post-war positions were an extension of those he had developed in the 1930s. During this earlier period, Warren's Agrarianism had placed him in opposition to forms of liberalism both inside and outside the South, forms which were distinguished by an uncritical promotion of industrial progress. However, he had been far more sympathetic to class politics and to Marxism than either Ransom or Tate had been. Both these political movements, he argued, were attempts to develop a concept of justice. This difference between Warren and the other two may have been related to the specific region of the South from which Warren came, one dominated by yeoman farming, with a populist, rather than a paternalist, political tradition. This social and political situation was also distinguished by a large amount of civil conflict, particularly in the case of the Black Patch Wars, which formed the basis of Warren's first novel, *Night Rider* (1939). This book concerns the involvement of a young Southerner, Percy Munn, within the political conflicts of his period; and while his involvement is associated with his need to rely upon abstractions in an attempt to compensate for his lack of self-definition, Warren does consider the political issues as significant. He is clearly concerned with the moral dilemmas of political action, rather than with a rejection of political action itself.[5]

These interests also affected Warren's consideration of literature throughout the 1940s. Literature, it was argued, examined the dilemmas and contradictions of human activity, and this involved the writer in complex social engagements and moral struggles. For example, in a discussion of Katherine Anne Porter published in 1942, Warren distinguishes between the artistic self of the writer, and the desire for mass appreciation through the popular magazines. Porter's inability to reach a large readership was, he argues, a result of her refusal to adopt the formulae of popular fiction and so compromise her writing. This argument defines aesthetic writing as a *process* of production. In fact, Warren not only distinguishes the aesthetic process of writing from the practice of professional writers – who define themselves as mere producers – but also from the opposite tendency which he associates with Rahv's 'redskins' – writers who ignore the creative activity of writing in favour of 'the pride of shutting your eyes and spilling your innards, in pouring out the pure spirit'.[6] In distinction to these two approaches, Warren claims that

Porter's fiction is distinguished by her style, but he supports popular reactions against many critical discussions of style.[7] In these types of criticism, style is discussed in a way which seems to have little to do with the way in which actual readers experience texts. Warren argues that the act of writing must be meaningful and significant, but he claims that Porter's style is not merely a pleasant effect or detail which is external to the meaning of her writing. It is the way in which that meaning is defined. It is the medium within which the contradictions and dilemmas of the social life are considered. Porter's fiction is composed of 'a tissue of contradictions, and the very phraseology takes us to those contradictions'.[8] For this reason, Porter's awareness of these contradictions, and her refusal to accept the formula solution, are not a rejection of social engagement, but the very means by which she engages with her society as a writer.[9] For Warren, Porter's use of irony and complexity is an engagement with social values.

Warren's case is that fiction, poetry, and the 'imagination' should not be seen as pleasant indulgences, but 'should have some significant relation to the world, some meaning'.[10] This claim is developed in relation to Coleridge's 'The Ancient Mariner' where he criticizes those writers who have either denied that the poem has a meaning, or merely seen the theme of redemption as a structural device which is used to hold the imaginative elements together. For Warren, both these positions reduce the imagination and the poem to the status of 'nothing more than a pleasant but meaningless dream'.[11] This type of criticism is claimed to contradict Coleridge's own views with regard to the imagination in which it was referred to as a creative and distinctly human process of knowing.[12] According to Warren, Coleridge distinguished between the primary imagination – in which human beings create their sense of the world – and the secondary imagination – in which human beings move beyond unconscious creation, and enter into a process of conscious creation which affirms their freedom. The process of aesthetic creation, it is argued, is an example of the secondary imagination, and poetic form and meaning are inseparable from that active process of production. The meaning of the poem is not defined by the conscious or unconscious intention of the poet, or by the responses of individual readers. It is not a position which can be abstracted from the text, but an aspect of the creative process itself. For Warren, the process of literary production may alter the original intentions and meanings of the poet, and the reader may be affected by those meanings without fully acknowledging or articulating those affects.

For Warren, the meaning of poetry could not be abstracted from its linguistic processes of production, but he insisted that 'the poem should not just be, but should also mean'. This position led Warren to distinguish between poetry as a form and specific poems: 'Poetry always wants to be pure, but poems do not.'[13] While poetry is always attempting to attain purity as a genre, the individual poem can only attain purity by earning it, by subjecting that purity to the experience of the world. For example, *Romeo and Juliet* is used to illustrate that poems must include base elements within themselves in order to make their metaphors prove themselves.[14] This position is developed directly from the New Critical concern with the use of language in literature and the forms of knowledge which it produces. It emphasizes that the poetic process investigates the limits of metaphor and human activity, and that while the impulse of poetry is to become all of one piece, the poem itself can only create and justify its unity through its process of production. This argument leads Warren to discuss the different uses of the term 'structure'. He challenges mechanistic uses of the term in which the structure is defined as an 'expression' of the poetic features or essence, rather than as the process of production itself.[15] As a result, Warren argues, as he had done in the 1930s, that it is specifically because poetry is concerned with significant meanings that it refuses to accept the abstract solutions available in mass forms. He claims that the poem is engaged in the struggle to investigate and improve both meanings and values, rather than simply expressing ones that had already been formulated.

These themes are developed in relation to Melville's poetry. According to Warren, the problems with Melville's poetry were not the result of a lack of ability. Melville was quite capable of producing the polished types of poetry which were produced by his contemporaries. Instead Melville's poetry is claimed to have confronted a more complex series of issues than that of his contemporaries. It examined 'the fundamental ironical dualities of existence'.[16] It may have run into difficulties, but these were only an indication of its ambition. An example of these ironic dualities is that despite a human will to act for Truth and Right, the force of circumstance can distort or contradict this will. Circumstance can turn human efforts against themselves. According to Warren, it is precisely Melville's consideration of these problems that led him to develop a new style, but it was one which avoided a pessimistic determinism. He did not present humanity as helplessly doomed by circumstance. Instead Melville presented the historical process as one which could not be escaped and had to be confronted. It was a process which could not only bring guilt and sin, but in which one could also earn a degree of salvation and redemption. This salvation could only be achieved through individuals' incorporation into the life of humanity as a whole, not through their attempt to affirm an independence from society and history.

For Warren, this process of incorporation requires individuals to define moral responsibilities for themselves, and for this reason, it was not the passive absorption of the self into an abstract wholeness or oneness. It was a recognition of the interrelations between the self and others. In the case of Conrad's *Nostromo*, for example, Warren argues that Gould's problem is that he fails to understand this distinction. He isolates himself from others by adopting the abstract role of an improver of mankind.[17] He is unable to acknowledge the dualities of existence. A solution to these dualities cannot be achieved through adherence to an abstract principle: good intentions can be incredibly destructive. A solution can only be achieved through a continual examination of one's relationships with others.[18] As a result, Warren's New Critical positions after the 1930s were not developed as a result of his abandonment of the Agrarian movement, but were an extension of the positions which he had developed in the 1930s. Nor did they see literary texts as entirely autonomous and self-contained objects. They saw literary forms as responses to their social and cultural contexts.

### Segregation and the South

By the mid-1950s, the debates concerning segregation and the situation of blacks within American society gave Warren a concrete image of the process of defining a moral identity, and of the interrelation between the self and others. In 1955, Warren published *Band of Angels*, a fascinating, though flawed, novel in which his themes of identity were developed through the figure of a female slave. This female slave, Amantha Starr, believes herself to be white until the death of her slaveowner father, when it is revealed that her mother was a black slave; that Amantha is legally both black and a slave; and that as her father's property, she must be sold to pay his debts. However, Amantha's problems are more complex than her legal status as property. They are related to her sense of racial and sexual identity. Her dilemma is that she is unable to define her own identity, and as she is exchanged between different male figures, she regards herself as a victim of others without a will of her own. This problem persists even after her legal freedom, which comes with the end of the Civil War, and in the novel, it is associated with her refusal to identify herself as black. In this way, the novel situates Warren's interest in the ironies and dualities of experience within the period of the Civil War and the reconstruction. It illustrates the ironies of emancipation and freedom. Warren does not suggest that emancipation was wrong in itself, but that in many cases it was implemented by people who had as little respect for blacks as those who opposed it. Blacks did achieve legal freedom in the post-bellum period, but this type of freedom created conditions which in many ways excluded them from an active involvement within American society as a whole.[19]

The novels which follow *Band of Angels* are very unsatisfying, and after 1955, Warren's most significant writings were forms of social and historical commentary. In this writing, Warren developed his positions through a mixture of dialogues and confessional passages where he wrestles with his conscience and his own sense of identity. These works drew directly upon the positions which Warren had developed throughout the 1930s – positions which had shaped his New Critical writings. In his writings from the 1950s onwards, Warren examined his own sense of self in relation to others. In *Segregation: the Inner Conflict of the South* (1956), for example, the conversations which compose the book are portrayed as a debate with the complexities of his own identity. For Warren, the 'inner conflict' of segregation was not merely within legal institutions, but within the individual's very sense of self.[20] For this reason, segregation is associated with a larger problem between the races. The black had been systematically denied human dignity – which Warren defines as the right to be seen as an active moral identity[21] – a denial which defined the black as an inferior who should not be involved in society as a citizen. It also defined the identity of the white. For Warren, the denial of others' humanity was a failure to exercise one's own humanity. By failing to define a self which could acknowledge the black as a human being of equal value to themselves, whites had repressed their own humanity. They had denied their own capacity for moral redefinition. They had denied their own ability to transform themselves. This argument brought Warren back to the problems of society and history. Despite his acknowledgement of the fact that racial antagonisms were the product of historical forces, he argues that human beings are not simply the prisoners of history. Humanity's unique and distinctive faculty is its ability to examine the meaning of the past and struggle to create a better future.[22] By denying that humans are the prisoners of history, Warren stresses that the issue of desegregation was only one stage in the longer struggle to define justice, and he identifies this struggle as the process of human development and liberation. It is a struggle to liberate the self from its own limitations which requires responsibility, commitment, self-discovery, and self-transformation.[23] For Warren, the human drama is a moral one through which the self redefines itself through a re-evaluation of its relations with others.

The New Criticism has often been described as a type of asocial formalism which came after these writers' interest in social criticism, but during this period, as his writing shows, Warren continued to be involved in critical social activity which was motivated by the same positions which had shaped his literary and cultural criticism. This becomes clear in his essay, 'Knowledge and the Image of Man' (1957), which maintains that human beings' right to existence is tied to their right to knowledge. This definition of knowledge draws directly upon his Agrarian and New Critical positions. It is seen as more than an accumulation of facts or instrumental information since it also involves an awareness of one's interpenetrations with others which is an essential part of human existence. It not only creates our sense of self, but also enables us to examine and redefine that sense. For Warren, the right to existence presupposes the right to knowledge because it permits human beings to exercise and affirm their distinctly human faculties.[24] In contrast to many post-structuralist theorists, Warren's recognition of difference, and the extent to which it is involved in the construction of identity, does not lead to a dissolution of identity into absence. Quite the reverse; it is such difference which enables the very definition of that identity, and affirms both individuality and communal relations at the same moment. Consequently, Warren claims that the problem of segregation is not solely about how whites can learn to live with blacks, but how whites can learn to live with themselves through an examination of their relationship with others and the redefinition of their sense of justice. As he stresses: 'I don't think you can live with yourself when you are humiliating the man next to you.'[25]

For Warren, the moral struggle to develop the sense of justice is a vitally important one, and one which requires the South to look carefully and critically at its own social relations. Through this process of self-examination, he argued, the South could also act as an example to the rest of the nation. It could enable America to acknowledge the complexities and paradoxes of human activity.[26] Warren's point was that American society had tended to avoid any serious evaluation of its own institutions and activities, a point which he discussed in 1961, in a book commemorating the centenary of the Civil War. The book argues that the war provided both the South and North with excuses for avoiding their moral responsibilities. These excuses are referred to as the 'Great Alibi' and the 'Treasury of Virtue'. The 'Great Alibi' allowed the South to explain away all its social problems with a reference to the Civil War and its treatment by the North. Southerners were never at fault and could not change matters. Their situation was determined by a history for which they were not responsible and over which they had no control. On the other hand, the 'Treasury of Virtue' allowed the North to ignore its own faults and associate itself with virtue. It had seen itself as being on the side of the angels in the war and had never investigated the dilemmas and contradictions of its own position. These two excuses thus also enabled the American nation as a whole to avoid an investigation of its own identity. The nation had failed 'to appreciate the difficulty of moral definition, the doubleness of experience – what [Reinhold Niebuhr] calls the "irony of history"'.[27] As a result, irony was not a specifically literary feature for Warren, but the actual condition of human existence which literature was required to acknowledge.

Consequently, Warren's opposition to forms of mass organization was not an elitist reaction against democracy. Instead he objected to political organizations which dominated their individual members and prevented them from exercising their own critical faculties. This objection drew upon the positions developed in the 1930s when he had argued that many modern mass movements prevented the majority from being actively involved with society. In the 1950s, this position is clearest in his attack on 'Common-manism' which, he argued, betrayed 'the right to knowledge, which should have meant the glorification of our common human capacity to move towards excellence, to define ourselves in a communal aspiration'.[28] As a result, Warren's reaction to mass forms was not opposed to forms of communal activity, or to the inclusion of all human beings within the citizenship of society. Rather, he attacked mass organizations for defining the mass in abstract terms, terms which failed to acknowledge the complex interrelations between people.

It was for this reason that Warren stressed that the problems of segregation went far beyond the legal issues surrounding the decisions of the Supreme Court. These problems went far beyond the constitutionality of specific laws, they were bound up with the nation's very definition of justice. The black struggle was part of a larger crisis in Western culture which required both North and South to redefine their sense of cultural identity. Warren's argument is that the black's struggle to include himself within the citizenship of society was an attempt to define himself as an active moral identity – as a maker of history – and that as such the black could redeem Western culture by struggling to redefine and extend its values.[29] Western culture had failed to attain its own standards through its denial of the black's humanity. It could only redeem itself by acknowledging this failure. It had to redefine its values and identity in order to enable the black to be actively involved within American society. Both the Southern and the Northern white needed to consider their own cultural identities.[30] Consequently, justice would not be served by a mere recognition of the black's legal rights as a citizen; it required a social reorganization. If Civil Rights were vital and important, Warren also drew attention to the economic and cultural deprivation which faced many blacks.[31] For Warren, the issue of citizenship concerns the active involvement of individuals within society, not simply a legal recognition of rights. As a result, it is necessary to confront the factors which limit involvement continually. For example, in 1965, Warren discusses the emergence of a growing group of poor Americans whose social and economic position has increasingly limited their involvement within American society since the 1960s. He claims that the development of this group requires the redefinition and extension of citizenship rights, rather than the contraction and erosion of these rights which distinguished the era of Reagan.[32]

## Conclusion: literature and the self

A concern with the relationship between the self and society was also a significant feature of Warren's literary criticism, even after the 1940s, and the institutionalization of the New Criticism within the academy: the New Criticism certainly did not develop out of a retreat from social criticism. This concern with the relation between the self and society is also important given the post-structural critique of the concept of self which it identifies with bourgeois individualism. As late as 1975, in his book *Democracy and Poetry*, Warren considers literature in relation to social and historical problems. The book argues that the self is defined through its relations to others, and that responsibility can only be defined by a being who is 'capable of action worthy of praise or blame'.[33] This position does acknowledge socially repressive and destructive constructions of the self, but it maintains that human beings are not simply the 'effects' of structures but are also able to struggle against these repressive constructions. The self is always defined dynamically through its relation to others, but Warren argues that people have lost a sense of this dynamic process. This loss is seen as part of a larger cultural and political crisis which is associated with the development of modernity and science.

As in the 1930s, Warren claims that modernity and science identify the self with abstractions. They limit an awareness of the self's relation to others. This limitation is also related to a loss of historical awareness. For Warren, America has identified itself with the new – it regards itself as a break with the past – and this position presents problems. It identifies the self with the process of human perfection and fails to acknowledge its faults. Literature is also associated with the sense of self, and is said to have both a diagnostic and a therapeutic role. It not only examines the ways in which social relations limit a sense of self, but also presents a concrete image of the human capacity to redefine itself. It celebrates the self's capacity for social engagement and moral struggle.

For example, in an examination of the diagnostic aspect of American literature, Warren maintains that writers such as Cooper and Melville discussed the ways in which entrepreneurial and industrial capitalism limited a sense of the self's relations to others. Writers such as Russell Reising have accused the New Criticism of devaluing realism and naturalism in favour of symbolic types of literature,[34] but Warren's criticism highly values these forms of writing. For example, Dreiser was a particularly important figure for Warren throughout his career. He is seen as emphasizing the complexity of historical determinations and processes. He is also said to illustrate that the goal of financial success negates an awareness that the self is part of a community to which it has a moral responsibility. Dreiser's novel, *An American Tragedy*, is also related to the rise of consumer culture. For Warren, while Cowperwood represents the man of the will in the novel *The Titan*, Clyde Griffiths is 'the born consumer with the passivity of the consumer, whose wishes are not only gratified, but created by the purveyor of goods'.[35] Even in the case of other realist writers, Warren stresses that their writing might be more interesting than their conscious intentions. The process of literary production could undercut a writer's explicit ideology. For example, the implications of Twain's writings are said to refute the writer's own explicit optimism in American society since they acknowledge the contradictory aspects of modernity and progress. This argument is developed in a discussion of *A Connecticut Yankee at King Arthur's Court*. The book, it is claimed, does not present the projects of modernization and imperialism as redeeming mankind, but as isolating the modernizer from others, and as slaughtering the very beings which they were supposed to have redeemed.[36]

While these discussions concern the 'diagnostic' aspect of literature, Warren claims there is also a 'therapeutic' aspect which is related to the process of literary production. This productive process, it is claimed, affirms the self's capacity for creative activity. None the less, this creative activity is not merely identified with the creation of meanings, but also with the materiality of language. Art, it is argued, acknowledges the material aspects of the self, and does not simply address their rational aspects. It gives pleasure to the senses with its material forms. These positions draw upon Warren's Agrarian positions of the 1930s. They argue that the creative activity presented by art involves a form of knowledge, but not one that is concerned with the communication of facts. Instead aesthetic activity involves an awareness of the context of human activity, an awareness which enables one to understand the *process* of human activity.[37] As a result, aesthetic activity is not an asocial or self-indulgent activity. On the contrary, it is presented as a process of creation which examines and evaluates social relations. As a result, when Warren writes that his own work represents 'the old, recurring reflex of art against the "real" world',[38] he is not implying that literature is not concerned with the 'real' world. Instead, he means that literature is a critical response to existing social relations. Consequently, the example of Warren not only highlights the continuity between the social criticisms of the Agrarian movement and the positions of the New Critics, it also illustrates that the New Criticism was not inherently reactionary in its politics, but that it also had the potential to produce a radical and socially engaged criticism.

# Modernism and postmodernism within the American Academy

## Introduction

According to contemporary wisdom, the New Criticism is dead. This is certainly true in so far as many of its key practitioners are now deceased: and with the recent death of Robert Penn Warren, all of the three critics dealt with in this book are now no longer with us. As a movement, the New Criticism is also dead; its missionary zeal dissipated by its own success. Even its critical positions are now the favourite whipping boy of most contemporary theorists. However, this continual need to repeat the dismantling of the New Criticism suggests a kind of presence which needs to be addressed. As we saw at the start of this book, Lentricchia argues that while the New Criticism is dead, 'it is dead in the way an imposing and repressive father figure is dead'.[1] Contemporary criticism's very sense of identity is defined through its opposition to the New Criticism which is therefore never absolutely absent. For Lentricchia, however, this is largely a matter of self-identification (or an 'anxiety of influence' to borrow Harold Bloom's phrase): after all, Lentricchia himself insists that 'in an offical sense, of course',[2] the New Criticism *is* dead!

As William E. Cain points out, this situation is misleading: if today the New Criticism seems to be dead (because everyone speaks against it and no one speaks for it), 'it seems so powerless only because its power is so pervasive that we are ordinarily not aware of it'.[3] Cain's argument on this point is very close to the one which I have been suggesting throughout this book: he claims that New Critical attitudes and activities are so deeply ingrained within the definition of literary study that most critics fail to even identify its legacy: 'we feel them to be natural and definitive conditions for criticism in general'.[4] The point is that, as we have seen, the attempt to establish the New Criticism within the universities was a conscious political tactic. Through this tactic Ransom, Tate, Warren, and others sought to define the terms of reference for literary study within the academy. They shifted the emphasis from historical scholarship and source hunting to a concentration upon the forms of language and style within the text. In so doing, they transformed their own particular approach into the general aims of the academic institution 'setting the norms for effective teaching and marking the boundaries within which nearly all criticism seeks to validate itself'.[5] The New Criticism thereby redefined the profession of English itself. It established not only the pedagogical methods by which students were trained, but also the criteria by which members of the profession were evaluated: 'It is not simply that the New Criticism has become institutionalized, but that it has gained acceptance as the institution itself. It has been transformed into "criticism", the essence of what we do as teachers and critics, the ground upon which everything else is based.'[6]

Consequently, while contemporary critics have criticized many aspects of the New Criticism, they have rarely challenged the concentration on the linguistic forms of the text. In fact, even critics such as Cain and Jonathan Culler, who have acknowledged the continuities between the New Criticism and contemporary critical modes, have associated these forms of criticism with the practice of 'close reading'. While Culler shifts his focus to an analysis of the linguistic structures within which *both* reading and writing are constructed, he still identifies the object of literary study with the textual, even if his textual analysis has been displaced from the individual text to an analysis of the textual system.[7] Where I differ from Cain, then, is over the 'inevitability' of this concentration on textuality. Whether it was a good or bad thing, literary study has not always been associated with the textual, nor need it be.[8] In fact, it is the contention of both Cain and myself that the concentration on the textual is the specific *innovation* of the New Criticism itself, an innovation which was defined in opposition to pre-existent and alternative forms of academic literary study.

# 13   The professionalization of literary study

In fact, the emergence of the professional academic is itself a relatively new phenomenon. As Gerald Graff has pointed out, departments of language and literature only really emerged in the last quarter of the nineteenth century 'as part of a larger process of professionalization by which the old "college" became the new "university"'.[1] Moreover, these departments of literature and language did not define their form of study as a professional discipline according to the same criteria as contemporary departments of literature. Instead they concentrated on 'scientific' research and the philological study of modern languages. When literature was used in these departments, it was studied etymologically and grammatically, as a way of documenting changes in language, not as an aesthetic form. As Graff puts it, 'the profession of "literary studies" was established before it began to consider literature its subject'.[2] However, while the philologists' emphasis on their discipline and training allowed them control over their recruitment and their curriculum, they did not go unchallenged. Graff has referred to a 'competing model' for the departments of language and literature which was proposed by a group of 'generalists'. These generalists maintained that philological study was too narrow and specialized for an understanding of culture. They thereby formed an alternative tradition which maintained that the study of literature should be concerned with cultural values not facts. They saw 'literature as a moral and spiritual force and a repository of "general ideas" which could be applied directly to the conduct of life and the improvement of national culture'.[3] But even this group did not really emphasize the linguistic forms of the text as the object of critical analysis.

For Graff, it was not the triumph of any one approach which was formative for the profession of literary study, but rather the conflicts which emerged from the attempt to reconcile the traditionalism of liberal culture with the criteria of professional secularism. The problem was that the very criteria which enabled the philologists to establish their credentials as professionals within the academy were at odds with the civic and humanistic claims which justified the study of language and literature to the rest of society. As a result, the debate over professionalism which 'had begun as a conflict between journalists and gentlemen amateurs *against* professionalism became increasingly a conflict *within* professionalism, a conflict for the right to define what professionalism in literary studies would mean. This debate continues today.'[4] For Graff, there never was a clear consensus on the aims of literary study within the academy, and its activities have always been contested. In fact, even some of the philologists realized that outside the academy, their scientific research had less appeal than the use of literature in a discussion of cultural values. What is more, as the universities continued to expand from the late nineteenth century and through the first half of the twentieth century, the philologists felt greater and greater pressure to shift the focus of their studies. It was one thing to defend their specialized forms of study at a time when the university population was small by 'protest[ing] that mass education was not their business', but 'as the universities expanded such disclaimers seemed irresponsible'.[5] It was the move towards mass education which finally forced the scholars' hands, and required them to justify their activities in social, rather than strictly technical, terms.

However, the profession found it hard to develop such a justification. It had based its claim to professional status on a distinction between research and criticism. It defined the former as the objective, scientific search for 'certifiable facts', and differentiated it from the latter which was dismissed as being merely a matter of 'subjective impressions'. Research scholars did attempt to revise their assessment of criticism by the end of World War I. They argued that it was not criticism which they found problematic, but criticism which was uninformed by the scholarly groundwork. However, as Graff claims, 'these concessions were hollow as long as most scholars still conceived of criticism as an affair of subjective impressions opposed to certifiable facts. As long as that assumption prevailed, there was little chance that criticism could become accepted as part of a literature student's necessary concerns.'[6] This distinction made it virtually impossible for the academic profession to incorporate the discussion of the cultural values within its discipline. The distinction enforced a division between the accumulation of historical information and the discussion of the literary text, and prevented any attempt to connect them significantly.

# 14    The New Critical intervention

It was this very problem which the New Critics addressed through a critique of scientific positivism in general, and literary scholarship in particular; a critique which challenged the division between the public and the private on which these forms of positivism were based. In his article, 'Miss Emily and the Bibliographer',[1] for example, Tate countered the scholars by attacking the very definition of 'criticism as an affair of subjective impressions opposed to certifiable facts'.[2] His objection was that this position limits the study of literature to the accumulation of historical information. The study of literary texts, he argued, could have little validity so long as reading was defined merely as a matter of the subjective response of individuals. The concentration on the text as a linguistic construct was offered as a basis for assessing the validity and significance of specific readings.[3] The attempt to identify the objectivity of the text was, at least in part, a way of overcoming the philologists' division between the objectivity of the historical background and the subjectivity of the reader's response. This concentration on the literary text as a linguistic process of production allowed Tate to distinguish the literary text from its background. He argued that it was not the text which had no meaning except as a transparent expression of its historical background, but that its background only had meaning for literary study in so far as it informed the process of literary production. Defining the literary process of production as a linguistic process also allowed Tate to define a basis for the evaluation of responses to literary texts. He was able to maintain that responses were not merely private and personal, but that they were defined in relation to a linguistic process that was both shared and social; and that, as a result, responses to the text could attain the status of claims about the meaning of that text whose validity and significance could be evaluated.

However, this focus on textuality was not intended to define criticism as a type of asocial formalism in which critics explicated texts within a vacuum. As Graff argues: 'Whatever one may think of their predominantly conservative politics, the fact remains that first-generation New Critics were neither aesthetes nor pure explicators but culture critics with a considerable "axe-to-grind" against the technocratic tendencies of modern mass civilization.'[4] In fact, Ransom, Tate, and Warren's critique of scientific positivism and literary scholasticism was only one aspect of a larger critique of capitalist relations which drew upon forms of Southern paternalism. These critics argued that just as capitalist relations reduce the individual labourer to their labour-power, and suppress other aspects of the labourer's social and material being, so the positivism of modern society relies on abstractions which suppress the limits to the rationalizing procedures of calculation and control.[5] For these writers, culture was defined as 'the whole way of life in which we live, act, think, and feel',[6] but they claimed that with the emergence of modern society, 'culture in the true sense was disappearing'.[7] Their argument was that the cash-nexus as a mode of social organization created a division between the way of living and the way of making a living, so that the latter appeared to be unconnected with the former, except as a means to an end. This situation, it was argued, resulted in the degradation of both aspects of life. The way of making a living became preoccupied with efficiency and control. It dehumanized the work-process and devalued its creative and pleasurable aspects. On the other hand, culture, which was the specific way of living, became associated with leisure rather than activity, and was seen as merely a series of decorative styles and objects with no relation to the whole context of human conduct.[8] This process also affected both language and literature. It created a division between meaning and form in which the meaning was associated with efficiency and control and was judged and valued as a positive statement, while the form was seen as a decorative addition with no intrinsic relationship to the meaning, except as a transparent expression of that meaning.[9]

It was for this reason that the New Critics argued that the literary process of production should be regarded as a specific, 'autonomous' activity which should not be 'judged by reference to criteria or considerations beyond itself'.[10] This argument did not seek to close the text off from history, or claim that literature was not a product of its social or historical context. Instead these critics argued that the process of literary production should be seen as an investigation of this context, not as a mere vehicle for a preformulated statement. Ransom, Tate, and Warren were therefore careful to emphasize that the meaning of a text must not be seen as a fixed object, or content, which could be abstracted from the linguistic processes of the text. Their critique of scientific positivism and literary scholasticism was specifically based on the claim that these forms suppressed the materiality and productivity of language. In opposition to these forms, the New Critics argued that the text could not be read as a transparent reflection of its background, or some fixed meaning, but that it involved a specific process of production which did not merely represent its context but reconsidered it as well. Furthermore, while this did lead them to maintain that the process of literary production did produce a form of knowledge, they emphasized that this knowledge was different from the form of knowledge associated with positivism. They stressed that it did not take the form of a statement or claim.[11]

If they argued that literature was a product of its social context, they also claimed that it was not merely a reflection or expression of that context. It was not only able to resist or respond to its situation, it should investigate its social and cultural context in a critical manner. To put it another way, they suggested that while the positivism of modern society produced literature which suppressed its materiality and its productivity, literature could also challenge that society by foregrounding its materiality and productivity. In this way, it could test the abstractions on which modern society was based. An emphasis on literature's texture of sound patterns, they claimed, could create a friction with its rational structure which worked against that structure, and forced the latter to particularize and justify itself.[12] The materiality of language was seen as a challenge to the positivistic emphasis on rational meaning, but they also argued that literature could resist positivism by foregrounding its figures of speech.[13] For example, Ransom claims that while 'science abhors the figurative, the tropical', art can resist positivism by making these forms its own 'object of knowledge, its designatum and denotatum'.[14] Rather than suppressing the productivity of these forms, literature could resist modern society by identifying the limitations and contradictions of positivist discourse through an investigation of the properties of language and meaning.

It was for this reason that these critics stressed the values of complexity and irony. They argued that these forms involved a critical process through which abstract propositions were tested and re-evaluated. They were not opposed to resolution itself, but argued that it must be legitimated through the linguistic processes of the text. It was for this reason that they opposed the 'heresy of paraphrase'. They claimed that the meaning of the text could not be reduced to a fixed object, and was inseparable from the linguistic processes of the text. The literary text was seen as capable of reasserting the limits of positivism and of emphasizing the historical and material contexts of human activity. These were seen by Tate in specifically religious terms as Original Sin, or the presence and limits of human nature, of the past, and of history.[15] His critique of modern society was that it had not come to terms with the presence of human nature, but saw it merely as something to be rationalized, controlled, and used. He claimed that modern society was in conflict with human nature, suppressing and denying it, and that literature could act as a challenge to modern society, if it offered 'communion', rather than 'communication'. Instead of concentrating on the rational exchange of information, literature should emphasize the presence of both rational and irrational elements in human existence. It should test the extent to which the abstractions of modern society do justice to human nature.[16]

If they claimed that the text was not reducible to a fixed content or meaning, they did stress that it was necessary to struggle to define a meaning. For these writers, literature must acknowledge that the modern world was complex and contradictory, but they still stressed that it was important to struggle to make sense of it.[17] Despite their critique of modern society, these critics were firmly a part of the project of aesthetic modernism. They sought out the contradictions of existing society and demanded the establishment of alternative ways of living. They stressed that the aesthetic was not inherently separate from human activity, but a form which should be fully integrated with all activities; that it should be established within a way of living that had acknowledged, and come to terms with, human nature. As a result, their literary criticism was not a form of scientism, but developed out of a reaction against positivist concepts of science. (Ransom did change his position in 1941, describing literary criticism as a form of science, but even he was careful to emphasize that its form was not the same as that of positivist science.)[18] Instead they argued that it was reductive to impose one reading upon the text, and argued that literary criticism should be an examination of the linguistic processes of the text, and as such, a form of activity itself.[19] For this reason, these critics were not solely the products of their context, unable to disentangle themselves from their historical situation; rather they analysed the text in relation to modern society, and examined the social situation within which the activity of writing takes place. However abstracted their historical framework, these critics did not ignore history: rather they made the critique of modern society the centre of their argument and approach, and emphasized the social context of literary texts.

While Graff acknowledges many of these features, he mistakenly suggests that the New Criticism sought to 'measure up to the institutional criteria set up by the scholarly opposition, which was still in control of the literature departments'.[20] Instead they attempted to redefine the literary institution and its claim to professional status. Despite Cain's claims, the New Critical shift in literary study to a concentration on the linguistic forms of the text was not inevitable, but the result of a struggle to displace the existing modes of scholarship with an oppositional set of professional criteria.[21] In fact, many of the New Critics were outsiders to the academy with little or no training in philological research. They were outsiders who found themselves alienated from the dominant modes of scholarship, and were consciously engaged in an attempt to redefine the teaching of literature. It is also the case that New Critics such as Ransom, Tate, and Warren clearly saw this redefinition as a political intervention through which they could counter modern society. Rather than failing to understand that reading practices were socially defined, as writers such as Terence Hawkes claim,[22] these New Critics consciously sought to transform the reading of literature through their teaching as a way of developing and distributing their own critique of modern society.

# 15    Cultural criticism and postmodernity

It was the New Critical identification of literary study with the analysis of the linguistic forms of the text which defined the preconditions for contemporary forms of literary criticism, such as post-structuralism. Both forms of criticism share an emphasis on the materiality and productivity of language, and a critique of the positivism of modern society. Consequently, despite the continual attacks on the New Criticism, it is this identification which has rarely been challenged. But if both New Critical and contemporary forms of criticism share the same assumptions about what the object of literary study should be, then what is it that differentiates these two forms? According to Fredric Jameson, contemporary criticism is distinguished by the emergence of 'a kind of writing simply called "theory"'.[1] He argues that the distinctive feature of this new kind of writing is its 'undecidability', and that this feature can be seen as a manifestation of its postmodernity. (Forms of criticism, such as the New Criticism, are identified as modernist by Jameson.) For Jameson, the 'undecidability' of postmodern criticism is a refusal to define itself within the terms of professional disciplines, but it is better understood if we examine Jameson's analysis of postmodernism more closely. After all, it is the forms of linguistic analysis offered by this new kind of discourse which have proved most attractive to its exponents within the departments of literature, Jameson himself included.[2]

According to Jameson, postmodernism is a reaction against the forms of modernism, and the concepts of unity on which they were based. He identifies postmodernism with the death of 'History', the 'Subject', and 'the unity of the text'. For Jameson, postmodernism is a periodizing concept which allows him to examine specific formal features of culture in relation to a specific type of social and economic order. The two significant features of this culture, it is argued, are pastiche and schizophrenia. Pastiche is distinguished from parody by Jameson who argues that while parody ridicules specific styles by comparing them with an ideal of normal language, pastiche comes into being with the loss of any sense of a linguistic norm. Pastiche is also supposed to be linked to the 'death of the subject'. High modernism, it is argued, was 'predicated on the invention of a personal, private style, as unmistakable as your finger print, as incomparable as your own body',[3] but with the death of the subject comes the end of any belief in the possibility of producing 'a unique vision of the world'.[4] Pastiche emerges and parody becomes impossible, according to Jameson, at the specific moment when 'stylistic innovation is no longer possible, [and] all that is left is to imitate dead styles, to speak through the voices of the styles in the imaginary museum'.[5] If the postmodern world is distinguished by the death of the subject, Jameson refuses to decide whether the subject no longer exists, or whether it was always an illusion. This refusal presents severe problems for Jameson. After all, these two positions are very different. It is one thing to claim that the self is an illusion which is now recognized as such, and quite another to claim that there were once individual subjects, but postmodern society prevents and denies the possibility of a unitary subjectivity.

In fact, it is debatable whether the postmodern world really is distinguished by the loss of subjectivity. After all, Jameson himself argues that the shift from parody to pastiche develops when the high modernist attempt to produce private languages reaches a point at which 'the very possibilities of any linguistic norm in terms of which one could ridicule private languages and idiosyncratic styles... vanish, and we... have nothing but stylistic diversity and heterogeneity'.[6] In a sense, what is lost is not so much the existence of private languages, but any sense of a public language which could relate private languages to one another. It is therefore significant that Jameson identifies postmodernity with the loss of a sense of history, and argues that postmodern culture is 'incapable of dealing with time and history'.[7] In this way, pastiche is linked to a nostalgic attempt to reproduce the experience of the past. However, it is an attempt to reproduce the past as style, not as history. Style has come to be seen as a part of 'some indefinable nostalgic past, an eternal 1930s, say, beyond history'.[8] For Jameson, postmodernism is therefore linked to the schizo-phrenic because the schizophrenic 'is condemned to live a perpetual present with which the various movements of his past have little connection and for which there is no conceivable future on the horizon'.[9] The schizophrenic has no fixed sense of personal identity, and it is for this reason that innovation is regarded as impossible. Lacking any sense of past and future, the schizophrenic can do nothing, 'since to have a project is to be able to commit oneself to a certain continuity over time'.[10]

What is particularly postmodern is not the loss of the private, but the isolation and alienation of the self. People still experience themselves as subjectivities, but they retreat from commitment to any long-term project and distrust all claims to authority.[11] In postmodern literary criticism this distrust of all claims to authority has only intensified the concentration on the linguistic forms of the text. The sign is broken free of any referential function and isolated from history. In this situation, the signifier 'becomes ever more material – or better still, *literal* – ever more vivid in sensory ways, whether the new experience is attractive or terrifying'.[12] The New Critical concern with the unity of the text, or the struggle for meaning, is replaced by a view of textuality as a perpetual process in which unity and meaning are impossible. In fact, the search for these forms is seen as 'a thing of the past', something to be rejected, and the literary text comes to be valued for its inability to commit itself. The text announces its own disunity, its lack of reference, its refusal of meaning. In this way, 'undecidability' *is* the distinctive feature of postmodern criticism.

This situation is most clearly seen in the case of deconstructive criticism where, even more than in the case of the New Criticism, the discussion of literature is limited to the analysis of linguistic processes. In fact, while the New Critics continued to discuss literary language in relation to modern society, deconstructive criticism refuses to see literature as a product of history. Instead it analyses literature as a form which does not refer to any realm beyond itself, but is entirely preoccupied with its own linguistic processes. Furthermore, any attempt to define a unity or meaning is seen as an attempt to limit or repress the 'free play' of language, an act which is claimed to be both impossible and undesirable. Deconstructive critics refuse to see criticism as an attempt to identify or define the meaning of the text. Rather they maintain that the critic uses the text as a way of considering the nature of linguistic processes. Even contemporary psycho-analytic criticism reproduces many of these arguments, despite its attempt to analyse the construction of gendered subjects within society. Again it limits the discussion of literature to an analysis of linguistic processes and refuses to see literature as either a product of history, or a form which refers to anything beyond language. In fact it defines the formation of the subject in a manner which is both transhistorical and universal. As Stuart Hall puts it, 'it addresses the subject-in-general, not historically-determinant social subjects, or socially determinant particular languages'.[13] Consequently, postmodern critical approaches to literature continue to focus on the language of the text. What finally distinguishes the New Criticism from postmodern criticism is that while the former continued to discuss literature in relation to history and valued the attempt to define a unified meaning within the text, the latter rejects the attempt to define unity or meaning, and defines literature as an entirely self-referring linguistic activity.

For Jameson, the break between modernism and postmodernism is not a 'complete change of content but rather the restructuration of a certain number of elements already given: features that in an earlier period or system were subordinate are now dominant, and features that had been dominant become secondary'.[14] Modernist forms had once been shocking, but their features have 'shifted [their] position fundamentally within our culture'.[15] The modernist text had attempted to resist its reduction to a commodity, but now it has become commercially successful. As a result, the postmodern period would appear to date from the 1960s when the works of modernism became established in the academy, and came to be seen as merely academic by a new generation. But Jameson also argues that one can also relate this break to other aspects of social life, and claims that 'postmodernism is closely related to the emergence of late, consumer, or multinational capitalism'.[16] Jameson draws his analysis of late capitalism from the work of Ernest Mandel,[17] but, as Mike Davis points out, there is a problem of 'establishing a ... fit between postmodernism and Mandel's concept of the late-capitalist stage'.[18] Mandel is quite specific that late capitalism refers to the rapid economic growth of the post-war period, a period which comes to an end in 1974–5 with the 'second slump'.[19] If postmodernism develops in the 1960s, it does so as late capitalism was coming to an end. In contrast to Jameson, Davis uses Mandel's periodization to examine postmodern architecture, and argues that it 'is a better grid to plot the relationship between cultural forms and economic phases'[20] than that of Jameson. Davis chooses to discuss architecture because of its centrality to debates concerning postmodernism.[21] In fact, Jameson's own position is largely developed through an analysis of the Bonaventure Hotel in Los Angeles, a construction which Jameson identifies as an exemplary instance of postmodernism. According to Davis, while modernism remained the major aesthetic in architecture during the long wave of late capitalism, the emergence of postmodernism coincides with two new features of American social and economic life: 'first, the rise of new international rentier circuits in the current crisis phase of capitalism; secondly the definitive abandonment of the ideal of urban reform as part of the new polarization taking place in the United States'.[22]

For Davis, it is necessary to relate postmodern styles and languages to these changes in American social and economic life, and he criticizes Jameson's analysis. His claim is that Jameson conflates contradictory forms and fails to specify the changes to which they relate. Davis' point is that despite Jameson's use of Mandel, his cultural analysis starts out from an investigation of cultural styles and languages, rather than the historical context in which they were produced. Jameson's problem is that despite his Marxist concern with history, he defines his cultural analysis very firmly within the terms of contemporary criticism. It is developed within the terms of the post-structuralist theory of the text. In his discussion of the

New Criticism, for example, he praises it for its similarities with contemporary criticism, the most central of which he sees as their shared attempt to disentangle 'the literary system from other extrinsic systems'.[23] He agrees with post-structuralist theory that literature should not be seen as a referential process, and that it should not be studied diachronically as the expression of its author or its history. Like other post-structuralist critics, his major objection to the New Criticism is that it is supposed to have had the 'tendency to resolve the literary work into a single technique or a single psychological impulse'.[24] Jameson's phrasing is misleading, but his criticism is directed against the value which the New Critics attributed to unity and meaning. Given this position, Jameson does not reject contemporary criticism's concentration on the linguistic forms of the text and replace texts within a historical framework. Instead he proposes a 'deductive' method of literary and cultural analysis in which

the data of the work are interrogated in terms of their formal and logical and most particularly, their *semantic* conditions of possibility. Such analysis thus involves the hypothetical *reconstruction* of the materials – content, narrative paradigms, stylistic and linguistic practices – which had to have been given in advance in order for that particular text to be produced in its unique historical specificity.[25]

Despite his Marxism, Jameson does not reject the post-structuralist concentration on the linguistic forms of the text, but attempts to subsume post-structuralism *within* Marxism.[26] An attempt which produces serious problems for both his Marxist and post-structuralist allegiances.

Similar problems are also a feature of those critics often referred to as the 'New Historicists'. Whatever the problems with this term, these critics are a part of American literary criticism's renewed interest in the role of history. After the heady days of 1970s deconstruction, many American critics have begun to address the relationship between various forms of literature and the forms of power and domination within their historical contexts. Many have drawn upon Gramsci's theory of hegemony as a way of avoiding mechanistic and deterministic accounts of this relationship, but like Jameson, most still remain focused on the linguistic forms of literary texts. For Raymond Williams, the importance of the concept of hegemony was that it did not see culture as a superstructural form. It emphasized that culture was a material process made up of means and relationships of production, institutions, formal and informal groupings, and so forth.[27] By contrast, while many of the New Historicists seek to avoid causal and mechanistic accounts of culture, they still tend to present it in superstructural terms. Literature is still defined as separate from other spheres of social activity. For example, while Jonathan Arac rejects a model of causality in which literature is determined by other social activities such as politics and economics, his alternative has severe problems. History becomes a network of relations in which activities such as economics, politics, and culture are 'not superimposed upon one another but rather juxtaposed'.[28] They are not layered in a causal hierarchy of base and superstructure, but spatially related as activities which are adjacent but connected. This may avoid the problems of determinism and causality, but it still maintains many of the problems which Williams and others identify with superstructural explanations. Arac's refusal to reduce literature to economics defines economic and political relations as external to it. It ignores the specific forms of social organization which are integral to literary activity. As a result, literature is once again a linguistic process which may be related to economic and political activities, but is also separate from them.

This is related to another problem. The failure to examine the social organization of literary production and consumption tends to misrepresent the workings of cultural power. The New Historicists' concept of power and domination is frequently abstract and total. As Peter Nichols puts it, 'for all its talk of dissensus and contestation [the New Historicism] is not much concerned with forms of antagonism and conflict'.[29] They overestimate the extent to which opposition can be incorporated, and underestimate the impact that such incorporations must have on a hegemonic formation. They tend to ignore Gramsci's presentation of hegemony as a complex and contradictory process which must continually be rewon, and tend to present it as a fixed structure which remains constant over time. They play down the different and even conflicting interests which the hegemony tries to reconcile, as well as the extent to which it must change over time through a process of contestation and struggle. In contrast to Williams and Gramsci, the New Historicists tend to present hegemony as an 'epochal structure', rather than a historical process.

They also fail to account for the differential distribution of cultural competences and dispositions.[30] The problem is that, as Janice Radway argues, while specific forms of 'literature might be taken as evidence for the beliefs of a particular section of the American population, assertions based upon it could not easily be extrapolated to wholly different classes or ethnic groups'.[31] It is also that, as a result, literary forms do not have *an* effect. As David Morley has argued in relation to the media, texts may have 'preferred readings', but actual audiences have a series of cultural resources which shape their readings of texts. Any reading is produced within a set of determinate conditions which are 'supplied by the text, the producing institution and the social history of the audience'.[32] The effect of the text is partially dependent on the competences and dispositions through which specific audiences decode it, but also through the continually changing state of the relationships and struggles between different audiences.

By contrast to the approaches offered by the New Historicists and post-structuralist Marxists such as Jameson, Davis examines the political and cultural significance of postmodern styles and languages through an account of the 'genealogy of [post]modern megastructures such as the Bonaventure'.[33] This genealogy is traced back to the Rockefeller Centre which was constructed between 1931 and 1940, and while Davis does discuss the limitations of the project's utopian dimensions, he stresses that the Centre 'interacted vitally with La Guardia's New York', and that 'its famous Plaza ... and mass amusements became a magnetic attraction for a varied and representative Manhattan public'.[34] For Davis, public spaces were central to the architecture of modernism, but he argues that with the crisis of the inner city and the ghetto rebellions of the 1960s, the presence of these spaces was redefined as a problem. In this situation, spatial separation was used to isolate and defend high property values. As a result, 'public spaces, whether as parks, streets, places of entertainment, or in urban transport, were devalued as amenities and redefined as planning problems to be eliminated or privatized'.[35] This analysis leads Davis to challenge Jameson's analysis of the Bonaventure. He argues that by characterizing the building as 'popular', Jameson 'miss[es] the point of its systematic segregation from the great Hispanic-Asian city outside'.[36] In fact, the supposedly popular character of the Bonaventure is referred to as the 'master illusion' of the hotel's architect, John Portman. For Davis, the Bonaventure is composed of 'large vivariums for the upper middle classes, protected by astonishingly complex security systems' within which Portman has attempted to recreate the popular texture of city life and 'a nostalgic Southern California in aspic'.[37]

Jameson's claim is that postmodernism is distinguished by the efface-ment of distinctions such as high and low culture, art and life – distinctions which, he maintains, were central to modernism. But if we accept Davis' periodization of postmodernist architecture, the stylistic features of postmodernism look somewhat different. In fact, as Berman suggests, the various forms of modernism can be seen as 'active orientations towards history, attempts to connect the turbulent present with a past and a future, to help men and women all over the contemporary world to make themselves at home in this world'.[38] However flawed, or limited by specific social and class interests, the forms of modernism were founded upon 'a largeness of vision and imagination'[39] which sought to address the conditions of human existence and to find ways of improving them. By contrast, postmodernism has displayed a wholesale rejection of this way of thinking. It overtly criticizes 'the large human connections that the idea of modernity entails'.[40] For example, postmodernism has been distinguished by its rejection of totalizing discourses in favour of endless diversity and difference. It maintains that the very grandness of modernist thought is founded upon domination and control. All appeals to unity are seen as repressing difference, and projects for the improvement of human life are criticized as attempts to dominate and control the world. As Berman claims: 'The eclipse of the problem of modernity in the 1970s has meant the destruction of a vital form of public space. It has hastened the disintegration of our world into an aggregation of private material and spiritual interest groups, living in windowless monads, far more isolated than we need be.'[41] As Davis argues, modernism with its use of public space was linked to an attempt to 'hegemonize the city', while post-modernism, with its cordoning off of private spaces, is linked to the polarization of groups within the urban landscape. Modernism was linked to public programmes of social improvement, such as urban renewal, but postmodernism is part of a retreat from collective movements for the improvement of the social world into an aggressive defence of the private.

Consequently, it would be wrong to see postmodernism as an effacement of the distinctions between high and low culture, or between art and life. Instead, if we return to an examination of literary and cultural criticism, we find that postmodern cultural forms are valued specifically because they differentiate themselves from supposedly 'ideological' popular forms. What has changed is that while modernism quoted popular forms while trying to transcend them, postmodernist texts frequently work from within popular forms. It 'deconstructs' them and foregrounds their devices. This latter option does not entail a collapse of the distinction between high and low culture, but if anything, it raises that distinction to a higher power. After all, modernism frequently saw popular forms as expressive, and used them in an attempt to develop upon them. Postmodernism, on the other hand, refuses to see them as expressive forms, and either attempts to deconstruct them from within, or reduces them to mere style. This latter strand of postmodernism does announce its love for popular culture, but it does so by denying it any meaningfulness. The popular is still defined as trash, even while the postmodernist emphasizes his love for this 'junk culture'. As Todd Gitlin points out, this love of popular culture is 'indistinguishable from contempt'.[42]

# Conclusion

What distinguishes postmodernist criticism from modernist criticism is that while modernism sought to achieve differentiation through the creation of alternative forms, postmodernism seeks to achieve it *without* producing an alternative. It deconstructs existing forms but refuses the project of reconstruction. The shift from the New Critical interpretation of the text as a 'struggle for unity and meaning' to the postmodern rejection of totalization or meaning is not a liberating one. Rather it constitutes a rejection of social engagement and a retreat from public discussion and debate. This reconceptualization of the difference between the New Criticism and contemporary critical modes is vital. It is necessary to acknowledge that the New Criticism is not distinguished from contemporary criticism by its failure to see the text as either a linguistic process of production or as a social product. Instead we should acknowledge that both modes of criticism define the object of literary study in much the same way. The difference is that the New Critics valued the 'struggle for meaning' as an attempt to define a position in relation to the modern world. Postmodern criticism, on the other hand, values the 'refusal of meaning', and maintains that any attempt to define a position limits the productivity of language. Whatever the strengths of postmodern critiques of totalizing discourses, we cannot 'leave open' the question of whether postmodernism resists the logic of consumer capitalism as Jameson does.[1] Instead we must recognize that postmodernism represents a retreat from collective social activity, and cannot provide the basis for new forms of collective struggle.

# Notes

1 CONTEMPORARY RESPONSES TO THE NEW CRITICISM

1 Frank Lentricchia, *After the New Criticism* (London: Methuen, 1983) p. xiii.
2 *Ibid.* p. xiii.
3 Terry Eagleton, *Against the Grain: Essays 1975–1985* (London: Verso, 1986) pp. 49–64.
4 Northrop Frye, *The Anatomy of Criticism* (Princeton University Press, 1957).
5 Geoffery Hartman, *Beyond Formalism* (New Haven, Conn.: Yale University Press, 1975).
6 W. K. Wimsatt, *The Verbal Icon: Studies in the Meaning of Poetry* (New York: Noonday, 1958).
7 R. P. Warren and C. Brooks, *Understanding Poetry* (New York: Holt, Rinehart and Winston, 1960).
8 Terry Eagleton, *Literary Theory: An Introduction* (Oxford: Blackwell, 1983) p. 44.
9 *Ibid.* p. 48.
10 Fredric Jameson, *The Prison House of Language* (Princeton University Press, 1974) p. 44.
11 *Ibid.* p. 44.
12 See, for example, Russell Reising, *The Unusable Past: Theory and the Study of American Literature* (London: Methuen, 1986).
13 Robert Scholes, *Semiotics and Interpretation* (New Haven, Conn.: Yale University Press, 1982) p. 23.
14 *Ibid.* p. 11.
15 'The linguistic model, therefore, helped to justify the desire to abandon literary history and biographical criticism; and if the notion that one was being scientific led on occasion to a misplaced arrogance, still the conclusion that literature could be studied as "un système qui ne connait que son ordre propre" – a system with its own order – has been eminently salutary, securing for the French some of the benefits of Anglo-American "New Criticism" without leading to the error of making the individual text an autonomous object that should be approached as a *tabula rasa*.' Jonathan Culler, *Structuralist Poetics* (London: Routledge and Kegan Paul, 1975) p. 255. See also Jonathan Culler, *The Pursuit of Signs* (London: Routledge and Kegan Paul, 1981) and Jonathan Culler, *On Deconstruction* (London: Routledge and Kegan Paul, 1983).
16 See David Bleich, *Subjective Criticism* (Baltimore: Johns Hopkins University

Press, 1978) and Stanley Fish, *Is There a Text in the Class?: The Authority of Interpretive Communities* (Cambridge, Mass.: Harvard University Press, 1980).
17 Terence Hawkes, *Structuralism and Semiotics* (London: Methuen, 1977) p. 155.
18 *Ibid.* p. 157.
19 *Ibid.* p. 157.
20 This term is used by Cleanth Brooks in *The Well-Wrought Urn: Studies in the Structure of Poetry* (London: Denis Dobson, 1968), but it is associated with the New Criticism in general.

## 2 THE HISTORICAL CONTEXT OF THE NEW CRITICISM

1 John Fekete, *The Critical Twilight: Explorations in the Ideology of Anglo-American Literary Theory from Eliot to McLuhan* (London: Routledge and Kegan Paul, 1978) p. 45.
2 *Ibid.* p. 45.
3 *Ibid.* p. 44.
4 Eugene Genovese, *The World the Slaveholders Made: Two Essays in Interpretation* (New York: Vintage Books, 1971) p. 99.
5 *Ibid.* p. 196.
6 *Ibid.* p. 16.
7 Karl Marx, *Capital Vol. 1* (Harmondsworth: Penguin, 1972).
8 *The World the Slaveholders Made* p. 5.
9 *Ibid.* p. 240.
10 Twelve Southerners, *I'll Take My Stand: The South and the Agrarian Tradition* (Baton Rouge: Louisiana State University Press, 1980).
11 Raymond Williams, *Culture and Society 1780–1950* (Harmondsworth: Penguin Books, 1961) p. 224.
12 Marshall Berman, *All That Is Solid Melts into Air: The Experience of Modernity* (London: Verso, 1983) p. 28.
13 'What is more surprising, and more disturbing, is the extent to which this perspective thrived among some of the participatory democrats of the recent New Left.' *Ibid.* p. 28.
14 'New Criticism had many defects, but the scientific reduction of literature to technical subtleties was not one of them. It is odd that the New Critics should be denounced for their arid scientific empiricism, since this was one of the chief cultural ills which the New Critics themselves sought to combat. The New Criticism stands squarely in the romantic tradition of the defense of the humanities as an antidote to science and positivism. The methodology of "close reading" was an attempt not to imitate science but to refute its devaluation of literature: by demonstrating the rich complexity of meaning within even the simplest poem, the New Critic proved to the "hard-boiled naturalist," as Cleanth Brooks called him, that literature had to be taken seriously as a rival mode of cognitive knowledge.' Gerald Graff, *Literature Against Itself: Literary Ideas in Modern Society* (University of Chicago Press, 1979) pp. 133–4.
15 'If one follows the New Critical argument against the heresy of paraphrase to its logical conclusion, one ends with a complete discontinuity between literature

and criticism; one may then follow those who reject interpretation as such, or one may turn interpretation into a kind of poetic creativity in itself, a Nietzschean "play" that makes no pretense of corresponding to any text but justifies itself as an existential gesture against an inhuman universe.' *Ibid.* p. 143.

16 Richard Gray, *Writing the South: Ideas of an American Region* (Cambridge University Press, 1986) p. 148.

17 *Ibid.* p. 161.

18 'Two civil wars finally opened the South fully for finance capital; where Ransom countered with ruah, and Faulkner with ▽, Tate offers an iconic horseman. Each icon, ontologically vehement through its impacted plots, is made to counter the narratives latent in a different kind of object – the commodity, as it sits in the ubiquitous shop window of a consumer culture. These three Southerners fought with one species of "image" (projected by a highly selective way of remembering) against what they saw as an intrusive, Northern amnesia. The Southern icon is "told" to block the telling of another object's story: the result are objects that Hemingway would not have begun to understand.' Richard Godden, *Fictions of Capital: The American Novel from James to Mailer* (Cambridge University Press, 1990) p. 169.

19 Umberto Eco, *A Theory of Semiotics* (London: Macmillan, 1977).

20 Raymond Williams, *Marxism and Literature* (Oxford University Press, 1977) p. 37.

21 Pierre Bourdieu, *Distinction: A Social Critique of the Judgement of Taste* (London: Routledge and Kegan Paul, 1984); see also Nicholas Garnham and Raymond Williams, 'Pierre Bourdieu and the Sociology of Culture' in Nicholas Garnham, *Capitalism and Communication: Global Culture and the Economics of Information* (London: Sage, 1990).

22 See writers such as Dwight MacDonald, *Against the American Grain* (London: Victor Gollancz, 1963).

23 Cleanth Brooks, 'The Christianity of Modernism', *AR* 6 (Feb. 1936) pp. 435–46.

24 See C. Brooks, *Modern Poetry and the Tradition* (New York: Oxford University Press, 1965); and *The Well-Wrought Urn*. There is also a very useful interview with Brooks in Lewis P. Simpson, ed., *The Possibilities of Order: Cleanth Brooks and His Work* (Baton Rouge: Louisiana State University Press, 1976).

25 Thomas Daniel Young, 'A Little Divergence: The Critical Theories of John Crowe Ransom and Cleanth Brooks' in Lewis P. Simpson, ed., *The Possibilities of Order.*

26 'A Conversation with Cleanth Brooks' in Lewis P. Simpson, ed., *The Possibilities of Order* p. 62.

27 *Ibid.* p. 62.

28 *Ibid.* p. 22.

3 BEFORE THE NEW CRITICISM

1 *The Fugitive*, Vols. 1–4 (1922–5).

2 For general histories of the 1920s, see the bibliography, but for material specifically concerned with the rise of corporate capitalism see: Alfred

Chandler, *The Visible Hand: The Managerial Revolution in American Business* (Cambridge, Mass.: Harvard University Press, 1977); William E. Leuchtenburg, *The Perils of Prosperity, 1914–1932* (University of Chicago Press, 1958).

3 See Stuart Ewen, *Captains of Consciousness: Advertising and the Roots of Consumer Culture* (New York: McGraw-Hill, 1977); Richard Godden, 'Money Makes Manners Makes Man Makes Woman', *Literature and History* 12: 1 (Spring 1986) pp. 16–37; Anne Firor Scott, *The Southern Lady From Pedestal to Politics, 1830–1930* (University of Chicago Press, 1970).

4 See Carl Degler, *At Odds: Women and the Family in America from the Revolution to the Present* (Oxford University Press, 1981); Estelle B. Freedman, 'Changing Views of Women in the 1920s', *JAH* 61 (1974) pp. 372–93; Scott, *The Southern Lady*.

5 See Harry Braverman, *Labor and Monopoly Capitalism: The Degradation of Work in the Twentieth Century* (New York: Monthly Review Press, 1974); Alfred Sohn-Rethel, *Intellectual and Manual Labour: A Critique of Epistemology* (London: Macmillan, 1978).

6 See Jonathan M. Wiener, 'Class Structure and Economic Development in the American South 1865–1955', *AHR* 84 (1979) pp. 970–1006; Jonathan M. Wiener, *The Social Origins of the New South: Alabama 1860–1885* (Baton Rouge: Louisiana State University Press, 1978); H. D. Woodman, 'Sequel to Slavery: The New History Views the Post Bellum South', *JSH* 43 (1977) pp. 529–54.

7 See G. B. Tindall, *The Emergence of the New South 1913–1945* (Baton Rouge: Louisiana State University Press, 1967); Wiener, 'Class Structure and Economic Development in the American South'.

8 J. M. Bradbury, *The Fugitives* (Chapel Hill: University of North Carolina Press, 1958) p. 10.

9 John Crowe Ransom, 'Waste Lands', *Evening Post's Literary Review* 3 (11 July 1923) pp. 825–6; Allen Tate, 'Waste Lands', *Evening Post's Literary Review* 3 (4 August 1923) p. 886; John Crowe Ransom, 'Mr. Ransom Replies', *Evening Post's Literary Review* 3 (11 August 1923) p. 902.

10 '[N]o art and no religion is possible until we make allowances, until we manage to keep quiet the *enfant terrible* of logic that plays havoc with the other faculties.' John Crowe Ransom, 'The Future of Poetry', *The Fugitive* (Feb. 1924) p. 3.

11 John Crowe Ransom, 'Thoughts on Poetic Discontent', *The Fugitive* (June 1925) p. 64.

12 *Ibid.* p. 64.

13 *The Third Moment* was never published.

14 John Crowe Ransom, *The Selected Letters of John Crowe Ransom* (Baton Rouge: Louisiana State University Press, 1985) p. 155.

15 *Ibid.* p. 157.

16 'Our fight is for survival; and it's got to be waged not so much against the Yankees as against the exponents of the New South. I see clearly that you are as unreconstructed and unmodernized as any of us, if not more so.' *Ibid.* p. 166.

17 John Crowe Ransom, 'The South – Old or New', *SeR* 36 (April 1928) p. 143.

18 See Bibliography.

19 Allen Tate, 'The Fallacy of Humanism', *Horn and Hound* 3 (Jan./March 1930) p. 252.

20 L. D. Rubin in *The Wary Fugitives* (Baton Rouge: Louisiana State University Press, 1978).

21 John Crowe Ransom, *God Without Thunder: An Unorthodox Defense of Orthodoxy* (London: Gerald Howe, 1931) p. 118.

22 '1. The formation of a society, or an academy of Southern *positive* reactionaries made up at first of people of our own group.

2. The expansion in a year or two of this academy to this size: fifteen active members – poets, critics, historians, economists – and ten inactive members – lawyers, politicians, private citizens – who might be active enough without being committed at first to direct agitation.

3. The drawing up of a philosophical constitution, to be issued and signed by the academy, as the groundwork of the movement. It should be ambitious to the last degree; it should set forth, under our leading idea, a complete social, philosophical, literary, economic and religious system. This will inevitably draw upon our heritage, but this heritage should be valued, not in what it actually performed, but in its possible perfection. Philosophically we must go the whole hog of reaction, and base our movement less upon the actual old South than upon its prototype – the historical social and religious scheme of Europe. We must be the last Europeans – there being no Europeans in Europe at the present.

4. The academy will not be a secret order: all the cards will be on the table. We should be *secretive*, however, in our tactics, and plan the campaign for the maximum of effect. All our writings should be signed "John Doe, of the ----- ----," or whatever we call it.

5. Organised publication should be looked to. A Newspaper, perhaps, to argue principles on the lower plane; then a weekly, to press philosophy upon the passing show; and thirdly, a quarterly devoted wholly to principles. This is a large scheme, but it must be held up constantly. We must do our best with what we get.' Thomas D. Young and John Tyree Fain, eds., *The Literary Correspondence of Donald Davidson and Allen Tate* (Athens: University of Georgia Press, 1974) pp. 229–30.

23 Tate argued that the title of the symposium 'emphasizes the fact of exclusiveness rather than its benefits; it points to a particular house but omits to say that it was the home of a spirit that may also have lived elsewhere and that this mansion was incidentally made with hands.' *I'll Take My Stand: The South and the Agrarian Tradition* (Baton Rouge: Louisiana State University Press, 1980) p. 155.

24 'Humanism, properly speaking, is not an abstract system, but a culture, the whole way in which we live, act, think, and feel. It is a kind of imaginatively balanced life lived out in a definite social tradition. And, in the concrete, we believe that this, the genuine humanism, was rooted in the agrarian life of the older South and of other parts of the country that shared in such a tradition. It was not an abstract moral "check" derived from the classics – it was not soft material poured in from the top. It was deeply founded in the way of life itself – in its tables, chairs, portraits, festivals, laws, marriage customs. We cannot recover our native humanism by adopting some standard of taste that is critical

enough to question the contemporary arts but not critical enough to question the social and economic life which is their ground.' *Ibid.* p. xliv.

25  *The World the Slaveholders Made*, p. 190.

26  'This modern mind sees only half of the horse – that half which may become a dynamo, or an automobile, or any other horsepowered machine. If this mind had much respect for the full-dimensioned, grass-eating horse, it would never have invented the engine which represents only half of him. The religious mind, on the other hand, has this respect; it wants the whole horse, and it will be satisfied with nothing less.' *I'll Take My Stand* p. 157.

27  *Ibid.* p. 166.

28  'They had a religious life, but it was not enough organized with a right mythology. In fact, their rational life was not powerfully united to the religious experience, as it was in medieval society, and they are a fine specimen of the tragic pitfall upon which the Western mind has always hovered. Lacking a rational system for the defence of their religous attitude and its base in feudal society, they elaborated no rational system whatever, no full-grown philosophy; so that, when the post-bellum temptations of the devil, who is the exploiter of nature, confronted them, they had no defence.' *Ibid.* p. 173.

29  Floyd C. Atkins and John T. Hiers, eds., *Robert Penn Warren Talking: Interviews 1950–1978* (New York: Random House, 1980) p. 35.

30  *I'll Take My Stand* p. 259.

31  'In the past [agriculture] has been accepted in most cases simply because no other was at hand, but now if it can be made attractive enough and can offer enough opportunity, it will serve as a ballast to an extravagant industrial expansion. If both the negro and the poor white can find a decent living, there will be no new crowded and clamoring slave auction ready for exploitation by the first bidder.' *Ibid.* pp. 261–2.

32  *Ibid.* p. 260.

33  John Crowe Ransom, 'The State and the Land', *NR* 66 (Feb. 1932) pp. 8–10 and 'Land!' *Harper's* 165 (July 1932) pp. 216–24.

34  'It is not by applying capitalism to the land that we can help ourselves; we have lately been trying that with all our might and know it to be a mistake. The capitalist landowner conceives of his land as a factory, producing goods exclusively for sale, and himself as the sort of consumer who must buy with money all that he consumes ... An agrarian economy does not conceive of the land as a capital to earn with, not primarily at least; but as a direct source of subsistence for its population.' John Crowe Ransom, 'The State and the Land' p. 9.

35  John Crowe Ransom, 'Happy Farmers', *AR* 1 (Oct. 1933) p. 514.

36  'The destiny of our broad acres is not to be the simple feed-bowl of the Western world, filled and steaming; nor even the simple feed-bowl of the United States, absurdly big for the job, and half-filled. It is to be hoped that its destiny is to support an excellent order of citizens, who will be economic dualists, men of unusual integrity and freedom even while they perform a professional function; farmers with more room, and more heart, than most of the farmers of the world; happy farmers.' *Ibid.* p. 531.

37  'As the community slowly adapts its life to the geography of the region, a thing happens which is almost miraculous; being no necessity of the economic

system, but a work of grace perhaps, a tribute to the goodness of the human heart, and an event of momentous consequence to what we call the genius of human "culture". As the economic patterns become perfected and easy, they cease to be merely economic and become gradually aesthetic. They are meant for efficiency, but they survive for enjoyment, and men who are only prosperous become also happy.' John Crowe Ransom, 'The Aesthetic of Regionalism', *AR* 2 (Jan. 1934) p. 296.

38  Thomas Daniel Young and John J. Hindle, eds., *The Republic of Letters in America: The Correspondence of John Peale Bishop and Allen Tate* (Lexington: University of Kentucky Press, 1981) p. 76.

39  Allen Tate, 'Where are the People?', *AR* 2 (Dec. 1933) p. 232.

40  *Ibid.* p. 233.

41  Allen Tate, 'A Traditionalist looks at Liberalism', *SR* 1 (Spring 1936) p. 740.

42  'The truly artistic life is surely that in which the aesthetic experience is not curtained off but is mixed up with all sorts of instruments and occupations pertaining to the round of daily life. It ranges all the way from pots and pans, chairs and rugs, clothing and houses, up to dramas publicly performed and government buildings.' Donald Davidson, 'A Mirror for Artists' in *I'll Take My Stand* pp. 39–40.

43  *Ibid.* p. 43.

44  Donald Davidson, 'The Political Economy of Regionalism', *SR* 6 (Feb. 1936) p. 410.

45  *Ibid.* p. 414.

46  Donald Davidson, 'Regionalism as Social Science', *SR* 3 (Autumn 1937) p. 213.

47  See, for example, Donald Davidson, 'A Sociologist in Eden', *AR* 8 (December 1936); 'Gulliver with Hayfever', *AR* 9 (Summer 1937); and 'The Class Approach to Southern Problems', *SR* 5 (Autumn 1939).

48  Thomas Daniel Young and John Tyree Fain, eds., *The Literary Correspondence of Donald Davidson and Allen Tate* (Lexington: University of Kentucky Press) p. 323.

49  *Ibid.* p. 323.

CONCLUSION

1  William E. Leuchtenburg, *Franklin D. Roosevelt and the New Deal, 1932–1940* (New York: Harper and Row, 1963).

4 JOHN CROWE RANSOM: THE SOCIAL RELATIONS OF AESTHETIC ACTIVITY

1  John Crowe Ransom, *The World's Body* (New York: Charles Scribner's Sons, 1938).

2  John Crowe Ransom, 'A Poem Nearly Anonymous: II The Poet and His Formal Tradition', *AR* 1 (Sept. 1933) p. 444.

3  John Crowe Ransom, 'Modern with a Southern Accent', *VQR* 11 (April 1935) pp. 184–5.

4  'There is a backwardness in the physical conduct of life here, and there is a backwardness lying much deeper in the Southern temper.' *Ibid.* p. 185.

5  In this discussion Ransom concentrates on the work of Dubose Heyward.
6  'Modern With a Southern Accent' p. 188.
7  '[A] writer may evidently have the juridical status of a Southerner without having the temper of one for the South cannot now be construed, under the legend, as a unified, powerful, ubiquitous spirit who imposes one habit of mind upon all her children.' *Ibid.* p. 191.
8  *Ibid.* pp. 191–2.
9  Henry James's 'habitual reference was to the formal society, and it determined his subject-matter and his sentence-structure'. *Ibid.* p. 192.
10  John Crowe Ransom, 'Flux and Blur in Contemporary Art', *SeR* 37 (July 1929) p. 362.
11  *Ibid.* p. 363.
12  John Crowe Ransom, 'Classic or Romantic', *Saturday Review of Literature* 6 (14 Sept. 1929) p. 125.
13  'A Poem Nearly Anonymous' p. 446.
14  *Ibid.* p. 444.
15  '[The invention of society cannot] have been simply to confirm the natural man as a natural man, or even simply to improve him in cunning and effectiveness by finishing him with its tried economic forms. It wanted to humanize him; which means, so far as his natural economy permitted, to complicate his natural functions with sensibility and make them aesthetic. The object of a proper society is to instruct its members how to transform instinctive experience into aesthetic experience.' *Ibid.* p. 456.
16  John Crowe Ransom, 'The Aesthetic of Regionalism', *AR* 2 (Jan. 1934) pp. 290–310.
17  'A Poem Nearly Anonymous: II' p. 126.
18  *Ibid.* p. 126.
19  '[The "cave-man"] is a predatory creature to whom every object is an object of prey and the real or individual object cannot occur; while the social man, who submits to the restraint of convention, comes to respect the object and to see it unfold at last in its individuality; which, if we must define it, is its capacity to furnish us with an infinite variety of innocent experience; that is, its character as a source, from which so many charming experiences have already flowed, and as a promise, a possibility of experience beyond all future prediction.' 'A Poem Nearly Anonymous: II', p. 449.
20  William R. Taylor, *Cavalier and Yankee* (London: W. H. Allen, 1963) p. 148.
21  John Crowe Ransom, 'The Poet as a Woman', *SR* 2 (Spring 1937) p. 784.
22  *Ibid.* p. 784.
23  John Crowe Ransom, 'Poetry: A Note on Ontology', *AR* 3 (May 1934) p. 173.
24  *Ibid.* p. 173.
25  *Ibid.* p. 175.
26  *Ibid.* pp. 180–1.
27  'The moralist, the scientist, and the prophet of idealism think evidently that they must establish their conclusions in poetry, though they reached these conclusions upon quite other evidence. The poetry is likely to destroy the conclusions with a sort of death by drowning, if it is free poetry.' *Ibid.* p. 185.
28  'Ontological interest would have to develop curiously, or wastefully and discontinuously, if men through their youth must cultivate the ideas so

passionately that upon its expiration they are done with ideas forever and ready to become little (and pre-logical) children. Because of the foolishness of idealists are ideas to be taboo for the adult mind?' *Ibid.* p. 188.

29 '[The poet] proposed to make virtue delicious. He compounded a moral effect with an aesthetic effect. The total effect was not a pure one, but was rich, and relished highly. The name of the moral effect was goodness; the name of the aesthetic effect was beauty. Perhaps they did not have to co-exist, but the planners of society saw to it that they should; they called upon the artists to reinforce morality with charm. The artists were obliged.' John Crowe Ransom, 'Poets without Laurels', *Yale Review* 24 (Autumn 1934) p. 505.

30 'When our critical theory is complete, perhaps we shall be able to distiguish various combinations of elements passing for poetry; thus, poetry by assemblage, poetry by mixture, and poetry by composition. The last of these sounds the best.' *Ibid.* p. 518.

31 'It will take a long time to change the philosophical set which has come over the practice of poets. The intellectual climate in which they live will have to be altered first.' *Ibid.* p. 518.

32 'Poetry: A Note on Ontology' p. 192.

33 '[T]he conceit is but a metaphor if the metaphor is meant; that is, if it is developed literally that it must be meant, or predicated so baldly that nothing else can be meant.' *Ibid.* p. 196.

34 '[Metaphysical poetry] is true enough. It is not true like history, but no poetry and only a poor science is true in this sense. It is true in the pragmatic sense in which some of the generalizations of science are true: it accomplishes precisely the sort of representation that it means to. It suggests to us that the object is perceptually or physically remarkable, and we had better attend to it.' *Ibid.* p. 200.

35 John Crowe Ransom, 'The Psychologist Looks at Poetry', *VQR* 11 (Oct. 1935) p. 581.

36 *Ibid.* p. 580.

37 '[The aesthetic experience] is a gigantic feat of ordering and organizing the system of clashing interests, setting a valuable example for the human economy to follow when it has real business to pursue.' *Ibid.* p. 581.

38 '[T]he one thing [interests] have in common is that they are all interests in an external reality. Inter-esse means to be environed, and interest means sensitiveness to the environment. To be interested is to try to obtain a cognition, to do what Mr. Richards forever denies to the poetic experience and grants exclusively to science: to seek the truth.' *Ibid.* p. 582.

39 'Poetry is creative, in the sense which science is not. It is such an eager cognitive impulse that it overreaches its object. That is its glory, and one of the causes of its delightfulness perhaps, and certainly the source of its bad reputation. This last may perhaps be improved if poetry will watch closely after its own innocence; that is, be careful not to perform by positive misrepresentation that compounded affair of our primary knowledge, the world. It makes a second version, perhaps a better one but still a new and not clearly authorised version of the world. And this is a matter which, with due respect to Coleridge and Mr. Richards, I do not think they have settled at all.' *Ibid.* p. 592.

40 'Many people think it ought to be as "realistic" as possible, with screams and

gore, so that the spectator may forget it is only an imitation; whereas the Greek population liked their plays produced under severe restrictions which did not permit the spectator to be so stupid even if he wanted to; plays then were imitations undisguised.' John Crowe Ransom, 'The Mimetic Principle', *AR* 5 (Oct. 1935) p. 538.

41 'The photograph is a mechanical imitation perhaps, but not a psychological one. It was obtained by the adjustment of the camera and the pressing of the button, actions so characterless that they indicate no attitude necessarily, no love; but the painting reveals the arduous pains of the artist. We are excited by these pains proportionately; they give the painting its human value; and carrying the principle a little further, we never discover in the work a single evidence of technique, discipline, deliberation, without having the value enhanced further. The pains measure the love.' *Ibid.* p. 549.

42 '[T]here cannot well be occasion for a cathartic without there being a nasty and toxic excrement somewhere, and a state of disease resulting from its presence within the system; nor can the joy of art be anything but the pleasure that attends the act of elimination; and all the fine notions which Europeans have so easily entertained about their arts and artists must be dissipated.' John Crowe Ransom, 'The Cathartic Principle', *AR* 5 (Summer 1935) p. 289.

43 'Do not the arts, with their discharge of love in so many harmless conventional forms, act as cathartics to purify the souls of citizens? I believe so; I mean that probably this was the action imputed to them by Aristotle, and also that it was imputed with reason. For the worst thing about our situation as civilized beings – it grows worse with the extent of our civilization – is that we vent our love of nature not in the usual action of living but in the random and occasional moments when we indulge ourselves in the special arts; that the arts are intercalary and non-participating in respect to the "serious" side of life; and that most of the time we are not human, so far as it is a work of the human dignity to respect and know the particularity by which we are so constantly environed. We live by inveterate habit now, abstractly. If we should take care to find aesthetic enjoyment in everything we are doing. But we should probably also have to do with less of science; that is, with an impure and less effective science.' 'The Mimetic Principle' p. 551.

44 'A good poem, even if it is signed with a full and well-known name, intends as a work of art to lose the identity of the author; that is, it means to represent him not as actualized, like an eye-witness testifying in court and held strictly by zealous counsel to the point at issue, but freed from his juridical or prose self and taking an ideal or fictitious personality; otherwise his evidence amounts to less than poetry.' John Crowe Ransom, 'A Poem Nearly Anonymous', *AR* 1 (May 1933) p. 180.

45 *Ibid.* p. 180.

46 *Ibid.* pp. 180–1.

47 '[P]robably we shall never find a better locus than *Lycidas* for exhibiting at once the poet and the man, the technique and the personal interest bound up tightly and contending all but equally; the strain of contraries, the not quite resolvable dualism, that is art.' *Ibid.* p. 182.

48 'If a whole series of artists in turn develop the same subject, it is to the last one's advantage that he may absorb the others, in addition to being in whatever

pointed or subtle manner his own specific self. His work becomes the climax of a tradition, and is better than the work of an earlier artist in the series. Unfortunately, there will come perhaps the effete day where there is no artist prepared to carry on the tradition; or more simply, if we prefer, the day when the tradition has gone far enough and is not worth carrying further; that is, when it is worn out as a "heuristic principle", and confines instead of freeing the spirit … On that day art will need its revolutionist, to start another tradition. It is a bold step for the artist to take, and Milton did not think it needful to take it here. The revolutionist who does not succeed must descend to the rating, for history, of rebel; the fool of the wrong *political* intuition.' [My emphasis.] *Ibid.* p. 194.

49  'Art was his deliberate career. It is a career, precisely as science is a career. It is serious, it has an attitude as official, it is as studied and consecutive, it is by all means as difficult, it is not less important.' 'A Poem Nearly Anonymous: II' p. 467.

50  'Those who will not undertake to gather what this involved for him will be finding themselves constantly rebuffed by the mountains of irrelevance raised against them in the body of his poetry. Milton is the poetry, and is lost to them if they do not know to make acquaintance there.' *Ibid.* p. 467.

51  John Crowe Ransom, 'The Content of the Novel', *AR* 7 (Summer 1936) p. 303.

52  'The business of the general critical theorist in any age is to define the patterns which have actually become stable in his art, and rationalize their common aesthetic ground so far as he can.' *Ibid.* p. 305.

5 ALLEN TATE: THE SOCIAL ORGANIZATION OF LITERATURE

1  Allen Tate, *Reactionary Essays on Poetry and Ideas* (New York: Scribner's Sons, 1936).

2  Allen Tate, 'Emily Dickinson' in *Essays of Four Decades* (London: Oxford University Press, 1970) p. 281.

3  *Ibid.* p. 283.

4  '[C]ulture, in the true sense, was disappearing.' *Ibid.* p. 283.

5  Tate argues that, for Emerson, 'man is greater than any idea and, being himself the Over-Soul, is innately perfect: there is not struggle because … there is no possibility of error. There is no human drama because there is no tragic fault.' *Ibid.* p. 285.

6  *Ibid.* pp. 285–6.

7  'If it were necessary to explain her seclusion with disappointment in love, there would remain the discrepancy between what the seclusion produced and the seclusion looked at as a cause. The effect, which is her poetry, would imply the whole complex anterior fact, which was the social and religious structure of New England.' *Ibid.* p. 286.

8  'These ideas, in her poetry, are momentarily assailed by the disintegrating force of Nature (appearing as Death) which, while constantly breaking them down, constantly redefines and strengthens them.' *Ibid.* p. 288.

9  *Ibid.* p. 288.

10  *Ibid.* p. 293.

11  *Ibid.* p. 293.

12 '[The] important thing is that [the code] shall tell the poet how people try to behave, and that it shall be too perfect, whether in good or evil, for human nature. The poet seizes one set of terms within the code ... and shows that the hero's application of the code to his own conduct is faulty, and doomed to failure. By adhering strictly to the code, the poet exhibits a typical action, and if he is a Shakespeare he exhibits it with finality.' Ashley Brown and Frances Neel Cheney, eds., *The Poetry Reviews of Allen Tate 1924–1944* (Baton Rouge: Louisiana State University Press, 1983) pp. 166–7.

13 Allen Tate, 'The Profession of Letters in the South' in *Essays of Four Decades* (London: Oxford University Press, 1970) p. 517.

14 *Ibid.* p. 519.

15 'Our books are sold on a competitive market; it is a book market, but it is a luxury market; and luxury markets must be fiercely competitive. It is not that the natural depravity of the writer as fallen man betrays him into imitating the tone and standards of the market; actually he cannot find a public at all, even for the most lost of lost causes, the *succès d'estime*, unless he is willing to enter the competitive racket of publishing. This racket, our society being what it is, is a purely economic process, and literary opinion is necessarily manufactured for its needs.' *Ibid.* p. 518.

16 *Ibid.* p. 529.

17 *Ibid.* p. 523.

18 '[T]he Southern man of letters, freed from it, has not seen the opportunities of his freedom. On the necessity of making Southern writers, and for that matter American writers, a professional class, bound together by ties of profession whose ethics consist in devotion to the craft – on the need of this, some writer should speedily write a tract, and no title could be better suited to it than *Up from Slavery.*' *The Poetry Reviews of Allen Tate* p. 143.

19 *Ibid.* p. 143.

20 'The Profession of Letters in the South' p. 532.

21 *Ibid.* p. 533.

22 'The prevailing economic passion of the age once more tempts, even commands, the Southern writer to go into politics. Our neo-communism is the new form in which the writer from all sections is dominated by capitalism, or "economic" society. It is the new political mania. And there is no escape from it. The political mind always finds itself in an emergency. And the emergency, this time real enough, becomes a pretext for ignoring the arts.' *Ibid.* p. 534.

23 *The Poetry Reviews of Allen Tate* p. 106.

24 *Ibid.* p. 106.

25 '[P]oetry, of all the arts, demands a serenity of view and a settled temper of the mind, and most of all the power to detach one's own needs from the experience set forth in the poem. A moral sense so organised sets limits to the human enterprise, and is content to observe them. But if the reader lacks this sense, the poem will be only a body of abstractions either useful or irrelevant to the body of abstraction already forming, but of uncertain direction, in the reader's mind. This reader will see the poem chiefly as biography, and he will proceed to deduce from it a history of the poet's case, to which he will attach himself if his own case resembles it; if it doesn't he will reject it. Either way, the quality of the poem is ignored.' *Ibid.* pp. 106–7.

26 *Ibid.* p. 107.

27 'It is not what a poet believes (Mr. Richards' theory) but rather what total attitude he takes towards all aspects of his conduct, that constitutes the "content" side of the aesthetic problem.' *Ibid.* p. 161.

28 Tate proposes 'to discuss three kinds of poetry that bring to focus three attitudes of the modern world. I do not say all three attitudes, because there are more than three attitudes, and there are more than three kinds of poetry.' Allen Tate, 'Three Types of Poetry' in *Essays of Four Decades* p. 173.

29 'The quality and intention of the allegorical will are the intention and quality of the will of science. With allegory the image is not a complete, qualitative whole; it is an abstraction calculated to force the situation upon which it is imposed towards a single direction.' *Ibid.* p. 180.

30 '[T]he poets, deprived of their magical fictions, and stripped of the means of affirming the will allegorically, proceed to revolt, pitting the individual will against all forms of order, under the illusion that all order is scientific order.' *Ibid.* p. 182.

31 'The [romantic] poet, instead of fixing his attention upon a single experience, instead of presenting dramatically the plight of human weakness – the subject of his poem – flies from his situation into a rhetorical escape that gives his will the illusion of power.' *Ibid.* p. 183. Tate also argues that 'the will of science and the will of the romantic poet (the frustrated allegorist) are the same will. Romanticism is science without the systematic method of asserting the will.' *Ibid.* p. 183.

32 Tate criticizes two claims by Wilson: '(1) that the only kind of imagination is that of the will, which best realizes its purposes in external constructions or in the control of the external relations of persons and things; (2) that this sole type of imagination will be disillusioned or optimistic, according to whether it is either imperfectly formed, as in mere poetry, or adequately equipped by science with "the fourfold forms of reason and consequent"'. *Ibid.* p. 186.

33 '[T]he recognition of that other half of experience, the realm of immitigable evil – or perhaps I had better say in modern abstraction, the margin of error in social calculation – has been steadily lost. The fusion of human success and human error in a vision of the whole of life, *the vision itself being its own goal*, has almost disappeared from the modern world.' *Ibid.* p. 188.

34 *Ibid.* p. 189.

35 'Two vastly different records or case-histories might give us, qualitatively speaking, very similar results: Baudelaire and Eliot have in common many qualities but no history.' *The Poetry Reviews of Allen Tate* p. 107.

36 *Ibid.* pp. 107–8.

37 *Ibid.* p. 109.

38 *Ibid.* p. 127.

39 *Ibid.* p. 127.

## 6 ROBERT PENN WARREN: AGAINST PROPAGANDA AND IRRESPONSIBILITY

1 Robert Penn Warren, 'John Crowe Ransom: A Study in Irony', *VQR* 11 (Jan. 1935) p. 93.

2 *Ibid.* p. 93.
3 *Ibid.* p. 95.
4 'A myth is a fiction, a construct, which expresses truth and affirms a value. It is not an illustration of doctrine. It differs from allegory in that its components, not to be equated with anything else, function in their own right. It is the dynamic truth, the dynamic value. The philosophy of a given myth may be defined, but the definition is no more the myth itself than the statement of the theme of a poem is the poem: in each instance the value becomes static, it may be discussed but not felt, the conviction of the experience is forfeited. (The position of the Platonic myth in relation to the particular topic of discussion is beautifully in point.) In other words, myth represents a primary exercise of sensibility in which thought and feeling are one: it is total communication.' *Ibid.* p. 96.
5 Warren argues that, for Ransom, Agrarianism 'would provide fuller opportunity for the play of man's sensibility, or in other words, for the play of his proper humanity. The essential qualities of that establishment – order, tradition, stability – are merely aspects of that sensibility.' *Ibid.* p. 100.
6 '[T]he objective is not the abolition, but the correction of industrialism, just as the objective on the theoretical side of Ransom's argument is not the abolition, but the correction of science; that is, the interpretation of science in the total context of human experience.' *Ibid.* pp. 99–100.
7 'I have named these four writers because they, perhaps more than any other Americans, have done work that is defined, in its theme and essence, by a powerful and coherent culture. Whatever the limits of New England culture may have been, it did propose that a man's experience and behaviour was not merely "interesting" as a case, or type, or illustration, but was important in itself as part of an eternal drama.' Robert Penn Warren, 'Literature as Symptom' in Allen Tate and Herbert Agar, eds., *Who Owns America: A New Declaration of Independence* (Boston: Houghton Mifflin, 1936) p. 266. Also published as 'Some Recent Novels', *SR* 1 (Winter 1936) pp. 624–49.
8 For Warren, the writer motivated in this way 'may engage himself in such an activity as a part, and perhaps the most significant part, of his role as a citizen and a human being. He is, then, motivated by the conviction that the study of human conduct is more important and positive because the human creature possesses an inalienable dignity and interest; and then, his effort to perform as an artist, to create from the premises of his speculations and the passions provoked by them, is in itself, finally, but a phase of his own conduct as a human being and, as a matter of fact, a citizen. His work, therefore, may more nearly achieve an objectivity and give an impression of fulfillment; it is not forever tied to his own personality, and the act of parturition is indeed complete. The work may be, therefore, a genuine creation.' *Ibid.* p. 267.
9 For Warren, the second type of writer has a different motive to the first type because he does not see his writing as 'a phase of his role as a human being or, perhaps, citizen. In that case, he may perform an abstraction, and may look about him merely in his role as an artist. That is, he is searching for a theme – something to give meaning to his impulse, a scaffolding or a stage on which he may parade, a device to permit the expression, ultimately, of his own personality. His speculative questions, then, are undertaken not because he

holds that they, in themselves, are finally important; they are a means to an end
... That end is self-expression; just that. He has defined himself as an artist – a
pard spirit, beautiful and swift and quite unlike other persons. His concerns are
not their concerns, and he is inclined, with egotism of frail morality, to set a
high valuation on his own concern. With his intelligence, his sensitivity, his
literary genius even, he may do a great deal to make that valuation appear not
too absurd. But he, our hypothetically contemporary writer, does not always
seem thoroughly content.' *Ibid.* pp. 267–8.

10  *Ibid.* p. 270.
11  *Ibid.* p. 273.
12  '[T]here is one important aspect which the two movements, as literary
    movements, share in common: both are revolutionary. Both the proletarian
    and regional writer are dissatisfied with the present relation of the writer to
    society.' *Ibid.* p. 276.
13  *Ibid.* p. 278.
14  Robert Penn Warren, 'Some Don'ts for Literary Regionalists', *AR* 8 (Dec.
    1936) pp. 142–50.
15  'The hick is not to be baited but pampered now, a process that may have its
    own dangers and many accomplish with a genial smile what ridicule and high-
    pressure salesmen left undone.' *Ibid.* p. 145.
16  *Ibid.* p. 149.
17  *Ibid.* p. 150.
18  'A Warlike, various, and a tragical age is best to *write of*, but worst to *write in*,
    said Abraham Cowley. When a people looks back on such an age in its own
    history, another question is raised as it evokes in memory those wars, the
    turbulent variety, and the tragedy. From such reflections they will ask: what
    have these tumults wrought? what relation have we, their product, to them?'
    Robert Penn Warren, 'Not Local Colour', *VQR* 8 (Jan. 1932) p. 153.
19  *Ibid.* p. 153.
20  Georg Lukacs, *The Historical Novel* (London: Merlin Press, 1962); *Essays in
    Realism* (London: Lawrence and Wishart, 1980); *Writer and Critic* (London:
    Merlin Press, 1978).
21  *Ibid.* p. 154.
22  'The historical novel, as ordinarily conceived, is equally deficient in the same
    respect; manners tend to be substituted for value, and costume and *décor* for an
    essential relationship between man and his background, both natural and
    social. The result is another form of the quaint, again incomplete and
    unphilosophical.' *Ibid.* p. 154.
23  For Warren, the transcription of historical particulars 'is incomplete and
    unphilosophical; it does not provide a framework in which human action has
    more than immediate and adventitious significance'. *Ibid.* p. 154. This position
    is also rehearsed in relation to the writings of T. S. Stribling in Robert Penn
    Warren's 'T. S. Stribling: A Paragraph in the History of Critical Realism', *AR*
    2 (Feb. 1934) pp. 463–86.
24  For Warren, MacLeish's 'poetry is a study in shading, not a study in resolution.
    In fact, his poetry is carefully purged of all opposing stresses; it is singularly
    undramatic. It is poetry of the single impulse, which requires no resolution.
    This implies a certain formlessness, a defect in logic. If the theme is vague (not

*difficult*), there can be no suspense or progression; there can be little more than the incidental excitement of the poetic perceptions at creating which MacLeish is adept.' Robert Penn Warren, 'Twelve Poets', *AR* 3 (May 1934) p. 214.

25 'In one poem MacLeish has said "a poem should not mean but be". This is perfectly true in one sense: the artist constructs a work which is self-contained, which does not demand external reference for its justification, in which idea is vindicated in terms of perception. Again he has asked: "Is it just to demand of us also to bear arms?" But the alternatives, as he puts them, are not necessary. The external reference of idea is propaganda; that is the poet bears arms. The option, the choice MacLeish has taken, is a poetry in which idea is reduced to a minimum, even as a structural element.' *Ibid.* p. 216.

26 'Irony, like wit, may be used because the writer happens to be enamoured of the effect divorced from any persistent point of view... the irony of Ransom's poetry is not one of irresponsible contrasts and negations.' 'John Crowe Ransom: A Study in Irony' pp. 102–3.

27 For Warren, Ransom's work involves 'a commentary on the situation, its irony deriving from the fact that these perhaps otherwise admirable people "cannot fathom nor perform their own nature." In general they represent a disorder contrary to the principles of order which the poet, in his more explicit, non-poetical work, has defended.' *Ibid.* p. 103.

28 'Eliot and Ransom have been concerned with the same problem. The method of irony in Ransom's poetry, for want of a better word, may be called psychological. Factors in the make-up of his heroes which might work for strength actually work toward weakness. Eliot's method may be called historical: the ignoble present is suddenly thrust into contrast with the noble past.' *Ibid.* p. 110.

CONCLUSION: THE ANALYSIS OF A SOUTHERN POET

1 Aubrey Harrison Starke, *Sidney Lanier, A Biography and Critical Study* (Chapel Hill: University of North Carolina Press, 1933).

2 'It is the desire to give Lanier a "rank" and to worry his poetry into some kind of "social significance" rather than the critical impulse to estimate the exact quality of his work, that has kept him from being justly placed in American letters.' Allen Tate, 'A Southern Romantic', *NR* 76 (Aug. 1933) p. 67.

3 *Ibid.* p. 70.

4 For details see *ibid.* p. 68.

5 'The conceit does not *represent* anything; it may be laid down as a principle of early seventeenth-century verse, that the conceit is no more than a simile or a metaphor. Where the symbol attempts to exhaust all the implication of the idea that it stands for, the conceit is only illustrative. The differences or identities of parallel images are exhibited, by intention of the poet, for the first time. The distinctive mark of the conceit, setting it apart from simple metaphor and simile, is its greater extent; the conceit is a single figure of speech earned through a long passage or an entire poem.' *Ibid.* p. 68.

6 *Ibid.* p. 68.

7 *Ibid.* p. 69.

8 'Having convinced himself, in an essay called "The New South", that the South would become, after the breakup of the plantations, a region of securely

rooted small farmers, he was at liberty to misunderstand the social and economic significance of the Civil War, and to flatter the industrial capitalism of the North ...' *Ibid.* p. 70.

9  *Ibid.* p. 70.
10  Robert Penn Warren, 'Sidney Lanier: The Blind Poet', *AR* 2 (Nov. 1933) p. 27.
11  *Ibid.* p. 34.
12  *Ibid.* p. 35.
13  *Ibid.* p. 35.
14  *Ibid.* p. 36.
15  Warren claims that, for Lanier, 'the poet is not only a special soul set apart, but a social prophet. That is, the business of the poet is twofold: he must "express" his own etherealizing personality and must perform the personalities of other people. Or perhaps it was not as paradoxical as it seems; the egoist imposes himself.' *Ibid.* pp. 37–8.
16  'The obvious criticism is that he is didactic. But more fundamentally, the trouble was that he never understood the function of idea in art. He regularly performed an arbitrary disjunction, both in creation and criticism, between the idea and the form in which it might be embodied. Painting etherealizes by freeing itself of the "purely material load of colour" ... The idea is never realized; it remains abstract; it does not achieve the status of experience.' *Ibid.* p. 18.
17  'After all, Mr. Starke may be right. Perhaps we should know Lanier. He may help us to assess our heritage.' *Ibid.* p. 45.
18  'Lanier did not have in him a normal degree of the sense of being placed or rooted anywhere. And yet it must be said that there is in him at any moment a natural piety in one sense; a love (nostalgia it amounts to when he is gone from it) for the specific physical nature of his own region.' John Crowe Ransom, 'Hearts and Heads', *AR* 2 (March 1933) p. 560.
19  'I am saying that sensibility to nature is an acquired faculty, and depends on having the right working relationship with nature, the right economy, rather than having tours and picnics.' *Ibid.* p. 560.
20  *Ibid.* p. 561.
21  'We gather that Trade is the enemy of chivalry and even of common honesty; and that the great fortunes, as they are acquired under the forms of capitalistic organisation, entail at the other end of the line, great destitution; two sound objections, neither an agrarian one.' *Ibid.* pp. 565–6.
22  *Ibid.* p. 566.

INTRODUCTION TO PART THREE

1  Charles William Morris was a leading figure among the Logical Positivists and he was the author of *Foundations of a Theory of Signs* which was published as *Encyclopedia of Unified Science No. 2, Vol. I* (University of Chicago Press, 1940).

7 THE ORIGINS OF ACADEMIC INVOLVEMENT

1  For a history of the *Southern Review*, see Thomas W. Cutrer, *Parnassus on the Mississippi: The Southern Review and the Baton Rouge Literary Community 1935–1942* (Baton Rouge: Louisiana State University Press, 1984).

2  An example of this is Kenneth Burke who was highly regarded by these writers, despite the fact that Ohmann and Lentricchia claim that he adopted positions which were repressed by the New Critics.
3  Allen Tate, 'The Function of the Critical Review', *SR* 1 (Winter 1936) p. 551.
4  'Doubtless our splitting off of information from understanding, this modern divorce of action from intelligence, is general, not particular to the arts of literature. It is a problem that on every hand confronts us, it must affect the policy of the critical review – and tremendously determine it. For the critical review stands for one half of the modern dilemma, the purer half – the intelligence thinking into the world a rational order of value.' *Ibid.* p. 552.
5  'The reader needs more than the mere news that a point of view exists; he must be initiated into the point of view, saturated with it. The critical program must, then, supply its readers with coherent standards of taste. Mere reporting enjoins the editor to glance at all points of view. The reader gets a "digest" of opinion, not critical thought; and he is encouraged to sample everything but to master nothing.' *Ibid.* p. 554.
6  *Ibid.* p. 552.
7  For a history of the *Kenyon Review*, see Marian Janssen, *The Kenyon Review, 1939–1970: A Critical History* (Baton Rouge: Louisiana State University Press, 1990).
8  See Thomas Daniel Young, *Gentleman in a Dustcoat: A Biography of John Crowe Ransom* (Baton Rouge: Louisiana State University Press, 1976).
9  John Crowe Ransom, *The Selected Letters of John Crowe Ransom* (Baton Rouge: Louisiana State University Press, 1985) p. 223.
10  John Crowe Ransom, *The World's Body* (New York: Charles Scribner's Sons, 1938).
11  Allen Tate, *Reactionary Essays on Poetry and Ideas* (New York: Charles Scribner's Sons, 1936) p. ix.
12  'There is a division of purpose, and the arrogance of facile "solution" that thinks it can get along without experience. The poet had better write his poetry first; examine it; then decide what he thinks; it will reveal all he thinks that is any good – for poetry. Poetry is one test of ideas; it is ideas tested by experience, by the act of direct appreciation.' *Ibid.* p. xi.
13  '[T]here is no large scheme of imaginative reference in which he has confidence. He must, in short, attach some irony to his use of "ideas" which tend to wither; he may look for new growth but with the reservation that it too may be subject to the natural decay.' *Ibid.* pp. xi-xii.
14  *The World's Body* p. vii.
15  *Ibid.* p. ix.
16  'In the labor we sacrificed nearly everything and naturally the reward is as tenuous as the labour. Where is the body and solid substance of the world? It seems to have retired into the fulness of memory, but out of this we reconstruct the fulness of poetry, which is a counterpart of the world's fulness.' *Ibid.* p. x.
17  *Ibid.* p. x.
18  'The race in its unconscious strategy pushes its sciences always harder, and they grow more and more exclusive as they prosper. But at the same time it devises the arts, and even sets them up in a sort of honor as an equal and opposite activity, and keeps them always changing their forms in order to have their full

effect. They are probably the best devices there could be for the purpose, and the way they work is the proper object of critical studies.' *Ibid.* p. xi.

19 For Tate, Eliot's criticism 'exhibits an insight into the poetry of the past that Mr. More, I believe, would call profound; but Mr. Eliot's own poetry seems to be quite different from the poetry that he admires. If Mr. Eliot is a traditionalist, and I think he notoriously is, why doesn't he write traditional poetry?' Allen Tate, 'Modern Poets and Conventions', *AR* 8 (Feb. 1937) p. 429.

20 'Whatever it is that stands powerfully under the language of Shakespeare, that centre of obscure luminosity that one penetrates only after a second reading, I admire at a distance, if I may be sure that I am entitled to admire it at all after thirty readings – I try to understand it as an archeologist, picking up a piece of chased bronze, marvels at the civilization of the sixth century of Troy.' *Ibid.* p. 431.

21 'We cannot penetrate the mind of another age deeply enough to repeat its experience: it is the task of poetry then to comprehend its awareness of the past in the experience of the present.' *Ibid.* p. 434.

22 'These critics, though not agreed on principles, are usually agreed in finding in modern poetry a certain reticence or unintelligibility. This agreement, however, is deceptive, for when their concealed disagreement on principles is brought into the open, one discovers that they are not agreed as to what should be communicated in any poetry whatsoever.' Robert Penn Warren and Cleanth Brooks, 'The Reading of Modern Poetry', *AR* 8 (Feb. 1937) p. 437.

23 *Ibid.* p. 438.

24 *Ibid.* p. 438.

25 Brooks and Warren argue that both forms of misreading neglect 'the fact that the poem, in so far as it is successful, is a unified construct, a psychological whole; and since a poem is an organism it is not only greater than, but different from, the sum of its parts. Indeed, it cannot be too highly emphasized that what we usually think of as the poetic quality resides in a functional combination of factors rather than the intrinsic nature of any single factor.' *Ibid.* p. 439.

26 *Ibid.* p. 441.

27 'The unity which the poet has attempted to attain is not an easily won unity, but one wrested from recalcitrant and discordant materials. Consequently such a poetry has been characterized by ironical devices, wretched rhymes, abrupt transitions, apparent discords, non-decorative metaphors, deficiency of statement, and when successful has attained its unity only in terms of a total intention. Such a poetry demands a fuller participation on the part of the reader. It is not an easy poetry, but it can claim to take its charter from Coleridge himself: for Coleridge admitted a theory of imagination that would accommodate this practice, and indeed described the imagination as a resolution of opposites.' *Ibid.* pp. 448–9.

28 John Crowe Ransom, 'Criticism Inc.', *VQR* 13 (Autumn 1937) p. 587.

29 'The department of English is charged with the understanding and communication of literature, an art, yet it has usually forgotten to inquire into the peculiar constitution and structure of its product.' *Ibid.* p. 592.

30 *Ibid.* p. 599.

31 *Ibid.* pp. 600–1.

32 *Ibid.* p. 601.
33 *Ibid.* p. 601.
34 *Ibid.* p. 602.
35 Ronald S. Crane, 'History Versus Criticism in the University Study of Literature', *The English Journal* 24 (Oct. 1935) pp. 635–67.
36 *The Selected Letters of John Crowe Ransom* p. 236.
37 *Ibid.* p. 236.


8 UNDERSTANDING LITERATURE: TEXTBOOKS AND THE DISTRIBUTION OF THE NEW CRITICISM

1 Robert Penn Warren and Cleanth Brooks, *Understanding Poetry* (New York: Holt, Rinehart and Winston, 1961) pp. 7–8.
2 *Ibid.* p. xiv.
3 *Ibid.* pp. 1–2.
4 *Ibid.* p. 2.
5 'The relationship among the elements in a poem is what is all important; it is not a mechanical relationship but one which is far more intimate and fundamental. If we must compare a poem to the make up of some physical object it ought not to be to a wall but to something organic like a plant.' *Ibid.* p. 16.
6 Robert Penn Warren and Cleanth Brooks, *Understanding Fiction* (New York: F. S. Crofts, 1947) p. xvii.
7 *Ibid.* pp. xviii–xix.
8 '[E]ven in this talking to one's self, there is a sense of audience, and a law imposed by that sense. One can express one's self to one's self, and thereby understand one's self, only by treating one's self as an audience – and that means respecting the form of what is said so that anyone quite distinct from the self might be able to get the full force and implication of what is being expressed.' *Understanding Poetry* p. 182.
9 'All our life and education is the preparation we bring to the poem which we can understand and appreciate today. If today we can read Shakespeare with pleasure, we can do so only because we have educated ourselves into it. A poem does not exist in isolation. It exists in history, we can appreciate it only in so far as we are acquainted with the relevant history – the world that brought it into being and the world to which it refers.' *Ibid.* p. 399.
10 *Ibid.* p. 519.
11 *Ibid.* p. 526.
12 *Ibid.* p. 526.
13 Gerald Graff, *Professing Literature: An Institutional History* (University of Chicago Press, 1987) p. 5.
14 *Ibid.* p. 6.
15 Out of a computer search which produced twenty-odd pages of material, I was only able to track down six relevant books – the rest were either republications of books from the period 1860–1900, or were not available in the British Library. In fact, of the six which I did track down, several were written and published in England. Furthermore, many of these books were not actually meant for use in the universities, but were written for the High School and the Junior High. The books which I did track down were the following: Emma

Miller Bolenius, *Literature in the Highschool II* (Boston: Houghton and Mifflin, 1927); Norman Callan, *Poetry in Practice: A Case Study for the Progressive Study of Poetry in Schools* (London: Lindsay Drummond, 1938); Ernest Hanes and Martha Joyce McCoy, *Manual to Readings in Literature* (New York: Macmillan, 1925); William Macpherson, *Principles and Method in the Study of English Literature* (Cambridge University Press, 1908); Howard Francis Seely, *On Teaching English* (New York: American Book Company, 1933); A. G. Tracey, *The Appreciation of Literature* (London: Sir Isaac Pitman and Sons, 1927).

16 *On Teaching English.*
17 *Poetry in Practice.*
18 *Principles and Method in the Study of English.*
19 *The Appreciation of Literature.*
20 *Understanding Fiction* p. viii.
21 '[A]ctually the process which leads him past the mere threshold interest to the fuller interests implicit in fiction causes an enlargement of the area of his potential enjoyment. As a human being, he has interests wider than baseball or Western adventure, and he may come to realize that, even in the shoddiest story dealing with baseball or the Wild West, his other more fundamental interests have been covertly engaged.' *Ibid.* p. x.
22 *Ibid.* p. x.

9 THE FORM OF CRITICISM

1 *The International Encyclopedia of Unified Science* was published at Chicago by the Logical Positivists and Vol. 1. No. 2 contained Charles William Morris' *Foundations of a Theory of Signs.*
2 *The Selected Letters of John Crowe Ransom* p. 256.
3 Paul de Man, *Allegories of Reading: Figural Language in Rousseau, Nietzsche, Rilke and Proust* (New Haven, Conn.: Yale University Press, 1979).
4 '[N]owhere can there be a case where the unification of different sciences will seem so violent as the attempt to unify the arts under the same rule with the sciences.' John Crowe Ransom, 'Editorial Note: The Arts and the Philosophers', *KR* 1 (Spring 1939) p. 194.
5 *Ibid.* p. 197.
6 'The Encyclopedists are talking about the language of science. I imagine that now is a splendid time for the aestheticians, inside or outside the Encyclopedia, to make an assertion which would be round, bold, metaphysical, just, and tactically perfect. To this effect: art has a language of its own; it is not the same as the language of science; its semantical meanings cannot be rendered in the language of science. Art fixes knowledge of which science has no understanding, and which gentlemen too confined within the scientific habit cannot approach intelligently.' *Ibid.* pp. 197–8.
7 'Thinking of the trope by which I attempted above to describe this meaning, I believe it may be suggested that the linguistic achievement of art is, as we see very clearly in poetry, just the *trope*. Its object of knowledge, its *designatum* and *denotatum*, is an object in the round, a figure of three dimensions, so to speak; in technical language a singular and individual object. That is not an object which scientific knowledge has, or affects, or desires. Science with its proportions, art

with its tropes. We are aware of how science abhors the figurative, the tropical, and that is significant. Art on its side abhors propositions, or it should. When the trope begins to reduce to a proposition we are coming out of the solid world of art into the abstract plane of science. We are also relapsing further from the world of actuality, of which art is the closest fiction that we have.' *Ibid.* p. 198.

8 John Crowe Ransom, 'The Pragmatics of Art', *KR* 2 (Winter 1940) p. 88.

9 *Ibid.* p. 82.

10 '[T]he value of the object denoted by the icon is to be looked for not necessarily "in itself" but in what it imitates; and here, in its affirmation of a structural or rational order.' *Ibid.* p. 86.

11 *Ibid.* p. 87.

12 Ransom argues that this group understand 'only that Joyce disdains the positive achievements of the race, and these they are prepared to defend for the sake of innumerable biological, political, moral, and material advantages; they are pensioners, not critics, of our opulent society. The others are persons of incorruptible innocence, unless they are actually in the green time of youth itself, and they believe that Joyce is really a writer with a positive attitude, and "difficult" only in being too difficult for ordinary readers to grasp.' John Crowe Ransom, 'Editorial Note: The Aesthetic of *Finnegans Wake*', *KR* 1 (Autumn 1939) p. 424.

13 'I believe that *Finnegans Wake* is the most comprehensive individual reaction we have yet seen to all that we have accomplished with our perverted ideal of perfect action.' *Ibid.* p. 425.

14 *Ibid.* p. 426.

15 'There is probably a poetry of feelings just as much as there is a poetry of knowledge; for we may hardly deny to a word its common usage, and poetry is an experience so various as to be entertained by everybody. But the poetry of feelings is not the one that the critic is compelled to prefer, especially if he can say that it taints us with subjectivism, sentimentality, and self-indulgence.' John Crowe Ransom, 'Shakespeare at Sonnets', *SR* 3 (Winter 1938) p. 537.

16 Allen Tate, 'Narcissus as Narcissus', *VQR* 14 (Winter 1938) p. 108.

17 'Poets, in their way, are practical men; they are interested in results. What is the poem, after it is written? That is the question. Not where it came from, or why. The Why and Where can never get beyond the questioning stage because, in the language of those who think it can, poetry cannot be brought to "laboratory conditions". The only real evidence that any critic may bring before his gaze is the finished poem.' *Ibid.* p. 110.

18 'A poem may be an instance of morality, of social conditions, of psychological history; it may instance all its qualities, but never be one of them alone, nor any two or three; nor even less all. In making women "instance" of sex we make them whores.' *Ibid.* p. 110.

19 '[Poetry] is merely a way of knowing something: if the poem is a real creation, it is a kind of knowledge that we did not possess before. It is not knowledge "about" something else; the poem is the fulness of that knowledge.' *Ibid.* p. 110.

20 'In metaphysical poetry the logical order is explicit; it must be coherent; the imagery by which it is sensuously embodied must have at least the look of logical determinism: I say look of logical determinism because the varieties of

ambiguity and contradiction possible beneath the surface are endless ...' Allen Tate, 'Tension in Poetry', *SR* 4 (Summer 1938) p. 108.

21 *Ibid.* p. 108.

22 *Ibid.* p. 108.

23 'I am not attacking the study or the writing of history for use in the criticism of literature. I am attacking the historical method. I trust everybody understands what this method is. It reflects at varying distances the philosophies of monism current in the nineteenth century and still prevailing today. Because the literary scholar in his monistic naturalism cannot discern the objectivity of the forms of literature, he can only apply to literature certain abstractions which he derives, two stages removed, from the naturalistic sciences; that is to say he gets these abstractions from the historians who got them from the scientists.' Allen Tate, 'Miss Emily and the Bibliographer' in *Essays of Four Decades* (London: Oxford University Press, 1970) p. 151.

24 'When the scholar assumes that he is judging a work of the past from a high and disinterested position, he is actually judging it from no position at all but is only abstracting from the work those qualities that his semiscientific method will permit him to see ...' *Ibid.* p. 152.

25 See Harold Bloom, *The Anxiety of Influence: A Theory of Poetry* (New York; London: Oxford University Press, 1973) and *A Map of Misreading* (New York; London: Oxford University Press, 1975).

26 'Miss Emily and the Bibliographer' p. 154.

27 *The Selected Letters of John Crowe Ransom* p. 268.

28 *Ibid.* p. 271.

29 John Crowe Ransom, 'Editorial Note: Mr. Tate and the Professors', *KR* 2 (Summer 1940) p. 349.

30 Introduction to 'Literature and the Professors: A Symposium', *SR* 6 (Summer 1940) p. 225.

31 The Symposium appeared in *SR* 6 (Summer 1940) and *KR* 2 (Summer 1940).

32 Ransom argues that the professors 'have been engaged faithfully together in a formidable and all together reputable work of collaboration, the enterprise of literary "scholarship". The range and volume of the literary evidence made to bear on this work, and the capabilities of the personel using it, have improved in our own time not so much steadily and satisfactorily as by leaps and bounds; by acceleration. The contribution of the American workers to the project is a matter, for the most part, of these last forty years. They have done well. They have done so well, in fact, that the job is about finished, and they must look for another job.' John Crowe Ransom, 'Strategy for English Studies', *SR* 6 (Autumn 1940) p. 226.

33 'The older generation of scholars may very honorably bask in its handsome achievements, but what is there for the younger generation to do? The younger generation at best is restive and discouraged. The older generation scarcely understands how ripe the times are for a revolutionary shift of strategy.' *Ibid.* p. 227.

34 *Ibid.* p. 227.

35 '[The professors of English] ought not to have contented themselves with knowing the famous critics, they should have tried some criticism of their own upon the critics. If they did try some they should try more. It scarcely seems too

daring to believe that the classics of criticism have not been of an excellence proportionate to the classics of creative literature, and that a great piety towards them makes in us an uncritical attitude and is a dangerous service to criticism.' *Ibid.* p. 229.

36  'Conspicuous in the symposium is a lack of value-judgements; it is another consequence of the historian's obligation to be sympathetic. The values missed would be not only the ethical but especially the aesthetic ones. The writers seem uncritically at home in the romantic atmosphere, and try to make us so.' *Ibid.* p. 232.

37  Allen Tate, 'The Function of the Critical Quarterly' in *Essays of Four Decades* p. 199.

38  Tate claims that for the educationalists and sociologists 'the greatest thing [is man's] adjustment to society (not to a good society): a mechanical society in which we were to be conditioned for the realization of a *bourgeois* paradise of gadgets and of consumption, not of the fruits of the earth, but of commodities.' *Ibid.* p. 199.

39  *Ibid.* pp. 201–2.

40  *Ibid.* p. 210.

10  JOHN CROWE RANSOM: THE ISOLATION OF AESTHETIC ACTIVITY

1  John Crowe Ransom, *Beating the Bushes: Selected Essays 1941–1970* (New York: New Directions, 1972).

2  'What is new is unsure, inconsistent, perhaps raw; even this new criticism. It makes errors in strategy, just as poetry and fiction may do. It does not usually have enough background in philosophy, and may rely on perfectly inadequate formulas, under which precise thinking cannot be effected. I approach these critics critically.' John Crowe Ransom, *The New Criticism* (Norfolk, Conn.: New Directions, 1941) pp. x–xi.

3  *Ibid.* p. xi.

4  *Ibid.* p. xi.

5  *Ibid.* p. 280.

6  *Ibid.* pp. 280–1.

7  *Ibid.* p. 291.

8  'The syntactical dimension is imperilled, upon the introduction of icons into discourse, along with the semantical. It will apparently be impossible for discourse to compel its icons to function in the strict logic which we have learned to expect from the symbols.' *Ibid.* p. 292.

9  'The world of art is the actual world which does not bear restriction; or at least is sufficiently defiant of the restrictiveness of science, and offers enough fullness of content, to give us the sense of the actual objects. A qualitative density, or value-density, such as is unknown to scientific understanding, marks the world of actual objects. The discourse which tries systematically to record this world is art.' *Ibid.* p. 293.

10  *Ibid.* p. 295.

11  *Ibid.* p. 295.

12  'Indeterminacy of this positive or valuable sort is introduced when the images make their entry. It looks as if there might be something very wise in the social, anonymous, and universal provision of metrical technique for poetry. The

meter seems only to harm the discourse, till presently it works a radical innovation: it induces the provision of icons among the symbols. This launches poetry upon its career.' *Ibid.* p. 316.

13 John Crowe Ransom, 'Editorial Note: Muses and Amazons', *KR* 3 (Spring 1941) p. 240.

14 'Political security and social stability are not identical with the substance of art, but they condition the form and the prosperity of the arts as much as building, marrying, and baking do.' *Ibid.* p. 242.

15 *The Selected Letters of John Crowe Ransom* p. 289.

16 John Crowe Ransom, 'Editorial Note: War and Publication', *KR* 4 (Spring 1942) p. 218.

17 John Crowe Ransom, 'Artists, Soldiers, and Positivists', *KR* 6 (Spring 1944) p. 278.

18 *The Selected Letters of John Crowe Ransom* p. 282.

19 *Ibid.* p. 282.

20 '[I]t is right that we should call something to the attention of the naturalists; a behaviour or two which appear rather different from these, with an outlook that does not deserve to be glozed. Sometimes the field does not seem to evoke from man the conquering action. It is as if some invincible residuum had asserted itself on nature's part, or else some scruple asserted itself in the conqueror.' John Crowe Ransom, 'Art Worries the Naturalists' in *Beating the Bushes: Selected Essays 1941–1970* pp. 95–6.

21 *Ibid.* p. 96.

22 *Ibid.* p. 81.

23 John Crowe Ransom, 'Positive and Near Positive Aesthetics' in *Beating the Bushes: Selected Essays 1941–1970* pp. 77–8.

24 'Unification is empire, in politics, in business and affairs. To unify an area of nature, if only in theory, is to grasp it firmly with one act of perfect understanding; and natural science acquires that grasp where it can, and sometimes it vaunteth itself, whereas the habit of art is discreetly, though willfully, to disperse the view, and to intimate that nature is too various to be unified, at least against her will.' 'Art Worries the Naturalists' p. 110.

25 *Ibid.* p. 92.

26 John Crowe Ransom, 'Art and the Human Economy' in *Beating the Bushes: Selected Essays 1941–1970* p. 128.

27 *Ibid.* p. 129.

28 Ransom claims that, for Adorno, a writer such as Proust 'knows the human heart because his own vision, his own experience, is complete. And it is because there will be in any society men strong enough to complete their experience eventually, and no society able to repress them permanently, that we say that art has an eternal vitality.' *Ibid.* p. 131.

29 *Ibid.* p. 132.

30 *Ibid.* p. 133.

31 *Ibid.* p. 135.

11 ALLEN TATE: THE MAN OF LETTERS AND THE COLD WAR

1 Godfrey Hodgson, *America in Our Time* (London: Macmillan, 1977).

2 For a history of the Congress of Cultural Freedom, see C. Lasch, 'The Cultural

Cold War: A Short History of the Congress of Cultural Freedom' in Barton J. Bernstein, *Towards a New Past* (London: Chatto and Windus, 1970).

3 Allen Tate, *Stonewall Jackson: The Good Soldier* (Ann Arbor: University of Michigan Press, 1957); *Jefferson Davis: His Rise and Fall* (New York: Minton Balch, 1929); the Lee biography was never completed.

4 'Our lives were eternally balanced upon a pedestal below which lay an abyss that I could not name. Within that invisible tension my father knew the moves of an intricate game that he expected everybody else to play. That, I think, was because everything he was and felt was in the game itself; he had no life apart from it and he was baffled by George Posey, by the threat of some untamed force that did not recognize the rules of the game.' Allen Tate, *The Fathers* (Baton Rouge: Louisiana State University Press, 1977) pp. 43–4.

5 'I know distinctly that I thought of him always boldly riding somewhere, and because I couldn't see where, I suppose I thought of a precipice.' *Ibid.* p. 10.

6 *Ibid.* p. 15.

7 *Ibid.* pp. 218–19.

8 Allen Tate, 'Notes on Southern Religion' in Twelve Southerners, *I'll Take My Stand: The South and the Agrarian Tradition* (Baton Rouge: Louisiana State University Press, 1980).

9 Louis Rubin, *The Wary Fugitives* (Baton Rouge: Louisiana State University Press, 1978).

10 Allen Tate, 'Literature and Knowledge', *SR* 6 (Spring 1941) p. 633.

11 Allen Tate, 'The Hovering Fly' in *Essays of Four Decades* (London: Oxford University Press, 1970) p. 110.

12 'If we think of the actual world as either a dead lump or a whirling wind somewhere outside us, against which we bump our heads or which whirls us around, we shall never be able to discover it: we have got to try to find it in terms of one of our chief interests. Let us call that interest the imagination.' *Ibid.* pp. 114–15.

13 Tate refers to the following passage which he quotes: '[Myshkin's] eyes were now accustomed to the darkness, so that he could make out the whole bed. Someone lay asleep on it, in a perfectly motionless sleep; not the faintest stir, not the faintest breath could be heard. The sleeper was covered from head to foot with a white sheet and the limbs were vaguely defined; all that could be seen was that a human figure lay there, stretched at full length. All around in disorder at the foot of the bed, on chairs beside it, and even on the floor, clothes had been flung; a rich white silk dress, flowers, and ribbons. On a little table at the head of the bed there was a glitter of diamonds that had been taken off and thrown down. At the end of the bed there was a crumpled heap of lace and on the white lace the toes of a bare foot peeped out from under the sheet; it seemed as though it had been carved out of marble and it was horribly still. Myshkin looked and felt that he had looked, the room became more and more still and death-like. Suddenly there was the buzz of a fly which flew over the bed and settled on the pillow.' Quoted in 'The Hovering Fly' pp. 118–19.

14 'We may *look* at the hovering fly; we can to a degree *know* the actual world. But we cannot know the actual world by looking at it; we know it by looking at the hovering fly.' 'The Hovering Fly' p. 117.

15 'Any sinister significance that the fly may create for us is entirely due to its

crossing our own path: by means of the fly the human order is compromised. But it is also extended, until through a series of similar conversions and correspondences of image the buzz of the fly distends, both visually and metaphorically, the body of the girl into the world. Her degradation and nobility are in that image. Shall we call it the actual world?' *Ibid.* p. 119.

16 'For if the drift of this essay have anything of truth in it, then our daily suffering, our best will towards the world in which we with difficulty breathe today, and our secret anxieties, however painful these experiences may be, must have something of the occult, something of the private, even something of the willful and obtuse, unless by a miracle of gift or character, and perhaps of history also, we command the imaginative power of the relation of things.' *Ibid.* p. 120.

17 'The battle is now between the dehumanized society of secularism, which imitates Descartes' mechanized nature, and the eternal society of the communion of the human spirit.' Allen Tate, 'The Man of Letters in the Modern World' in *Essays of Four Decades* pp. 4–5.

18 *Ibid.* p. 8.

19 *Ibid.* p. 8.

20 'Our unexamined theory of literature as communication could not have appeared in an age in which communion was still possible for any appreciable majority of persons. The word communication presupposes the victory of the secularized society of means without ends. The poet, on the one hand, shouts to the public, on the other (some distance away), not the rediscovery of the common experience, but a certain pitch of sound to which the well-conditioned adrenals of humanity obligingly respond.' *Ibid.* p. 12.

21 'The poet was saddled with the total responsibility for the moral, political, and social well-being; it was pretty clearly indicated that had he behaved differently at some definite time in the near or remote past the international political order itself would not have been in jeopardy, and we should not perhaps be at international loggerheads today. We should not have had the Second World War, perhaps not even the first.' Allen Tate, 'To Whom is the Poet Responsible?' in *Essays of Four Decades* p. 17.

22 'Reason – in the sense of moderate unbelief in the difficult truths about human nature – and belief in the perfectibility of man-in-the-gross, were the great liberal dogmas which underlay much of our present trouble. The men in charge of nature never told me that I ought to try to perfect myself; that would be done for me by my not believing that I could do anything about it, by relying on history to do it, by the invocation of ideals that many of us thought were democratic, by the resolutions of committees, conventions, and associations; and not least by condescending affirmations of faith in the Common Man, a fictitious person with whom neither philosopher-scientist nor I had even a speaking acquaintance. Will it not be borne in upon us in the next few years that Hitler and Stalin *are* the Common Man, and that one of the tasks of democracy is to allow as many men as possible to make themselves uncommon?' *Ibid.* pp. 24–5.

23 'We have virtually turned the argument of the attack around upon itself. For it was an irresponsible demand to ask the poet to cease to be a poet and become the propagandist of a political ideal, even if he himself thought it a worthy ideal.

If the report of the imagination on the realities of western culture in the past century was as depressing as the liberal mind said it was, would not the scientist, the philosopher, and the statesman, have done well to study it? They might have got a clue to what was wrong.' *Ibid.* p. 28.

24 '[T]he true province of the man of letters is nothing less (as it is nothing more) than culture itself. The state is the mere operation of society, but culture is the way society lives, the material medium through which men receive the one lost truth which must be perpetually recovered: the truth of what Jacques Maritain calls the "supra-temporal destiny" of man. It is the duty of the man of letters to supervise the culture of language, to which the rest of culture is subordinate, and to warn us when our language is ceasing to forward the ends proper to man. The end of social man is communion in time through love, which is beyond time.' 'The Man of Letters in the Modern World' p. 16.

25 '[I]t should be pointed out, I think, to these same European brothers, that the darkness of barbarism still shows forth at least one light which even the black slaves of the Old South were permitted to keep burning, but which the white slaves of Russia are not: I mean the inalienable right to talk back of which I cite the present discourse as an imperfect example.' *Ibid.* p. 15.

26 Allen Tate, 'A Note on Critical "Autotelism"' in *Essays of Four Decades* p. 169.

27 *Ibid.* p. 172.

28 Allen Tate, 'The Symbolic Imagination: The Mirrors of Dante' in *Essays of Four Decades*.

29 'Poe understood the spiritual disunity that had resulted from the rise of the demi-religion of scientism, but by merely opposing its excesses with equally excessive claims for the "poetic intellect" he subtly perpetuated the disunity in another direction.' Allen Tate, 'The Angelic Imagination: Poe as God' in *Essays of Four Decades* p. 415.


12 ROBERT PENN WARREN: LITERATURE AND SOCIAL ENGAGEMENT

1 Comer Vann Woodward, *Thinking Back: The Perils of Writing History* (Baton Rouge: Louisiana State University Press, 1986).

2 Raymond Williams, *Keywords: A Vocabulary of Culture and Society* (London: Fontana, 1976) p. 150.

3 Raymond Williams, *Culture and Society 1780–1950* (Harmondsworth: Penguin, 1961).

4 In the present era, it is important to acknowledge the strengths of this form of liberalism because many of its gains are presently being limited and eroded both in England and America, where large sections of the population are becoming excluded from social involvement. See Mike Davis, *Prisoners of the American Dream* (London: Verso, 1986) and *The Year Left: A Socialist Yearbook* (London: Verso, 1985).

5 Robert Penn Warren, *Night Rider* (New York: Random House, 1939).

6 Robert Penn Warren, 'Katherine Anne Porter (Irony with a Center)', *KR* 4 (Winter 1942) pp. 31–2.

7 Warren argues that the discussions of Katherine Anne Porter's style 'in the

reviews, have chilled the heart of the potential reader, who – and I believe quite rightly – does not want to be lulled or titillated exquisitely by "beautiful style". He is put off by the reviewers' easy abstracting of style for comment and praise; his innocence repudiates the fallacy of "agreeable style". Style does not come to his attention as style.' *Ibid.* p. 32.

8  *Ibid.* p. 34.

9  'The skeptical and ironical basis is, I think, important in Miss Porter's work, and it is true that her work wears an air of detachment and contemplation. But I should say, her irony is an irony with a center, never irony for irony's sake. It simply implies, I think, a refusal to accept the code, the formula, the ready-made solution, the hand-me-down morality, the word for the spirit. It affirms, rather, the constant need for exercising discrimination, the arduous obligation of the intellect in the face of conflicting dogmas, the need for a dialectical approach to matters of definition, the need for exercising as much of the human faculty as possible.' *Ibid.* p. 42.

10  Robert Penn Warren, 'Pure and Impure Poetry' in *Selected Essays* (New York: Random House, 1958) p. 199.

11  *Ibid.* p. 204.

12  'I am inclined to believe that they take the word imagination here at their own convenience and not in Coleridge's context and usage. They take it, as a matter of fact, in the casual and vulgar sense, as equivalent to meaninglessness and illusion; or if they don't take it in the casual and vulgar sense, they take it in terms of a poetic theory of illusion for illusion's sake which, as stated, denies significance to the word as fully as does the casual and vulgar sense.' *Ibid.* p. 205.

13  *Ibid.* p. 229.

14  'The Lady distrusts "pure" poems, nature spiritualized into forgetfulness. She has, as it were, a rigorous taste in metaphor, too; she brings a logical criticism to bear on the metaphor which is too easy; the metaphor must prove itself to her, must be willing to subject itself to scrutiny beyond the moment's enthusiasm. She infects the purity of an intellectual style into her lover's pure poem.' *Ibid.* p. 232.

15  For Warren, 'the poet is like a juijitsu expert: he works by utilizing the resistance of his opponent – the material of the poem. In other words, a poem, to be good, must earn itself. It is a motion towards a point of rest, but if it is not a resisted motion, it is a motion of no consequence.' *Ibid.* p. 251.

16  Robert Penn Warren, 'Melville the Poet' in *Selected Essays* p. 214.

17  'Gould himself is a kind of cousin to Kurtz of *Heart of Darkness*, though Gould is doomed to his isolation, not like Kurtz by avarice, vanity, and violence, by refusing his mission as a light-bringer, by repudiating the idea, but by accepting his mission as a light-bringer and bearer of the idea. He accepts his mission, but ironically enough he falls a victim to the impersonal logic of "material interests" and in the end is the slave of his silver, not by avarice, not by vanity, certainly not vanity in the simple sense, but because he has lost love to the enormous abstraction of his historical role.' Robert Penn Warren, 'Nostromo' in *Selected Essays* p. 35.

18  'Man must make his life somehow in the dialectical process of these terms and in so far as he is to achieve redemption, he must do so through an awareness of

his condition that identifies him with the general human communion, not in abstraction, not in mere doctrine but immediately. The victory is never won, the redemption must be continually reearned.' *Ibid.* p. 54.

19  *Band of Angels* (New York: Random House, 1955).

20  'I was going back to look at the landscapes and streets I had known – Kentucky, Tennessee, Arkansas, Mississippi, Louisiana – to look at the faces, to hear the voices, to hear in fact the voices in my own blood. A girl from Mississippi had said to me: "I feel it's all happening inside of me, every bit of it. It's all there."' Robert Penn Warren, *Segregation: the Inner Conflict of the South* (New York: Random House, 1956) pp. 3–4.

21  'I ask my question of the Negro scholar. His reply is immediate: "It's not so much what the Negro wants as what he doesn't want. The main point is not that he has poor facilities. It is that he must endure the constant assault on his ego. He is denied human dignity."' *Ibid.* p. 72.

22  '*it ain't our hate, it's the hate hung on us by the old folks dead and gone. Not I mean to criticize the old folks, they done the best they knew, but that hate, we don' know how to shuck it. We got that God-damn hate stuck in our craw and can't puke it up. If white folks quit shoving the nigger down and calling him nigger he could maybe get to be a asset to the South and the country. But how stop shoving?* We are the prisoners of our history. Or are we?' *Ibid.* p. 109.

23  For Warren, 'desegregation is just one small episode in the long effort for justice. It seems to me that that perspective, suddenly seeing the business as little, is a liberating one. It liberates you from yourself.' *Ibid.* p. 113.

24  'It assumes the right because only by knowledge does man achieve his identity. I do not mean that the mere implements of knowledge – books, libraries, laboratories, seminars – distinguish man from the brute. No, knowledge gives him his identity because it gives him an image of himself. And the image of himself, necessarily has a foreground and a background, for man is in the world not as a billiard ball placed on a table, not even as a ship on the ocean with a location determinable by latitude and longitude. He is, rather, in the world with continual and infinite interpenetration, and inevitable osmosis of being, which in the end does not deny, but affirms, his identity. It affirms it, for out of a progressive understanding of this interpenetration, this texture of relation, man creates new perspectives, discovers new values – that is, a new self – and so the identity is a continually emerging, an unfolding, a self-affirming and, we hope, a self-corrective creation.' Robert Penn Warren, 'Knowledge and the Image of Man' in John L. Longley, *Robert Penn Warren: A Collection of Critical Essays* ( New York University Press, 1965) p. 241.

25  *Segregation: the Inner Conflict in the South* p. 111.

26  'If the South is really able to face up to itself and its situation, it may achieve identity, moral identity. Then in a country where moral identity is hard to come by, the South, because it has had to deal concretely with a moral problem, may offer some leadership. And we need any we can get. If we are to break out of the national rhythm, the rhythm between complacency and panic.' *Ibid.* p. 115.

27  Robert Penn Warren, *The Legacy of the Civil War* (New York: Random House, 1961) p. 71.

28  'Knowledge and the Image of Man' p. 240.

29 Warren argues that 'if [the black] is to redeem America, he will do so as a creative inheritor of the Judeo-Christian and American tradition – that is, by applying the standards of that tradition – the standards of Western civilization developed and elaborated here. He will point out – as he is now pointing out with anger and irony, with intelligence, devotion, and distinguished courage – that the white man is to be indicted by his own self-professed, and self-created, standards. For the Negro is a Negro-American, and is "more American than the Americans". He is, shall we say, the "existentialist" American. He is a fundamentalist of Western culture. His role is to dramatize the most inward revelation of that culture.' Robert Penn Warren, *Who Speaks for the Negro?* (New York: Random House, 1965) p. 442.

30 'It would be sentimentality to think that our society can be changed easily and without pain. It would be worse sentimentality to think that it can be changed without some pain to our particular selves – black and white. It would be realism to think that that pain would be a reasonable price to pay for what we all, selfishly, might get out of it.' *Ibid.* p. 444.

31 '[T]he myth of progress and the hymn to the redemptive modernity winds up with the Boss and his Janizaries victorious but fatally imprisoned by ramparts of the putrescent dead. They wind up with Hank sunk in the cynical contempt for what he now calls "human muck", the very people he hoped to redeem by reason and technology; and with the phrase "human muck" we find the death knell of the faith in the common sense of the common man.' *Ibid.* p. 169.

32 *Prisoners of the American Dream.*

33 Robert Penn Warren, *Democracy and Poetry* (Cambridge, Mass.: Harvard University Press, 1975) p. xiii.

34 Russell Reising, *The Unusable Past: Theory and the Study of American Literature* (London: Methuen, 1986).

35 *Democracy and Poetry* p. 26.

36 *Ibid.* p. 20.

37 For Warren, 'art ... provides the most perfect example of self-fulfilling activity, the kind of activity of which gratuitous joy in the way of the doing is the mark, and in which the doer pursues the doing as a projection of his own nature upon objective nature, thereby discovering both the law of the medium in which he chooses to work and his own nature.' *Ibid.* p. 85.

38 *Ibid.* p. xvi.

INTRODUCTION TO THE CONCLUSION

1 Frank Lentricchia, *After the New Criticism* (London: Methuen, 1983) p. xiii.

2 *Ibid.* p. xiii.

3 William E. Cain, *The Crisis in Criticism: Theory, Literature and Reform in English Studies* (Baltimore: Johns Hopkins University Press, 1984) p. 105.

4 *Ibid.* p. 105.

5 *Ibid.* p. 105.

6 *Ibid.* p. 106.

7 Jonathan Culler, *Structuralist Poetics* (London: Routledge and Kegan Paul, 1975); *The Pursuit of Signs* (London: Routledge and Kegan Paul, 1981); and *On Deconstruction* (London: Routledge and Kegan Paul, 1983).

8  Even if we accept that culture can be defined as a 'signifying process', we do not have to limit the study of culture to an analysis of the language, or linguistic processes, of the text. Instead, as Raymond Williams illustrates in his book, *Culture*, the process of signification involves both forces and relations of production; it is organized by institutions with historically determinant political economies, institutions such as the publishing industry. And this is as true of 'high culture' as it is of 'popular culture'. Thus, when we study literature, we should not limit the analysis of the process of literary production to an analysis of the linguistic features of the text or the textual system. See Raymond Williams, *Culture* (London: Fontana, 1981).

13  THE PROFESSIONALIZATION OF LITERARY STUDY

1  Gerald Graff, *Professing Literature: An Institutional History* (University of Chicago Press, 1987) p. 55.
2  Gerald Graff and Michael Warner, 'Introduction' in Gerald Graff and Michael Warner, eds., *The Origins of Literary Study: A Documentary History* (London: Routledge, 1989) p. 5.
3  *Ibid.* p. 6.
4  *Ibid.* p. 6.
5  Gerald Graff, *Professing Literature* p. 144.
6  *Ibid.* p. 137.

14  THE NEW CRITICAL INTERVENTION

1  'The historical method will not permit us to develop a critical instrument for dealing with works of literature as existent objects; we see them as expressive of substances beyond themselves. At the historical level the work expresses its place and time, or the author's personality, but if the scholar goes further and says anything about the work, he is expressing himself. Expressionism is here a sentiment, forbidding us to think and permitting us to feel as we please.' Allen Tate, 'Miss Emily and the Bibliographer' in *Essays of Four Decades* (London: Oxford University Press, 1970) pp. 146–7.
2  Gerald Graff, *Professing Literature* p. 137.
3  'The question in the end comes down to this: What as literary critics are we to judge? As literary critics we must first of all decide in what respect the literary work has a specific objectivity. If we deny its specific objectivity then not only is criticism impossible but literature also. We have got to decide what it is about the whole of a work of literature which distinguishes it from its parts – or rather the parts we can abstract from this whole and then distribute over the vast smudge of history, whence they presumably were derived. It is a question of knowing before we talk what as critics we are talking about.' Allen Tate, 'Miss Emily and the Bibliographer' p. 149.
4  Gerald Graff, *Professing Literature* p. 149.
5  Allen Tate, 'The Man of Letters in the Modern World' in *Essays of Four Decades*.
6  Twelve Southerners, *I'll Take My Stand: The South and the Agrarian Tradition* (Baton Rouge: Louisiana State University Press, 1980) p. xliv.

7 Allen Tate, 'Emily Dickinson' in *Essays of Four Decades* p. 89.
8 Allen Tate, 'A Traditionalist Looks at Liberalism', *SR* 1 (Spring 1936) p. 740.
9 John Crowe Ransom, 'Positive and Near Positive Aesthetics' in *Beating the Bushes: Selected Essays 1941–70.*
10 Terence Hawkes, *Structuralism and Semiotics* (London: Methuen, 1977) p. 152.
11 Cleanth Brooks and Robert Penn Warren, *Understanding Fiction* (New York: F. S. Crofts, 1947) p. xvii.
12 John Crowe Ransom, *The New Criticism* (Norfolk, Conn.: New Directions, 1941).
13 John Crowe Ransom, 'Poetry: A Note on Ontology', *AR* 3 (May 1934) and Allen Tate, 'Three Types of Poetry' in *Essays of Four Decades* p. 173.
14 John Crowe Ransom, 'Editorial Note: The Arts and the Philosophers', *KR* 1 (Spring 1939) p. 198.
15 For an excellent discussion of the Agrarian/New Critical preoccupation with concepts of History and Original Sin, see Richard Gray, *Writing the South: Ideas of an American Region* (Cambridge University Press, 1986).
16 Allen Tate, 'To Whom is the Poet Responsible?' in *Essays of Four Decades.*
17 Robert Penn Warren, 'Twelve Poets', *AR* 3 (May 1934).
18 John Crowe Ransom, *The Selected Letters of John Crowe Ransom* (Baton Rouge: Louisiana State University Press, 1985) p. 289.
19 Allen Tate, 'The Symbolic Imagination: The Mirrors of Dante' in *Essays of Four Decades.*
20 Gerald Graff, *Professing Literature* p. 145.
21 William E. Cain, *The Crisis in Criticism.*
22 Terence Hawkes, *Structuralism and Semiotics* (London: Methuen, 1977).

15 CULTURAL CRITICISM AND POSTMODERNITY

1 Fredric Jameson, 'Postmodernism and Consumer Society' in Hal Foster, ed., *Postmodern Culture* (London: Pluto, 1985) p. 112.
2 In fact, as Jameson himself points out, structuralism and post-structuralism are distinguished by their attempt to 'rethink everything once again in terms of linguistics!' (Fredric Jameson, *The Prison House of Language: A Critical Account of Structuralism and Russian Formalism* (Princeton University Press, 1972) p. vii.) Rather than bringing history, economics, or social relations to an explanation of the linguistic processes of the text, history, economics, and social relations are themselves reread as linguistic texts. Jameson does refuse the fashionable attempt to define History itself as a text, but he insists that History 'is inaccessible to us except in textual form, and that our approach to it and to the Real itself necessarily passes through our prior textualization, its narrativization in the political unconscious.' (Fredric Jameson, *The Political Unconscious: Narrative as a Socially Symbolic Act* (London: Methuen, 1983) p. 35.) Thus, the task of the literary critic is to analyse the language of texts to discover History as the great unsaid. Moreover, even though writers such as Fredric Jameson, Frank Lentricchia, and even Christopher Norris use Foucault to counter what they see as the possible excesses of post-structuralism, claiming his post-structuralism to be 'worldly' or 'historical', Foucault's actual writing concentrates on the analysis of discoursive formations, or epistemes. He

analyses social institutions in terms of their discourses, not their forces and relations of production and not their relations to other institutions. In this way, his approach is only historical in so far as it allows the literary critic to analyse the linguistic forms of the text in an attempt to identify the discourses which construct it.

3  'Postmodernism and Consumer Society' p. 114.
4  *Ibid.* p. 114.
5  *Ibid.* p. 115.
6  *Ibid.* p. 114.
7  *Ibid.* p. 117.
8  *Ibid.* p. 117.
9  *Ibid.* p. 119.
10  *Ibid.* p. 120.
11  Christopher Lasch, *The Minimal Self: Psychic Survival in Troubled Times* (London: Pan, 1985).
12  Fredric Jameson, 'Postmodernism and Consumer Society' p. 120.
13  Stuart Hall, 'Cultural Studies: Two Paradigms' in Tony Bennett et al., eds., *Culture, Ideology and Social Process* (London: Batsford, 1981) p. 34.
14  Fredric Jameson, 'Postmodernism and Consumer Society' p. 123.
15  *Ibid.* p. 123.
16  *Ibid.* p. 125.
17  Ernest Mandel, *Late Capitalism* (London: Verso, 1978).
18  Mike Davis, 'Urban Renaissance and the Spirit of Postmodernism', *NLR* 151 (1985) pp. 107.
19  Ernest Mandel, *The Second Slump: A Marxist Analysis of the Recession in the 1970s* (London: New Left Books, 1978).
20  Mike Davis, 'Urban Renaissance and the Spirit of Postmodernism' p. 108.
21  See Fredric Jameson, 'Postmodernism or the Cultural Logic of Late Capital', *NLR* 146 (1984) pp. 53–92.
22  Mike Davis, 'Urban Renaissance and the Spirit of Postmodernism' p. 108. For Davis, postmodernist architecture differs from modernist architecture because it is no longer linked to the functionalism of industrial Fordism, but has 'loosened the commodity-form of the building from its use-value supports', and 'given freer expression than ever before to the spirit of fictitious capital'. *Ibid.* p. 108. He claims that postmodernism in architecture is specific to the period since 1974 in which 'a reckless overbuilding of commercial space' has been 'inflated, not by expanding civilian industrial production, but by oil rents, third-world debts, military outlays, and the global flight of capital to the safe harbour of Reagan's America'. *Ibid.* p. 109. Rather than seeing postmodernism as a feature of the triumph of late capitalism, Davis therefore sees it as a symptom of a system which is undergoing breakdown and crisis, and he argues that it develops alongside a decay of the urban infrastructure and the immigration of an estimated one million 'undocumented Asians, Mexicans, and Central Americans' into the urban landscape. *Ibid.* p. 110.
23  Fredric Jameson, *The Prison House of Language* p. 44.
24  *Ibid.* p. 44.
25  Fredric Jameson, *The Political Unconscious* p. 57.
26  *Ibid.* p. 47.

27 See Raymond Williams, *Culture*.
28 Jonathan Arac, 'The Politics of *The Scarlet Letter*' in Sacvan Bercovitch and Myra Jehlen, ed., *Ideology and Classic American Literature* (Cambridge University Press, 1986) p. 262.
29 Peter Nichols, 'Old Problems and the New Historicism', *Journal of American Studies* 23: 3 (December 1989) p. 428.
30 See Pierre Bourdieu, *Distinction: A Social Critique of the Judgement of Taste* (London: Routledge and Kegan Paul, 1984).
31 Janice Radway, *Reading the Romance: Women, Patriarchy, and Popular Literature* (London: Verso, 1987) p. 3.
32 David Morley, 'Changing Paradigms in Audience Studies' in Ellen Seiter et al., eds., *Remote Control: Television, Audiences, and Culture Power* (London: Routledge, 1990) p. 19. See also Mark Jancovich, 'David Morley, The *Nationwide* Studies' in Martin Barker and Anne Beezer, eds., *Reading into Cultural Studies* (London: Routledge, 1992).
33 Mike Davis, 'Urban Renaissance and the Spirit of Postmodernism' p. 110.
34 *Ibid.* p. 110.
35 *Ibid.* p. 111.
36 *Ibid.* p. 112.
37 *Ibid.* p. 112.
38 Marshall Berman, *All That Is Solid Melts into Air: The Experience of Modernity* (London: Verso, 1983) p. 33.
39 *Ibid.* p. 33.
40 *Ibid.* p. 33.
41 *Ibid.* p. 34.
42 Todd Gitlin, 'Postmodernism: Roots and Politics' in Ian Angus and Sut Jhally, eds., *Cultural Politics in Contemporary America* (London: Routledge, 1989) p. 360.

CONCLUSION

1 Jameson 'Postmodernism and Consumer Society' p. 125.

# Bibliography

## PRIMARY SOURCES

### GENERAL

Twelve Southerners, *I'll Take My Stand: The South and the Agrarian Tradition*. Baton Rouge: Louisiana State University Press, 1980

Tate, Allen and Herbert Agar, eds., *Who Owns America: A New Declaration of Independence*. Boston: Houghton Mifflin, 1936

### JOHN CROWE RANSOM

*God Without Thunder: An Unorthodox Defense of Orthodoxy*. London: Gerald Howe, 1931

*The World's Body*. New York: Charles Scribner's Sons, 1938

*The New Criticism*. Norfolk, Conn: New Directions, 1941

*Poems and Essays*. New York: Random House, 1955

*Beating the Bushes: Selected Essays 1941–1970*. New York: New Directions, 1972

*The Selected Letters of John Crowe Ransom*. Baton Rouge: Louisiana State University Press, 1985

'Waste Lands', *Evening Post's Literary Review* 3 (11 July 1923) pp. 825–6

'Mr. Ransom Replies', *Evening Post's Literary Review* (11 August 1923) p. 902

'The Future of Poetry', *The Fugitive* (February 1924)

'Freud and Literature', *Saturday Review of Literature* 1 (4 October 1924) pp. 161–2

'Thoughts on Poetic Discontent', *The Fugitive* (June 1925)

'A Man Without a Country', *SeR* 33 (July 1925) pp. 301–7

'The Poet and the Critic', *NR* 51 (June 1927) pp. 125–6

'The South – Old or New', *SeR* 36 (April 1928) pp. 139–47

'The South Defends its Heritage', *Harper's* 159 (June 1929) pp. 108–18

'Flux and Blur in Contemporary Art', *SeR* 37 (July 1929) pp. 353–66

'Classic or Romantic', *Saturday Review of Literature* 6 (14 September 1929) pp. 125–7

'The State and the Land', *NR* 66 (February 1932) pp. 8–10

'Land!' *Harper's* 165 (July 1932) pp. 216–24

'Shall We Complete the Trade?' *SeR* 45 (April 1933) pp. 182–90

'A Poem Nearly Anonymous', *AR* 1 (May 1933) pp. 179–203

'A Poem Nearly Anonymous: II The Poet and His Formal Tradition', *AR* 1 (September 1933) pp. 444–67

'Happy Farmers', *AR* 1 (October 1933) pp. 513–35
'A Capital for the New Deal', *AR* 2 (December 1933) pp. 129–42
'The Aesthetic of Regionalism', *AR* 2 (January 1934) pp. 290–310
'Hearts and Heads', *AR* 2 (March 1934) pp. 554–71
'Poetry: A Note on Ontology', *AR* 3 (May 1934) pp. 172–200
'Poets without Laurels', *Yale Review* 24 (Autumn 1934) pp. 503–18
'Sociology and the Black Belt', *AR* 4 (December 1934) pp. 147–54
'Modern with a Southern Accent', *VQR* 11 (April 1935) pp. 184–200
'The Cathartic Principle', *AR* 5 (Summer 1935) pp. 287–300
'The Mimetic Principle', *AR* 5 (October 1935) pp. 536–51
'The Psychologist Looks at Poetry', *VQR* 11 (October 1935) pp. 575–92
'The Tense of Poetry', *SR* 1 (Autumn 1935) pp. 221–38
'Autumn of Poetry', *SR* 1 (Winter 1936) p. 609
'Characters and Character: A Note on Fiction', *AR* 6 (January 1936) pp. 271–88
'What does the South Want?', *VQR* 12 (April 1936) pp. 180–94
'The South as Bulwark', *Scribner's* 99 (May 1936) pp. 299–303
'The Content of the Novel: Notes Towards a Critique of Fiction', *AR* 7 (Summer 1936) pp. 301–18
'Fiction Harvest', *SR* 2 (Autumn 1936) p. 399
'Sentimental Exercise', *Yale Review* 26 (December 1936) pp. 353–68
'The Poet as a Woman', *SR* 2 (Spring 1937) pp. 783–8
'Art and Mr. Santayana', *VQR* 13 (Summer 1937) pp. 420–36
'Criticism Inc.', *VQR* 13 (Autumn 1937) pp. 586–602
'Shakespeare at Sonnets', *SR* 3 (Winter 1938) p. 531–41
'Mr. Empson's Muddles', *SR* 4 (Autumn 1938) pp. 322–39
'Editorial Note: Was Shakespeare a Philosopher?', *KR* 1 (Winter 1939) pp. 75–80
'Editorial Note: The Teaching of Poetry', *KR* 1 (Winter 1939) pp. 81–3
'Editorial Note: The Arts and the Philosophers', *KR* 1 (Spring 1939) pp. 194–9
'Editorial Note: The Aesthetic of *Finnegans Wake*', *KR* 1 (Autumn 1939) pp. 424–8
'The Pragmatics of Art', *KR* 2 (Winter 1940) pp. 76–87
'Editorial Note', *KR* 2 (Winter 1940) pp. 92–3
'Editorial Note: Old Age of a Poet', *KR* 2 (Summer 1940) pp. 345–7
'Editorial Note: Mr. Tate and the Professors', *KR* 2 (Summer 1940) pp. 348–50
'Editorial Note: Concerning the Symposium', *KR* 2 (Autumn 1940) pp. 476–7
'Strategy for English Studies', *SR* 6 (Autumn 1940) pp. 226–35
'Editorial Note: Ubiquitous Moralists', *KR* 3 (Winter 1941) pp. 95–100
'Editorial Note: Muses and Amazons', *KR* 3 (Spring 1941) pp. 240–2
'Editorial Note: Moholy-Nagy's New Arts', *KR* 3 (Summer 1941) pp. 372–4
'Editorial Note: The Younger Poets', *KR* 3 (Autumn 1941) pp. 491–4
'Editorial Note: The Aesthetic of Music', *KR* 3 (Autumn 1941) pp. 494–7
'Criticism as Pure Speculation' in *The Intent of the Critic* (Donald A. Stauffer ed.) Princeton University Press, 1941
'Editorial Note: War and Publication', *KR* 4 (Spring 1942) pp. 217–18
'Editorial Note: An Address to Kenneth Burke', *KR* 4 (Spring 1942) pp. 219–37
'Editorial Note: We Resume', *KR* 4 (Autumn 1942) pp. 405–6
'Editorial Note: Mr. Russell and Mr. Schorer', *KR* 4 (Autumn 1942) pp. 406–7

'Inorganic Muses', *KR* 5 (Spring 1943) pp. 278–300
'Positive and Near Positive Aesthetics', *KR* 5 (Summer 1943) pp. 443–7
'Editorial Note: The James Number', *KR* 5 (Autumn 1943) p. 618
'Editorial Note: EM Forster', *KR* 5 (Autumn 1943) pp. 618–23
'Art Needs a Little Separating', *KR* 6 (Winter 1944) pp. 114–22
'Artists, Soldiers, and Positivists', *KR* 6 (Spring 1944) pp. 276–81
'Editorial Note: The Severity of Mr. Savage', *KR* 7 (Winter 1945) pp. 114–17
'Art Worries the Naturalists', *KR* 7 (Spring 1945) pp. 282–99
'Art and the Human Economy', *KR* 7 (Autumn 1945) pp. 683–8
'Poetry: I The Final Analysis', *KR* 9 (Summer 1947) pp. 436–56
'Poetry: II The Final Cause', *KR* 9 (Autumn 1947) pp. 640–58
'The Literary Criticism of Aristotle (Reconsiderations No. X)', *KR* 10 (Summer
    1948) pp. 382–403
'The Understanding of Fiction', *KR* 12 (Spring 1950) pp. 189–218
'William Wordsworth: Notes Towards an Understanding of Poetry', *KR* 12
    (Summer 1950) pp. 498–519
'The Poetry of 1900–1950', *KR* 13 (Summer 1950) pp. 445–54
'Why Critics Don't Go Mad', *KR* 14 (Spring 1952) pp. 331–9
'Humanism at Chicago', *KR* 14 (Autumn 1952) pp. 647–59
'The Concrete Universal: Observations on the Understanding of Poetry', *KR* 16
    (Autumn 1954) pp. 554–64
'The Concrete Universal II', *KR* 17 (Summer 1955) pp. 383–407


ALLEN TATE

*Stonewall Jackson: The Good Soldier.* New York: Minton, Balch and Co, 1928
*Jefferson Davis: His Rise and Fall.* New York: Minton Balch, 1929
*Reactionary Essays on Poetry and Ideas.* New York: Charles Scribner's Sons, 1936
*The Fathers.* New York: G. P. Putnam's Sons, 1938 [republished Baton Rouge:
    Louisiana State University Press, 1977]
*Reason in Madness: Critical Essays.* New York: G. P. Putnam's Sons, 1941
*Poems 1920–1945: A Selection.* London: Eyre and Spottiswood, 1947
*On the Limits of Poetry: Selected Essays 1928–1948.* New York: Swallow, 1948
*The Forlorn Demon: Didactic and Critical Essays.* Chicago: Regnery, 1953
*The Man of Letters in the Modern World: Selected Essays: 1928–1955.* New York:
    Meridian Books, 1955
*Essays of Four Decades.* London: Oxford University Press, 1970
*Memoirs and Opinions 1926–1974.* Chicago: Swallow Press, 1975
Young, Thomas Daniel and John Tyree Fain, eds., *The Literary Correspondence of
    Donald Davidson and Allen Tate.* Athens: University of Georgia Press, 1974
Young, Thomas Daniel and John J. Hindle, eds., *The Republic of Letters in
    America: The Correspondence of John Peale Bishop and Allen Tate.* Lexington:
    University of Kentucky Press, 1981
Brown, Ashley and Frances Neel Cheney, eds., *The Poetry Reviews of Allen Tate
    1924–1944.* Baton Rouge: Louisiana State University Press, 1983
'Waste Lands', *Evening Post's Literary Review* 3 (4 Aug. 1923) p. 886
'The Persistent Illusion', *Na* 119 (November 1924) p. 549
'Last Days of a Charming Lady', *Na* 121 (October 1925) pp. 485–6

'Good Prose', *Na* 122 (February 1926) pp. 160–1
'Distinguished Minor Poetry', *Na* 122 (March 1926) pp. 237–8
'Complex Melancholy', *Na* 122 (April 1926) pp. 416–18
'A Philosophical Critic', *NR* 46 (April 1926) p. 281
'Fundamentalism', *Na* 72 (May 1926) pp. 532–3.
'A Poetry of Ideas', *NR* 47 (June 1926) pp. 172–3
'Literary Criticism in America', *NR* 47 (July 1926) p. 283
'The Spirituality of Roughnecks', *Na* 133 (July 1926) pp. 89–90
'The Holy War', *Na* 123 (December 1926) p. 694
'Poetry and the Absolute', *SeR* 35 (January 1927) pp. 41–52
'Towards Objectivity', *Na* 123 (February 1927) pp. 185–6
'The Revolt against Literature', *NR* 49 (February 1927) pp. 329–30
'Critical Responsibility', *NR* 51 (August 1927) pp. 339–40
'Beyond Imagism', *NR* 54 (March 1928) pp. 165–6
'A Defense of Order', *NR* 54 (16 May 1928) pp. 395–6
'Lincoln, Lee', *NR* 55 (June 1928) pp. 75–6
'The Presidents' Wives', *NR* 60 (June 1928) p. 127
'The Irrepressible Conflict', *Na* 124 (September 1928) p. 274
'Mr. More, the Demon', *NR* 57 (December 1928) pp. 116–17
'Life in the Old South', *NR* 59 (July 1929) pp. 211–12
'Poetry in the Laboratory', *NR* 61 (December 1929) pp. 111–13
'Mr Cabell's Farewell', *NR* 61 (January 1930) pp. 31–6
'The Fallacy of Humanism', *Horn and Hound* 3 (Jan./March 1930) pp. 234–57
'The Same Fallacy of Humanism', *Bo* 71 (March 1930) pp. 31–6
'Confusion and Poetry', *SeR* 38 (April 1930) pp. 133–49
'More about the Reconstruction', *NR* 63 (August 1930) pp. 376–7
'The BiMillennium of Virgil', *NR* 64 (October 1930) pp. 296–8
'Regionalism and Sectionalism', *NR* 69 (December 1931) pp. 158–61
'A New English Criticism', *NR* 70 (March 1932) pp. 89–90
'The Problem of the Unemployed', *AR* 1 (May 1933) pp. 129–49
'A Southern Romantic', *NR* 76 (August 1933) pp. 67–70
'Where are the People?' *AR* 2 (December 1933) pp. 231–7
'A View of the Whole South', *AR* 2 (February 1934) pp. 411–32
'Spengler's Tract against Liberalism', *AR* 3 (April 1934) pp. 41–7
'The Profession of Letters in the South', *SeR* 11 (April 1935) pp. 161–76
'The Function of the Critical Review', *SR* 1 (Winter 1936) pp. 556–9
'Notes on Property and Liberty', *AR* 6 (March 1936) pp. 596–611
'A Traditionalist looks at Liberalism', *SR* 1 (Spring 1936) pp. 731–44
'Mr. Burke and the Historical Environment', *SR* 1 (Autumn 1936) pp. 353–62
'What is a Traditional Society?' *AR* 7 (September 1936) pp. 376–87
'Modern Poets and Conventions', *AR* 8 (February 1937) pp. 427–35
'R. P. Blackmur and Others', *SR* 3 (Summer 1937) pp. 183–98
'Tension in Poetry', *SR* 4 (Summer 1938) pp. 101–15
'Narcissus as Narcissus', *VQR* 14 (Winter 1938) pp. 108–22
'The Present Function of Criticism', *SR* 6 (Autumn 1940) pp. 236–46
'Literature and Knowledge', *SR* 6 (Spring 1941) p. 629

ROBERT PENN WARREN

*John Brown: The Making of A Martyr.* New York: Payson and Clarke, 1929
*Understanding Poetry* (with Cleanth Brooks). New York: Henry Holt and Co.,
     1938 [republished New York: Holt Rinehart and Winston, 1960]
*Night Rider.* New York: Random House, 1939
*At Heaven's Gate.* New York: Random House, 1943
*Understanding Fiction* (with Cleanth Brooks). New York: Appleton-Century-
     Crofts, Inc., 1943 [republished New York: F. S. Crofts, 1947]
*All the King's Men.* New York: Harcourt, Brace and Co., 1946
*World Enough and Time.* New York: Random House, 1950
*Brother to Dragons: A Tale in Verse and Voices.* New York, Random House, 1953
*Band of Angels.* New York: Random House, 1955
*Segregation: The Inner Conflict in the South.* New York: Random House, 1956
*Selected Essays.* New York: Random House, 1958
*Remember the Alamo.* New York: Random House, 1958
*The Cave.* New York: Random House, 1959
*The Legacy of the Civil War: Meditations on the Centennial.* New York: Random
     House, 1961
*Wilderness.* London: Eyre and Spottiswood, 1962
*Flood.* London: Collins, 1964
*Who Speaks for the Negro?.* New York: Random House, 1965
*Meet Me in the Green Glen.* New York: Random House, 1971
*Homage to Theodore Dreiser, August 27th, 1871 – December 28th, 1945 on the
     Centennial of his Birth.* New York, Random House, 1971
*Democracy and Poetry.* Cambridge, Mass: Harvard University Press, 1975
*Selected Poems 1923–1975.* London: Secker and Warburg, 1976
*A Place to Come to.* London: Secker and Warburg, 1977
*Jeff Davis gets his Citizenship Back.* Lexington: University of Kentucky Press, 1980
Atkins, Floyd C. and John T. Hiers, eds., *Robert Penn Warren Talking: Interviews
     1950–1978.* New York: Random House, 1980
'The Romantic Strain', *NR* 53 (23 November 1927) pp. 23–4
'Sacheverell Sitwell's Poems', *NR* 54 (29 February 1928) p. 76
'The Bright Doom', *NR* 54 (4 April 1928) p. 227
'Guinea-Fowl', *NR* 54 (2 May 1928) pp. 330–1
'Hawthorne, Anderson and Frost', *NR* 54 (16 May 1928) pp. 399–401
'Not Local Colour', *VQR* 8 (January 1932) pp. 153–60
'Two Poets', *NR* 70 (24 February 1932) pp. 51–2
'Sidney Lanier: The Blind Poet', *AR* 2 (November 1933) pp. 27–45
'T. S. Stribling: A Paragraph in the History of Critical Realism', *AR* 2 (February
     1934) pp. 463–86
'Twelve Poets', *AR* 3 (May 1934) pp. 212–27
'John Crowe Ransom: A Study in Irony', *VQR* 11 (January 1935) pp. 92–112
'A Note on the Hamlet of Thomas Woolf', *AR* 5 (May 1935) pp. 191–208
'Some Recent Novels', *SR* 1 (Winter 1936) pp. 624–49
'Dixie Looks at Mrs. Geroud', *AR* 6 (March 1936) pp. 585–95
'Some Don'ts for Literary Regionalists', *AR* 8 (December 1936) pp. 142–50

with Cleanth Brooks, 'The Reading of Modern Poetry', *AR* 8 (February 1937)
pp. 435–49
'Arnold vs. the 19th Century', *KR* 1 (Spring 1939) pp. 217–26
'The Present State of Poetry: In the United States', *KR* 1 (Autumn 1939)
pp. 384–98
'The Snopes World', *KR* 3 (Spring 1941) pp. 253–7
'Katherine Anne Porter (Irony with a Center)', *KR* 4 (Winter 1942) pp. 29–42
'Homage to Oliver Allston', *KR* 4 (Spring 1942) pp. 259–63
'Pure and Impure Poetry', *KR* 5 (Spring 1943) pp. 228–54
'Love and Separateness in Miss Welty', *KR* 6 (Spring 1944) pp. 246–59
'Melville the Poet', *KR* 7 (Spring 1946) pp. 208–23
'A Poem of Pure Imagination (Reconsiderations VI)', *KR* 8 (Summer 1946)
pp. 391–427
'Hemingway', *KR* 9 (Winter 1947) pp. 1–28
'Knowledge and the Image of Man', *SeR* 62 (Winter 1955) pp. 182–92


DONALD DAVIDSON

*The Attack on Leviathan.* Chapel Hill: University of North Carolina Press, 1938
*Still Rebels, Still Yankees and Other Essays.* Baton Rouge: Louisiana State
University Press, 1957
*Southern Writers in the Modern World.* Athens: University of Georgia Press, 1958
Fain, John Tyree, ed., *The Spyglass, 1924–1930.* Nashville: Vanderbilt University
Press, 1963
'Artist as Southerner', *Saturday Review of Literature* 2 (15 May 1926) pp. 781–83
'First Fruits of Dayton', *Forum* 89 (June 1928) pp. 896–907
'Criticism Outside New York', *Bo* 73 (May 1931) pp. 247–56
'The Rise of the American City', *AR* 1 (April 1933) pp. 100–4
'Agrarianism for Commuters', *AR* 1 (May 1933) pp. 238–42
'Still Rebels, Still Yankees I', *AR* 2 (November 1933) pp. 58–72
'Still Rebels, Still Yankees: II Brother Jonathan of Vermont and Cousin Roderick
of Georgia', *AR* 2 (December 1933) pp. 175–88
'Restoration of the Farmer', *AR* 3 (April 1934) pp. 96–101
'A Novel in Verse', *AR* 3 (June 1934) pp. 526–30
'A Case in Farming', *AR* 3 (September 1934) pp. 526–61
'Lands that were Golden', *AR* 3 (October 1934) pp. 545–61
'Lands that were Golden: II The Two Old Wests', *AR* 4 (November 1934)
pp. 29–55
'Waldo Frank', *AR* 4 (December 1934) pp. 233–8
'Regionalism and Education', *AR* 4 (January 1935) pp. 310–25
'The Returning Frontier', *AR* 4 (March 1935) pp. 622–7
'Regionalism and Nationalism in American Literature', *AR* 5 (April 1935)
pp. 48–61
'The First Agrarian Economist', *AR* 5 (April 1935) pp. 106–12
'An Innocent at Home', *AR* 5 (May 1936) pp. 234–8
'I'll Take My Stand: A History', *AR* 5 (Summer 1935) pp. 301–21
'A Note on American Heroes', *SR* 1 (Winter 1936) pp. 436–48

'The Political Economy of Regionalism', *SR* 6 (February 1936) pp. 410–34
'Six Poets', *SR* 1 (Spring 1936) p. 875
'The Shape of Things and Men', *SR* 7 (Summer 1936) pp. 225–48
'Humor of the South', *SR* 7 (Summer 1936) pp. 335–41
'A Sociologist in Eden', *AR* 8 (December 1936) pp. 177–201
'Howard Odum and the Sociological Proteus', *AR* 8 (February 1937) pp. 385–417
'Expedients and Principles', *SR* 2 (Spring 1937) p. 645
'Gulliver with Hayfever', *AR* 9 (Summer 1937) pp. 152–72
'Regionalism as Social Science', *SR* 3 (Autumn 1937) p. 209
'Where are the Laymen?', *AR* 9 (October 1937) pp. 456–81
'Erskine Caldwell's Picture Book', *SR* 4 (Summer 1938) p. 15
'The Class Approach to Southern Problems', *SR* 6 (Autumn 1939) p. 261
'Mr. Babbitt in Philadelphia', *SR* 6 (Spring 1941) p. 695
'Mr. Cash and the ProtoDorian South', *SR* 7 (Summer 1941) p. 1


CLEANTH BROOKS

*Understanding Poetry* (with Robert Penn Warren). New York: Holt Rinehart and
    Winston, 1960
*Understanding Fiction* (with Robert Penn Warren). New York: F. S. Crofts, 1947
*Modern Poetry and the Tradition*. New York: Oxford University Press, 1965
*The Well-Wrought Urn: Studies in the Structure of Poetry*. London: Denis Dobson,
    1968
'A Note on Symbol and Conceit', *AR* 3 (May 1934) pp. 201–11
'The Modern Southern Poet and Tradition', *VQR* 11 (April 1935) pp. 305–20
'The Christianity of Modernism', *AR* 6 (Feb. 1936) pp. 435–46
'The Reading of Modern Poetry' (with Robert Penn Warren), *AR* 8 (Feb. 1937)
    pp. 427–56
'My Credo: The Formalist Critic', *KR* 13 (Winter 1951) pp. 72–81


SECONDARY SOURCES

Aaron, Daniel, *Writers on the Left*. New York: Octagon, 1979
    *The Unwritten War: American Writers and the Civil War*. London: Oxford
    University Press, 1975
Adorno, Theodor, *Minima Moralia*. London: Verso, 1978
Adorno, Theodor and Max Horkheimer, *Dialectic of Enlightenment*. London:
    Verso, 1976
Aglietta, Michel, *The Theory of Capitalist Regulation*. London: Verso, 1979
Althusser, Louis, *Reading Capital*. London: NLB, 1970
    *Lenin and Philosophy and Other Essays*. London: NLB, 1971
    *Politics and History*. London: NLB, 1972
    *Essays in Self-Criticism*. London: NLB, 1976
    *For Marx*. London: NLB, 1977
Ambrose, Steven E., *Rise to Globalism: American Foreign Policy Since 1938*.
    Harmondsworth: Penguin, 1983

Angus, Ian and Sut Jhally, *Cultural Politics in Contemporary America*. London, Routledge, 1989

Applebee, A. N., *Tradition and Reform in the Teaching of English: A History*. Urbana, Ill.: National Council of Teachers of English, 1974

Arato, Andrew and Paul Breines, *The Young Lukacs*. New York: The Seabury Press, 1979

Aronowitz, Stanley, *False Promises: The Shaping of American Working Class Consciousness*. New York: McGraw-Hill, 1973

'Marx, Braverman, and the Logic of Capital', *Essays on the Social Relations of Work and Labour: Special Issue of The Insurgent Sociologist* ed. O. Clark, J. Lemtoke, S. Marotto, Vol. 7 No. 2 & 3 (Fall 1978) pp. 126–46

'The End of Political Economy', *Social Text* 2 (1980) pp. 3–52

*The Crisis in Historical Materialism: Class Politics, and Culture in Marxist Theory*. New York: Praeger, 1981

Aronson, Ronald, *Jean-Paul Sartre: Philosophy in the World*. London: NLB, 1980

Bailyn, Bernard, *Education in the Framing of American Society*. Chapel Hill: University of North Carolina Press, 1960

Bakhtin, M. M., *Problems in Dostoevski's Poetics*. Michigan: Ardis/Ann Arbor, 1973

*The Dialogical Imagination*. Austin: University of Texas Press, 1981

*Rabelais and His World*. Bloomington: Indiana University Press, 1984

Barratt, Michele, *Women's Oppression Today*. London: Verso, 1980

Barratt, Michele and Mary McIntosh, *The Anti-Social Family*. London: Verso, 1982

Barthes, Roland, *Writing Degree Zero*. New York: Hill and Wang, 1968

*Mythologies*. London: Granada, 1973

*Image/Music/Text*. London: Fontana 1977

Barzun, Jacques, *Teacher in America*. Boston: Little, Brown and Co, 1946

Baudrillard, Jean, *The Mirror of Production*. St. Louis: Telos Press, 1975

*For a Critique of the Political Economy of the Sign*. St. Louis: Telos Press, 1981

Bell, Daniel, *The End of Ideology*. New York: Collier-Macmillan, 1965

*The Cultural Contradictions of Capitalism*. New York: Basic Books, 1975

Benjamin, Walter, *Illuminations*. New York: Schocken, 1969

*Charles Baudelaire: a Lyric Poet in the Era of High Capitalism*. London: Verso, 1983

*Understanding Brecht*. London: Verso, 1983

Bennett, Tony, *Formalism and Marxism*. London: Methuen, 1979

Bennett, Tony, Graham Martin, Colin Mercer and Janet Woollacott, eds., *Culture, Ideology and Social Process*. London: Batsford Academic and Educational, 1981

Bercovitch, Sacvan and Myra Jehlen, eds., *Ideology and Classic American Literature*. Cambridge University Press, 1986

Berger, John, *Art and Revolution*. London: Writers and Readers Publishing Cooperative, 1969

*Ways of Seeing*. London: British Broadcasting Corporation, 1972

*The Success and Failure of Picasso*. London: Writers and Readers Publishing Cooperative, 1980

*About Looking*. London: Writers and Readers Publishing Cooperative, 1980

*Another Way of Telling.* London: Writers and Readers Publishing Cooperative, 1982

Berman, Marshall, *All That Is Solid Melts into Air*: *The Experience of Modernity*. London: Verso, 1983

Bernstein, Barton J., ed., *Towards a New Past*. London: Chatto and Windus, 1970

Bernstein, J. M., *The Philosophy of the Novel*: *Lukacs, Marxism, and the Dialectics of Form*. Brighton: Harvester, 1984

Bishop, Ferman, *Allen Tate*. New York: Twayne, 1967

Blackburn, Robin, ed., *Ideology in Social Science*: *Readings in Critical Social Theory*. London: Fontana, 1972

Bledstein, B. J., *The Culture of Professionalism*: *The Middle Class and the Development of Higher Education in America*. New York: W. W. Norton, 1976

Bleich, David, *Subjective Criticism*. Baltimore: Johns Hopkins University Press, 1978

Bloch, Ernst et al., *Aesthetics and Politics*. London: Verso, 1977

Bloom, Harold, *The Anxiety of Influence*: *A Theory of Poetry*. New York: Oxford University Press, 1973

*A Map of Misreading*. New York: Oxford University Press, 1975

*Deconstruction and Criticism*. London: Routledge and Kegan Paul, 1979

*Kabbalah and Criticism*. New York: Seabury Press, 1979

Bohner, C. H., *Robert Penn Warren*. New York: Twayne, 1964

Bourdieu, Pierre, *Distinction*: *A Social Critique of the Judgement of Taste*. London: Routledge and Kegan Paul, 1984

Bourdieu, Pierre and Jean-Claude Passerson, *Reproduction in Education, Society and Culture*. London: Sage Publications, 1977

Bove, Paul, *Intellectuals in Power*: *A Genealogy of Critical Humanism*. New York: Columbia University Press, 1986

'Agriculture and Academe: America's Southern Question', *Boundary* 2 14: 3 (Spring 1986) pp. 169–95

Bowles, Samuel and Herbert Gintis, *Schooling in Capitalist America*: *Educational Reform and the Contradiction of Economic Life*. London: Routledge and Kegan Paul, 1976

Bowles, Samuel, D. M. Gordon and Thomas E. Weisskopf, *Beyond the Wasteland*: *A Democratic Alternative to Economic Decline*. London: Verso, 1984

Bradbury, J. M., *The Fugitives*. Chapel Hill: North Carolina University Press, 1958

*Renaissance in the South*. Chapel Hill: North Carolina University Press, 1963

Brantlinger, Patrick, *Crusoe's Footprints*: *Cultural Studies in Britain and America*. London: Routledge, 1990

Braudel, Ferdinand, *Afterthoughts on Material Civilization and Capitalism*. Baltimore: Johns Hopkins University Press, 1977

Braverman, Harry, *Labor and Monopoly Capitalism*: *The Degradation of Work in the Twentieth Century*. New York: Monthly Review Press, 1974

Brinley, Alan, *Voices of Protest*: *Huey Long, Father Coughlin and the Great Depression*. New York: Alfred Knopf, 1982

Brookeman, Christopher, *American Culture and Society since the 1930s*. London: Macmillan, 1984

Burke, Kenneth, *Attitudes towards History*. New York: New Republic, 1937

*The Philosophy of Literary Form*. Baton Rouge: Lousiana State University Press, 1941

Burt, John, *Robert Penn Warren and American Idealism*. New Haven, Conn.: Yale University Press, 1988

Cain, William E., *The Crisis in Criticism: Theory, Literature and Reform in English Studies*. Baltimore: Johns Hopkins University Press, 1984

*F. O. Matthiessen and the Politics of Criticism*. Madison: University of Wisconsin Press, 1988

Callinicos, Alex, *Althusser's Marxism*. London: Pluto, 1976

Campbell, Jeremy, *Grammatical Man: Information, Entropy, Language and Life*. Harmondsworth: Penguin, 1984

Carol, P. N. and D. W. Nobel, *The Free and the Unfree*. Harmondsworth: Penguin, 1977

Cash, W. J., *The Mind of the South*. New York: Alfred Knopf, 1941

Casper, L., *The Dark and Bloody Ground*. Seattle: Washington State University Press, 1960

Castells, Manuel, *The Economic Crisis and American Society*. Oxford: Blackwell, 1980

Centre for Contemporary Cultural Studies, *Resistance through Ritual*. London: Hutchinson, 1976

*On Ideology*. London: Hutchinson, 1978

*Working Class Culture*. London: Hutchinson, 1979

*Culture, Media, and Language*. London: Hutchinson, 1980

Chambers, Robert H., *Twentieth-Century Interpretations of All the King's Men: A Collection of Critical Essays*. Englewood Cliffs: Prentice Hall, 1977

Chandler, Alfred, *Strategy and Structure*. Cambridge, Mass: Harvard University Press, 1962

*The Visible Hand: The Managerial Revolution in American Business*. Cambridge, Mass.: Harvard University Press, 1977

Chiodi, P., *Sartre and Marxism*. Brighton: Harvester, 1978

Chodorow, Nancy, *The Reproduction of Mothering*. Berkeley; Los Angeles: University of California Press, 1978

Colletti, Lucio, *From Rousseau to Lenin*. London: NLB, 1972

Conkin, Paul K., *The Southern Agrarians*. Knoxville: University of Tennessee Press, 1988

Connerton, Paul, *Critical Theory*. Harmondsworth: Penguin, 1976

Conrad, D. E., *The Forgotten Farmers*. Urbana, Ill.: University of Illinois Press, 1965

Couch, W. T., ed., *Culture in the South*. Chapel Hill: University of North Carolina Press, 1935

Cowan, Louise, *The Fugitives*. Baton Rouge: Louisiana State University Press, 1959

Coward, Rosalind and John Ellis, *Language and Materialism: Developments in Semiology and the Theory of the Subject*. Boston; London: Routledge and Kegan Paul, 1977

Cox, Geoff, 'Literary Pragmatics', *Literature and History* 12: 1 (Spring 1986) pp. 79–96

Craig, David, *Marxists and Literature*. Harmondsworth: Penguin, 1975

Crane, Ronald S., 'History Versus Criticism in the University Study of Literature', *The English Journal* 24 (Oct. 1935) pp. 635–67

Cremin, Lawrence, *The Transformation of the School*. New York: Alfred Knopf, 1961

Crunden, Robert M., *From Self to Society*. Englewood Cliffs: Prentice Hall, 1972

Culler, Jonathan, *Structuralist Poetics*. London: Routledge and Kegan Paul, 1975

*The Pursuit of Signs*. London: Routledge and Kegan Paul, 1981

*On Deconstruction*. London: Routledge and Kegan Paul, 1983

*Barthes*. London: Fontana, 1983

*Saussure*. London: Fontana, 1983

Curran, James, Michael Gurevitch, and Janet Woollacott, eds., *Mass Communications and Society*. London: Edward Arnold, 1977

Cutler, A., et al., *Marx's Capital and Capital Today*. London: Routledge and Kegan Paul, 1977

Cutrer, Thomas W., *Parnassus on the Mississippi: The Southern Review and the Baton Rouge Literary Community 1935–1942*. Baton Rouge: Louisiana State University Press, 1984

Danto, Arthur C., *Sartre*. London: Fontana, 1975

Davenport, F. G., *The Myth of Southern History: Historical Consciousness in Twentieth-Century Southern Literature*. Nashville, Tenn.: Vanderbilt University Press, 1970

Davis, Mike, *Prisoners of the American Dream*. London: Verso, 1986

'Urban Renaissance and the Spirit of Postmodernism', *NLR* 151 (1985) pp. 106–13

*The Year Left: A Socialist Yearbook*. London: Verso, 1985

*City of Quartz: Excavating the Future in Los Angeles*. London: Vintage, 1992

De Bord, Guy, *Society of the Spectacle*. Detroit: Red and Black, 1973

Debray, Regis, *Teachers/Writers/Celebrities: The Intellectuals of Modern France*. London: Verso, 1981

De George, R. and F., *The Structuralists: From Marx to Levi-Strauss*. New York: Doubleday, Anchor, 1972

Degler, Carl, *Place over Time: The Continuity of Southern Distinctiveness*. Baton Rouge: Louisiana State University Press, 1977

*At Odds: Women and the Family in America from the Revolution to the Present*. Oxford University Press, 1981

*Out of Our Past: The Forces that Shaped Modern America*. 3rd edition, New York: Harper and Row, 1984

De Hart Mathews, Jane, 'Arts and People: The New Deal and the Quest for Cultural Democracy', *JAH* 64 (1975) pp. 316–55

De La Haye, Y., *Marx and Engels on the Means of Communication*. New York: International General, 1980

Deleuze, Gilles and Feliz Guattari, *Anti-Oedipus: Capitalism and Schizophrenia*. New York: Viking, 1977

Della Volpe, G., *Critique of Taste*. London: Verso, 1978

de Man, Paul, *Blindness and Insight: Essays in the Rhetoric of Contemporary Criticism*. New York: Oxford University Press, 1971

*Allegories of Reading: Figural Language in Rousseau, Nietzsche, Rilke and Proust*. New Haven, Conn.: Yale University Press, 1979

Derrida, Jacques, *Of Grammatology*. Baltimore: Johns Hopkins University Press, 1977

*Writing and Difference*. London: Routledge and Kegan Paul, 1978

Diggins, J. P., 'Flirtations with Fascism: American Pragmatic Liberals and Mussolini's Italy' *AHR* 71 (1965–66) pp. 487–506

'The American Writer and Fascism and the Liberation of Italy', *AQ* 18 (1966) pp. 599–614

*Up From Communism: Conservative Odysseys in American Intellectual History*. New York: Harper and Row, 1977

Dollard, John, *Caste and Class in a Southern Town*. New York: Harper's, 1949

Dowling, William C., *Jameson/Althusser/Marx: An Introduction to The Political Unconsciousness*. London: Methuen, 1984

DuBois, W. E. B., *The Souls of Black Folk*. New York: Signet, 1969

Duffus, R., *Books, Their Place in Our Democracy*. New York: Houghton, Mifflin and Co., 1930

Dupree, Robert S., *Allen Tate and the Augustan Imagination: A Study of The Poetry*. Baton Rouge: Louisiana State University Press, 1983

Eagleton, Terry, *Criticism and Ideology*. London: NLB, 1976

*Marxism and Literary Criticism*. London: Methuen, 1976

'Review of *The Critical Twilight*', *JAS* Vol. 13 (1979) pp. 304–5

*Walter Benjamin: Towards a Revolutionary Criticism*. London: Verso, 1981

*Literary Theory: An Introduction*. Oxford: Blackwell, 1983

*The Function of Criticism: From the Spectator to Post-Structuralism*. London: Verso, 1984

*Against the Grain: Essays 1975–1985*. London: Verso, 1986

Eco, Umberto, *Theory of Semiotics*. London: Macmillan, 1977

*The Role of the Reader*. Bloomington: Indiana University Press, 1984

Egbert, Donald, 'The Idea of the Avant-Garde in Art and Politics', *AHR* 73 (1967–68) pp. 339–66

Eisinger, C. E., *Fictions of the Forties*. University of Chicago Press, 1963

Eliot, T. S., *After Strange Gods: A Primer of Modern Heresy*. London: Faber and Faber, 1934

*Selected Essays*. London: Faber and Faber, 1976

Engels, F., *The Origins of the Family, Private Property and the State*. New York: Pathfinder, 1972

Enzensberger, H. M., *The Consciousness Industry*. New York: Seabury Press, 1974

Ewen, Stuart, *Captains of Consciousness: Advertising and the Roots of Consumer Culture*. New York: McGraw-Hill, 1977

*Channels of Desire: Mass Images and the Shaping of American Consciousness*. New York: McGraw-Hill, 1982

Fanon, Franz, *The Wretched of the Earth*. Harmondsworth: Penguin, 1967

Fass, Paula, *The Damned and the Beautiful: American Youth in the 1920's*. New York: Oxford University Press, 1977

Faust, Drew Gilpin, *The Sacred Circle: The Dilemma of the Intellectual in the Old South, 1840–1860*. Baltimore: Johns Hopkins University Press, 1977

Fekete, John, *The Critical Twilight: Explorations in the Ideology of Anglo-American Literary Theory from Eliot to McLuhan*. London: Routledge and Kegan Paul, 1978

*The Structuralist Allegory: Reconstructive Encounters with New French Thought.* Manchester University Press, 1984

Fiedler, L., *Love and Death in the American Novel.* London: Jonathan Cape, 1967

Fish, Stanley, *Is There a Text in the Class?: The Authority of Interpretive Communities.* Cambridge, Mass.: Harvard University Press, 1980

Foner, Eric, *Politics and Ideology in the Age of the Civil War.* New York: Oxford University Press, 1980

*Nothing but Freedom: Emancipation and its Legacy.* Baton Rouge: Louisiana State University Press, 1983

Foster, Hal, ed., *Post-Modern Culture.* London: Pluto, 1985

Foster, R. J., *The New Romantics: A Reappraisal of the New Criticism.* Bloomington: Indiana University Press, 1962

Foucault, Michel, *Madness and Civilization.* New York: Pantheon, 1965

*Discipline and Punish.* London: Allen Lane, 1977

*The History of Sexuality, Vol. 1: An Introduction.* London: Allen Lane, 1979

*Power/Knowledge: Selected Interviews and Other Writings.* Brighton: Harvester, 1980

Fowler, Roger, *Linguistics and the Novel.* London: Methuen, 1977

Frascina, Francis, *Pollock and After: the Critical Debate.* London: Harper and Row, 1985

Freedman, Estelle B., 'Changing Views of Women in the 1920s', *JAH* 61 (1974) pp. 372–93

Freire, Pablo, *Pedagogy of the Oppressed.* New York: Herder and Herder, 1972

Freud, Sigmund, *On Dreams.* New York: W. W. Norton, 1952

Frye, Northrop, *Anatomy of Criticism.* Princeton University Press, 1957

Fuller, Peter, *Art and Psychoanalysis.* London: Writers and Readers Publishing Collective, 1980

Gadamer, Hans-Georg, *Truth and Method.* New York: Continuum, 1975

Galbraith, Kenneth, *The New Industrial Estate.* Harmondsworth: Penguin, 1969

Garnham, Nicholas, 'Towards a Political Economy of Culture', *New Universities Quarterly* (Summer 1977) pp. 341–57

'Information Society as a Class Society', Paper presented to EEC Conference on the Information Society, Dublin 18–20 November 1981

*Capitalism and Communication: Global Culture and the Economics of Information.* London: Sage, 1990

Gatlin, R., *American Women Since 1945.* London: Macmillan, 1987

Geertz, Clifford, *The Interpretation of Culture: Selected Essays.* London: Hutchinson, 1975

Genovese, Eugene, *The Political Economy of Slavery.* New York: Vintage, 1966

*The World the Slaveholders Made: Two Essays in Interpretation.* New York: Vintage Books, 1971

*In Red and Black: Marxian Explorations in Southern and Afro-American History.* New York: Pantheon, 1971

*Roll, Jordan, Roll: The World the Slaves Made.* New York: Vintage, 1974

*From Rebellion to Revolution: Afro-American Slave Revolts in the Making of the Modern World.* Baton Rouge: Louisiana State University Press, 1979

Geras, Norman, *Marx and Human Nature.* London: Verso, 1983

Giddens, Antony, *Durkheim.* London: Fontana, 1978

*Central Problems in Social Theory: Action, Structure and Contradiction in Social Analysis.* London: Macmillan, 1979

Gilbert, James Burhart, *Writers and Partisans: A History of Literary Radicalism in America.* New York: John Wiley, 1968

*Another Chance: Post-War America.* New York: Alfred Knopf, 1981

Glad, Paul W., 'Progressives and the Business Culture of the 1920s', *JAH* 53 (1966) pp. 75–89

Gloversmith, Frank, *The Theory of Reading.* Brighton: Harvester, 1984

Godden, Richard, 'Some Slight Shifts in the Manner of the Novel of Manners' in *Henry James: Fiction As History,* ed. Ian Bell. London: Vision, 1984, pp. 156–83

'Money Makes Manners Makes Man Makes Woman' *Literature and History,* 12: 1 (Spring 1986) pp. 16–37

'What Did You Do in the Study Daddy ...' (review of T. Eagleton, *The Function of Criticism*), *Poetics Today* 7: 1 (1986) pp. 147–56

*Fictions of Capital: The American Novel from James to Mailer.* Cambridge University Press, 1990

Godelier, Maurice, *Perspectives in Marxist Anthropology.* Cambridge University Press, 1977

Goldfield, Daniel R., 'The Urban South: A Regional Framework', *AHR* 86 (1981) pp. 1009–34

Goldman, Lucien, *Immanuel Kant.* London: NLB, 1971

*Power and Humanism.* Nottingham: Bertrand Russell Peace Foundation for 'The Spokesman', 1974

*Lukacs and Heidegger: Towards a New Philosophy.* London: Routledge and Kegan Paul, 1979

*Method in the Sociology of Literature.* Oxford: Blackwell, 1981

Goldsmith, Arnold L., *American Literary Criticism 1905–1965.* Boston: Twayne, 1979

Gorz, Andre, *Socialism and Revolution.* London: Allen Lane, 1975

*The Division of Labour: The Labour Process and Class Struggle in Modern Capitalism.* Hassocks: Harvester, 1976

*Farewell to the Working Class: An Essay on Post-Industrial Socialism.* London: Pluto, 1982

*Paths to Paradise: The Liberation from Work.* London: Pluto, 1985

Graff, Gerald, *Literature Against Itself: Literary Ideas in Modern Society.* University of Chicago Press, 1979

*Professing Literature: An Institutional History.* Chicago University Press, 1987

Graff, Gerald and Michael Warner, eds., *The Origins of Literary Study: A Documentary History.* London: Routledge, 1989

Gramsci, Antonio, *Selections from the Prison Notebooks.* London: Lawrence and Wishart, 1971

*Letters from Prison.* London: Quartet, 1979

Grantham, Dewey, *The Regional Imagination: The South and Recent American History.* Nashville, Tenn.: Vanderbilt University Press, 1979

Gray, Richard, *The Literature of Memory: Modern Writers of the American South.* Baltimore: Johns Hopkins University Press, 1977

*Writing the South: Ideas of an American Region.* Cambridge University Press, 1986

Gray, Virginia, 'Anti-evolution Sentiment and Behaviour: The Case of Arkansas', *AS* 57 (1970) pp. 352–66

Guattari, Felix, *Molecular Revolution.* Harmondsworth: Penguin, 1984

Guilbaut, Serge, *How New York Stole the Idea of Modern Art: Abstract Expressionism, Freedom and the Cold War.* University of Chicago Press, 1983

Habermas, Jurgen, *Knowledge and Human Interests.* Boston: Beacon, 1971

*Theory and Practice.* London: Heinemann, 1974

*Towards a Rational Society.* London: Heinemann, 1974

*Legitimation Crisis.* London: Heinemann, 1976

Hahn, S., *Roots of Southern Populism: Yeoman Farmers and the Transformation of the Georgia Upcountry 1850–1890.* New York: Oxford University Press, 1983

Hall, Stuart, 'Culture, Media and the "Ideological Effect"' in James Curran et al., eds., *Mass Communications and Society.* London: Edward Arnold, 1977

'Deconstructing the Popular' in Raphael Samuel, ed., *People's History and Socialist Theory.* London: Routledge and Kegan Paul, 1981

'Cultural Studies: Two Paradigms' in Richard Collins et al., eds., *Media, Culture and Society: A Critical Reader.* London: Sage, 1986

Hammen, Oscar J., 'Marxism and the Agrarian Question', *AHR* 77 (1972) pp. 679–704

Harding, S. and M. B. Hintikka, *Discovering Reality: Feminist Perspectives on Epistemology, Metaphysics, Methodology, and Philosophy of Science.* Dordrecht: Reidel, 1983

Harrison, Helen A., 'American Art and the New Deal', *JAS* 6 (1973) pp. 289–96

Hartman, Geoffery, *Beyond Formalism.* New Haven, Conn.: Yale University Press, 1975

*The Fate of Reading and Other Essays.* University of Chicago Press, 1975

*Criticism in the Wilderness.* New Haven, Conn.: Yale University Press, 1980

*Saving the Text: Literature/Derrida/Philosophy.* Baltimore: Johns Hopkins University Press, 1981

Harvey, David, *The Limits to Capital.* Oxford: Blackwell, 1982

*The Condition of Postmodernity: An Enquiry into the Origins of Cultural Change.* Oxford: Blackwell, 1989

Hauser, Arnold, *The Sociology of Art.* London: Routledge and Kegan Paul, 1982

Havard, William C., 'The Politics of *I'll Take My Stand*', *SR* 16 (1980) pp. 757–75

Havard, William C. and Walter Sullivan, *A Band of Prophets: the Vanderbilt Agrarians After Fifty Years.* Baton Rouge: Louisiana University Press, 1982

Hawkes, Terence, *Structuralism and Semiotics.* London: Methuen, 1977

Hebdige, Dick, *Subculture: The Meaning of Style.* London: Methuen, 1979

Heidegger, Martin, *Being and Time.* Oxford University Press, 1967

Hemphill, George, *Allen Tate.* Minneapolis: University of Minnesota Press, 1964

Higham, John and Paul Conkin, *New Directions in American Intellectual History.* Baltimore: Johns Hopkins University Press, 1979

Hirsch, E. D., *Validity in Interpretation.* New Haven: Yale, 1967

*Aims of Interpretation.* University of Chicago Press, 1976

Hirst, Paul, *Durkheim, Bernard and Epistemology.* London: Routledge and Kegan Paul, 1975

*On Law and Ideology.* London: Macmillan, 1979
*Social Relations and Human Attitudes.* London: Tavistock, 1982
Hobsbawm, Eric J., *The Age of Revolution, 1789–1848.* London: Weidenfeld and Nicholson, 1962
*Industry and Empire.* Harmondsworth: Penguin, 1968
*Bandits.* London: Weidenfeld and Nicholson, 1969
*Revolutionaries: Contemporary Essays.* London: Weidenfeld and Nicholson, 1973
*The Age of Capital, 1848–1875.* London: Weidenfeld and Nicholson, 1975
*Labouring Men: Studies in the History of Labour.* London: Weidenfeld and Nicholson, 1986
Hodgson, Godfrey, *America in Our Time.* London: Macmillan, 1977
Hofstadter, Richard, *Anti-Intellectualism in American Life.* New York: Random House, 1963
Hoggart, Richard, *The Uses of Literacy.* London: Chatto and Windus, 1957
Hohendahl, Peter, *The Institution of Criticism.* Ithaca: Cornell University Press, 1982
Holland, L. V., *Counterpoint: Kenneth Burke and Aristotle's Theories of Rhetoric.* New York: Philosophical Library, 1959
Hollinger, David, 'Ethnic Diversity, Cosmopolitanism and the Emergence of American Liberal Intellectuals', *AQ* 27 (1975) pp. 133–51
Holub, Robert C., *Reception Theory.* London: Methuen, 1984
Howe, Irving, *Politics and the Novel.* New York: Horizon, 1957
Hyman, Stanley Edgar, *The Armed Vision.* New York: Alfred A. Knopf, 1952
Ingarden, Roman, *The Literary Work of Art: An Investigation on the Borderlines of Ontology, Logic and the Theory of Literature.* Evanston, Ill.: Northwestern University Press, 1973
*Cognition in the Literary Work of Art.* Evanston, Ill.: Northwestern University Press, 1973
Iser, Wolfgang, *The Implied Reader: Patterns of Communication in Prose Fiction from Bunyan to Beckett.* Baltimore; London: Johns Hopkins University Press, 1974
*The Act of Reading: A Theory of Aesthetic Response.* Baltimore: Johns Hopkins University Press, 1978
Jackson, George, *Soledad Brother: The Prison Letters of George Jackson.* Harmondsworth: Penguin, 1971
Jameson, Fredric, *Marxism and Form.* Princeton University Press, 1974
*The Prison House of Language.* Princeton University Press, 1974
'Imaginary and Symbolic in Lacan: Marxism, Psycho-analytic Criticism and the Problem of the Subject' in *Psychoanalysis and Literature, Yale French Studies* 55/56 (1977) pp. 338–95
*The Political Unconscious: Narrative as a Socially Symbolic Act.* London: Methuen, 1981
*Fables of Aggression: Wyndham Lewis, the Modernist as Fascist.* Berkeley; Los Angeles: University of California Press, 1981
'Post Modernism, or the Cultural Logic of Late Capitalism', *NLR* (July/August 1984) pp. 53–92

Jancovich, Mark, 'David Morley, The *Nationwide* Studies' in Martin Barker and Anne Beezer, eds., *Reading into Cultural Studies*. London: Routledge, 1992

Janssen, Marian, *The Kenyon Review 1939–1970: A Critical History*. Baton Rouge: Louisiana State University Press, 1990

Jauss, Hans R., *Towards an Aesthetic of Reception*. Brighton: Harvester, 1982
*Aesthetic Experience and Literary Hermeneutics*. Minneapolis: University of Minnesota Press, 1982

Jay, Martin, *The Dialectical Imagination: A History of the Frankfurt School and the Institute of Social Research 1923–1950*. London: Heinemann Education, 1976
*Adorno*. London: Fontana, 1984
*Marxism and Totality: The Adventures of a Concept from Lukacs to Habermas*. Cambridge: Polity, 1984

Jefferson, Ann and David Robey, eds., *Modern Literary Theory: A Comparative Introduction*. London: Batsford Academic, 1982

Jencks, Christopher, *Inequality*. New York: Basic Books, 1972

Joll, James, *Gramsci*. London: Fontana, 1977

Joyce, Davis and Michael Kraus, *The Writing of American History*. Norman: University of Oklahoma Press, 1985

Justus, James H., *The Achievement of Robert Penn Warren*. Baton Rouge; London: Louisiana State University Press, 1981

Kampf, Louis and Paul Lauter, eds., *The Politics of Literature: Dissenting Essays on the Teaching of English*. New York: Vintage, 1973

Karabel, Jerome and A. H. Halsey, eds., *Power and Ideology in Education*. New York: Oxford University Press, 1977

Karanikas, Alexander, *The Tillers of Myth: Southern Agrarians as Social and Literary Critics*. Madison: University of Wisconsin Press, 1966

Karier, C., *Shaping the American Educational State 1900–Present*. New York: The Free Press, 1975

Katz, Barry, *Herbert Marcuse and the Art of Liberation: An Intellectual Biography*. London: Verso, 1982

Katz, M. B., *Class Bureaucracy and Schools*. New York: Praeger, 1971

Kermode, Frank, *The Romantic Image*. London: Fontana, 1971

Kerr, Clark, *The Uses of the University*. Cambridge, Mass.: Harvard University Press, 1963

Key, V. O., *Southern Politics in State and Nation*. Knoxville: University of Tennessee Press, 1984

King, Richard, *A Southern Renaissance: The Cultural Awakening of the American South, 1930–1955*. London: Oxford University Press, 1980
'The South and Cultural Criticism' in *American Literary History* 1:2 (Fall 1989) pp. 699–714

Krieger, Murray, *The New Apologists for Poetry*. Minneapolis: University of Minnesota Press, 1956
*The Classic Vision*. Baltimore: Johns Hopkins University Press, 1971

Kristeva, Julia, *Desire in Language*. Oxford: Blackwell, 1980

Lacan, Jacques, *Ecrits: A Selection*. London: Tavistock, 1977
'Seminar on "The Purloined Letter"' in *Psychoanalysis and Literature*, *Yale French Studies* 55/56 (1977) pp. 39–72

Laclau, Ernesto, *Politics and Ideology in Marxist Theory*. London: Verso, 1977

Landes, David, *The Unbound Prometheus*. Cambridge University Press, 1970
Lasch, C., *The Agony of the American Left: One Hundred Years of Radicalism*. Harmondsworth: Pelican Books, 1973
*The Culture of Narcissism: American Life in an Age of Diminishing Expectations*. New York: W. W. Norton, 1978
*The Minimal Self: Psychic Survival in Troubled Times*. London: Pan Books, 1985
*The New Radicalism in America 1889–1963: The Intellectual as a Social Type*. New York: Norton, 1986
Leach, Edmund, *Levi-Strauss*. London: Fontana, 1970
*Culture and Communication: The Logic by which Symbols are Connected*. Cambridge University Press, 1976
Lefebvre, Henri, *Everyday Life in the Modern World*. London: Allen Lane, 1971
*The Survival of Capitalism*. London: Allison and Busby, 1976
Lenin, V., *Imperialism, the Highest Stage of Capitalism*. Peking: Foreign Languages Press, 1975
*The State and Revolution*. Peking: Foreign Languages Press, 1976
Lentricchia, Frank, *Literature and Social Change*. Chicago University Press, 1983
*After the New Criticism*. London: Methuen, 1983
Leuchtenburg, William E., *The Perils of Prosperity, 1914–1932*. University of Chicago Press, 1958
*Franklin D. Roosevelt and the New Deal, 1932–1940*. New York: Harpers and Row, 1963
Leverette, William E. and David E. Shi, 'Herbert Agar and Free America: A Jeffersonian Alternative to the New Deal', *JAS* 16 (1982) pp. 189–206
Levi-Strauss, Claude, *The Savage Mind*. London: Weidenfeld and Nicholson, 1966
*Structural Anthropology*. London: Allen Lane, 1968
*Triste Tropiques*. London: Cape, 1973
Lichtman, Richard, *The Production of Desire*. New York: Free Press, 1982
Longley, John L., *Robert Penn Warren: A Collection of Critical Essays*. New York University Press, 1965
Lukacs, Georg, *The Historical Novel*. London: Merlin Press, 1962
*History and Class Consciousness: Studies in Marxist Dialectics*. London: Merlin Press, 1971
*Writer and Critic*. London: Merlin Press, 1978
*Essays in Realism*. London: Lawrence and Wishart, 1980
Lyotard, J. F., *The Postmodern Condition: A Report on Knowledge*. Manchester University Press, 1984
Lytle, Andrew, *Southerners and Europeans: Essays in a Time of Disorder*. Baton Rouge: Louisiana State University Press, 1988
MacCarthy, Thomas, *The Critical Theory of Jurgen Habermas*. Cambridge: Polity, 1984
McCoy, Donald, *Coming of Age: The United States During the 1920s and 1930s*. Harmondsworth: Penguin Books, 1973
MacDonald, Dwight, *Against the American Grain*. London: Victor Gollancz, 1963
MacKethan, L. H., *The Dream of Arcady: Place and Time in Southern Literature*. Baton Rouge: Louisiana State University Press, 1980
McLellan, David, *Marx's The Grundrisse*. London: Macmillan, 1971
*Karl Marx: His Life and Thought*. London: Macmillan, 1973

MacLennan, Gregor, *Marxism and the Methodologies of History*. London: Verso, 1981

*The State in Contemporary Britain*. Oxford: Polity, 1984

McLuhan, Marshall, *Understanding Media: The Extensions of Man*. London: Routledge and Kegan Paul, 1964

*The Medium is the Message*. Harmondsworth: Allen Lane, 1967

Machery, Pierre, *Theory of Literary Production*. London: Routledge and Kegan Paul, 1978

Machery, Pierre and E. Balibar, 'On Literature as an Ideological Form: Some Marxist Propositions', *Oxford Literary Review* 3: 1 (1978)

Mandel, Ernest, *Late Capitalism*. London: Verso, 1978

*The Second Slump: A Marxist Analysis of Recession in the Seventies*. London: Verso, 1980

Mangione, Jerry, *The Dream and the Deal: The Federal Writers Project 1935–1943*. Boston: Little, Brown, 1972

Mannheim, Karl, *Utopia and Ideology*. London: Routledge and Kegan Paul, 1936

Marcuse, Herbert, *One Dimensional Man: Studies in the Ideology of Advanced Industrial Society*. Boston: Beacon Press, 1964

Marx, Karl, *Capital Vol. I*. Harmondsworth: Penguin, 1972

*Surveys from Exile*. Harmondsworth: Penguin, 1973

*The Grundrisse*. Harmondsworth: Penguin, 1973

Marx, Karl and F. Engels, *The German Ideology*. London: Lawrence and Wishart, 1970

Marx, Leo, *The Machine in the Garden*. New York: Oxford University Press, 1964

Matejka, L. and K. Pomoroska, *Readings in Russian Poetics*. Cambridge, Mass.: MIT Press, 1971

Mathews, F. H., 'The Americanization of Sigmund Freud before 1917', *JAS* 1 (1967–8) pp. 39–62

Mattelart, Armand, *Multinational Corporations and the Control of Culture: The Ideological Apparatus of Imperialism*. Brighton: Harvester, 1979

Mattelart, Armand et al., *Communications and Class Struggle, 1: Capitalism and Imperialism*. New York: International General, 1979

*Communications and Class Struggle, 2: Liberation, Socialism*. New York: International General, 1983

Matthews, Betty, *Marx 100 Years On*. London: Lawrence and Wishart, 1983

May, H. F., 'Shifting Perspectives on the 1920s', *MVHR* 43 (1956) pp. 405–27

May, Lary, ed., *Recasting America: Culture and Politics in the Age of the Cold War*. University of Chicago Press, 1989

Mehlman, Jeffery, 'The Floating Signifier from Levi-Strauss to Lacan' in *French Freud: Structural Studies in Psychoanalysis* in *Yale French Studies* 48 (1975) pp. 10–37

Meiners, R. K., *The Last Alternatives: A Study of the Works of Allen Tate*. Denver: Allen Swallow, 1963

Melody, W. H., L. Salter, and P. Heyer, *Culture Communication and Dependency: The Tradition of H. A. Innis*. Norwood, NJ: Ablex Publishing, 1981

Miller, Jonathan, *McLuhan*. London: Fontana, 1971

Miller, Mark S., *Working Lives: The Southern Exposure History of Labor in the South*. New York: Random House, 1980

Milliband, Ralph, *Marxism and Politics*. Oxford: Oxford University Press, 1977

Mills, C. Wright, *The Power Elite*. New York: Oxford University Press, 1956

*Power, Politics and People: Collected Essays of C. Wright Mills*. New York: Oxford University Press, 1963

Mitchell, Juliet, *Women's Estate*. London: Penguin, 1971

*Psychoanalysis and Feminism*. Harmondsworth: Penguin Books, 1975

Moi, Toril, *Textual/Sexual Politics*. London: Methuen, 1985

Montgomery, David, *Workers' Control in America: Studies in the History of Work, Technology and Labour Struggles*. Cambridge University Press, 1979

Moore, Barrington, *Social Origins of Dictatorship and Democracy*. Harmondsworth: Penguin Books, 1969

Morley, David, *The 'Nationwide' Audience: Structure and Decoding*. London: BFI, 1980

*Family Television: Cultural Power and Domestic Leisure*. London: Comedia, 1986

Morley, David and Charlotte Brunsdon, *Everyday Television: 'Nationwide'*. London: BFI, 1978

Morley, David and Ken Worpole, *The Republic of Letters: Working Class Writing and Local Publishing*. London: Comedia, 1982

Moretti, Franco, *Signs Taken as Wonders: Essays in the Sociology of Literary Forms*. London: Verso, 1983

Mosco, Vincent, *Broadcasting in the United States: Innovation Challenge and Organizational Control*. Norwood, NJ: Ablex Publishing, 1979

*Pushbutton Fantasies: Critical Perspectives on Videotext and Information Technology*. Norwood, NJ: Ablex Publishing, 1982

Mottram, Eric, 'Living Mythically: the Thirties', *JAS* 6 (1972) pp. 267–87

Mulgan, Geof and Ken Worpole, *Saturday Night or Sunday Morning?: From Arts to Industry – New Forms of Cultural Policy*. London: Comedia, 1986

Mulhern, Francis, *The Moment of Scrutiny*. London: NLB, 1979

Murdock, Graham and Peter Golding, 'For a Political Economy of Mass Communications', *Socialist Register* (1973) pp. 205–34

Murphy, B., *The World Wired Up: Unscrambling the New Communications Puzzle*. London: Comedia, 1983

Murphy, Paul L., 'Sources of Intolerance in the 1920s', *JAH* 51 (1964) pp. 60–76

Murray, Robin and Tom Wengraf, 'The Political Economy of Communications', *The Spokesman* 1 (Summer 1970) pp. 8–14

Nichols, Peter, 'Old Problems and the New Historicism', *JAS* 23: 3 (December 1989) pp. 423–34

Nietzsche, Friedrich, *The Pocket Nietzsche*. New York: Viking, 1954

Norris, Christopher, *Deconstruction: Theory and Practice*. London: Methuen, 1982

O'Brien, Michael, 'C. Vann Woodward and the Burden of Southern Liberalism', *AHR* 78 (1973) pp. 589–603

'W. J. Cash, Hegel and the South', *JSH* 44 (1978) pp. 379–98

*The Idea of the American South 1920–1941*. Baltimore: Johns Hopkins University Press, 1979

*Rethinking the South: Essays in Intellectual History*. Baltimore: Johns Hopkins University Press, 1988

O'Conner, James, *The Fiscal Crisis of the State*. New York: St Martin's Press, 1973
    *Accumulation Crisis*. Oxford: Blackwell, 1986
Ohmann, Richard, *English in America: A Radical View of the Profession*. New York: Oxford University Press, 1976
Ong, Walter, *Orality and Literacy: The Technologizing of the Word*. London: Methuen, 1982
Parsons, T. H., *John Crowe Ransom*. New York: Twayne, 1969
Pashukanis, E. B., *Law and Marxism: A General Theory*. London: Ink Links, 1978
Patterson, James T., 'The New Deal and the States', *AHR* 73 (1967–8) pp. 70–84
Pecheux, Michel, *Language, Semantics and Ideology*. London: Macmillan, 1982
Pelling, Henry, *American Labor*. University of Chicago Press, 1960
Pells, Richard H., *Radical Visions and American Dreams: Culture and Social Thought in the Depression Years*. New York: Harper and Row, 1973
    *The Liberal Mind in a Conservative Age: American Intellectuals in the 1940s and 1950s*. Middleton, Conn.: Wesleyan University Press, 1989
Perkinson, H. J., *The Imperfect Panacea: American Faith in Education, 1865–1965*. New York: Random House, 1968
Polenberg, Richard, *One Nation Divisible: Class, Race, and Ethnicity in the United States Since 1938*. Harmondsworth: Penguin Books, 1980
Post, Charles, 'The American Road to Capitalism', *NLR* 133 (May/June 1982) pp. 30–51
Poster, Mark, *Existential Marxism in Post War France: From Sartre to Althusser*. Princeton University Press, 1975
    *Foucault, Marxism and History: Mode of Production versus Mode of Information*. Cambridge: Polity, 1984
Radway, Janice, *Reading the Romance: Women, Patriarchy, and Popular Literature*. London: Verso, 1987
Rahv, Philip, *Literature and the Sixth Sense*. Boston: Houghton Mifflin, 1970
Reich, R. B., *The New American Frontier: A Provocative Program for Economic Renewal*. Harmondsworth: Penguin Books, 1984
Reising, Russell, *The Unusable Past: Theory and the Study of American Literature*. London: Methuen, 1986
Richards, I. A., *Practical Criticism: A Study of Literary Judgement*. London: Routledge and Kegan Paul, 1929
    *Poetry and Science*. London: Routledge and Kegan Paul, 1970
    *Principles of Literary Criticism*. London: Routledge and Kegan Paul, 1976
Ricoeur, Paul, *Freud and Philosophy: An Essay on Interpretation*. New Haven: Yale University Press, 1970
    *Hermeneutics and the Human Sciences*. Cambridge University Press, 1981
Riesman, David, *The Lonely Crowd: A Study of the Changing American Character*. New Haven: Yale University Press, revised edition, 1970
Rosenblatt, Louise, *Literature as Exploration*. London: Heinemann, 1970
    *The Reader, the Text, the Poem: The Transactional Theory of the Literary Work*. Carbondale: Feffer and Simons, 1970
Ross, Andrew, *No Respect: Intellectuals and Popular Culture*. London: Routledge, 1989
Rowbotham, Sheila, *Women, Resistance, and Revolution*. London: Allen Lane, 1972

*Hidden from History.* London: Pluto, 1973
*Women's Consciousness, Man's World.* Harmondsworth: Penguin, 1973
*Dreams and Dilemmas: Collected Writings.* London: Virago, 1983
Rowbotham, Sheila, Lynne Segal and Hilary Wainwright, *Beyond the Fragments:
    Feminism and the Making of Socialism.* London: Merlin, 1979
Rubin, Louis D., *Writers of the Modern South: The Faraway Country.* Seattle:
    University of Washington Press, 1963
*The Wary Fugitives.* Baton Rouge: Louisiana State University Press, 1978
*The American South: Portrait of a Culture.* Baton Rouge: Louisiana State
    University Press, 1980
Sabel, C. F., *Work and Politics: The Division of Labour in Industry.* Cambridge
    University Press, 1982
Saloutos, Theodore, 'New Deal Agricultural Policy: An Evaluation', *JAH* 61
    (1974) pp. 374–416
Samuel, Raphael, ed., *People's History and Socialist Theory.* London: Routledge
    and Kegan Paul, 1981
Sartre, Jean Paul, *The Question of Method.* London: Methuen, 1963
*What is Literature?* New York: Harper and Row, 1965
*Being and Nothingness.* New York: Washington Square Press, 1966
*Critique of Dialectical Reason.* London: NLB, 1976
Saussure, Ferdinand De, *Course in General Linguistics.* London: Fontana, 1974
Schiller, Dan, *Telematics and Government.* Norwood, NJ: Ablex Publishing, 1982
Schiller, Herbert I., *Mass Communications and American Empire.* Boston: Beacon
    Press, 1971
*The Mind Managers.* Boston: Beacon Press, 1973
*Who Knows?: Information in the Age of Fortune 500.* Norwood, NJ: Ablex
    Publishing, 1981
*Information and the Crisis Economy.* Norwood, NJ: Ablex Publishing, 1984
Schlesinger, A. M., *The Crisis of the Old Order, 1919–1933.* London: Heinemann,
    1957
Scholes, R., *Structuralism in Literature: An Introduction.* New Haven: Yale
    University Press, 1974
*Semiotics and Interpretation.* New Haven: Yale University Press, 1982
*Textual Power: Literary Theory and the Teaching of Literature.* New Haven:
    Yale University Press, 1985
Scott, Anne Firor, *The Southern Lady: From Pedestal to Politics, 1830–1930.*
    University of Chicago Press, 1970
Seiter, Ellen, et al., eds., *Remote Control: Television, Audiences, and Cultural
    Power.* London: Routledge, 1990
Shapiro, Edward S., 'Southern Agrarians and the Quest for Southern Identity',
    *AS* 13: 2 pp. 75–91
'Decentralist Intellectuals and the New Deal', *JAH* 58 (1971) pp. 938–57
Sharratt, Bernard, *Reading Relations: Structures of Literary Production: A
    Dialectical Text/Book.* Brighton: Harvester, 1982
*The Literary Labyrinth.* Brighton: Harvester, 1985
Sheridan, Alan, *Michel Foucault: The Will to Truth.* London: Tavistock, 1980
Showalter, Elaine, *The New Feminist Criticism: Essays on Women, Literature and
    Theory.* London: Virago, 1985

Shugg, R., *The Origins of Class Struggle in Louisiana*: *A Social History of White Farmers and Labourers During Slavery and After*. Baton Rouge: Louisiana State University Press, 1939

Silverman, David and B. Torode, *The Material Word*: *Some Theories of Language and its Limits*. London: Routledge and Kegan Paul, 1980

Simpson, Lewis P., ed., *The Possibilities of Order*: *Cleanth Brooks and His Work*. Baton Rouge: Louisiana State University Press, 1976

Simpson, Lewis P., *The Brazen Face of History*. Baton Rouge: Louisiana State University Press, 1980

Singal, Daniel Joseph, *The War Within*: *From Victorian to Modernist Thought in the South, 1919–1945*. Baton Rouge: Louisiana State University Press, 1982

Slater, Phil, *The Origins and Significance of the Frankfurt School*: *A Marxist Perspective*. London: Routledge and Kegan Paul, 1977

Smith, David N., *Who Rules the Universities?*: *An Essay in Class Analysis*. New York: Monthly Review Press, 1974

Smith, Roger H., *The American Reading Public*: *What it Reads and Why it Reads*. New York: R. R. Bowher, 1963

Sohn-Rethel, Alfred, *Intellectual and Manual Labour*: *A Critique of Epistemology*. London: Macmillan, 1978

Spring, Joel H., *Education and the Rise of Corporate Order*. Boston: Beacon Press, 1972

Squires, R., *Allen Tate*: *A Literary Biography*. New York: Pegasus, 1971

Stauffer, D. H., *The Intent of the Critic*. Princeton University Press, 1941

Steiner, George, *In Bluebeard's Castle*: *Some Notes Towards a Redefinition of Culture*. London: Faber and Faber, 1971
*Heidegger*. Brighton: Harvester, 1978

Stern, J. P., *Nietzsche*. London: Fontana, 1978

Stewart, John L., *John Crowe Ransom*. Minneapolis: University of Minnesota Press, 1963
*The Burden of Time*: *The Fugitives and Agrarians*. Princeton University Press, 1965

Suliman, S. and I. Crosman, eds., *The Reader in the Text*: *Essays on Audience and Interpretation*. Princeton University Press, 1980

Sweezy, Paul M., *The Theory of Capitalist Development*: *Principles of Marxian Political Economy*. New York: Monthly Review Press, 1970

Tallack, Douglas, *Twentieth-Century America*: *The Intellectual and Cultural Context*. London: Longman, 1991

Taylor, William R., *Cavalier and Yankee*. London: W. H. Allen, 1963

Thompson, E. M., *Russian Formalism and Anglo-American New Criticism*. The Hague: Mouton, 1971

Thompson, E. P., 'Review of *The Long Revolution*', *NLR* 9 and 10 (1961) pp. 24–33 and 34–9
*The Making of the English Working Class*. Harmondsworth: Penguin Books, 1968
*Whigs and Hunters*. London: Allen Lane, 1975
*William Morris*: *Romantic to Revolutionary*. New York: Pantheon Books, 1976
*The Poverty of Theory*. London: Merlin, 1978

Thompson, John B. and David Held, *Habermas: Critical Debates*. London: Macmillan, 1982

Timpanaro, S., *The Freudian Slip: Psychoanalysis and Textual Criticism*. London: NLB, 1976

*On Materialism*. London: NLB, 1976

Tindall, G. B., *The Emergence of the New South 1913–1945*. Baton Rouge: Louisiana State University Press, 1967

*The Ethnic Southerners*. Baton Rouge: Louisiana State University Press, 1976

Toffler, Alvin, *Future Shock*. London: Pan Books, 1971

*The Third Wave*. New York: Bantam, 1981

Tompkins, Jane, ed., *Reader-Response Criticism: From Formalism to Post-Structuralism*. Baltimore: Johns Hopkins University Press, 1980

Trilling, Lionel, *Beyond Culture: Essays on Literature and Learning*. Harmondsworth: Penguin Books, 1967

*The Liberal Imagination: Essays on Literature and Society*. Harmondsworth: Penguin Books, 1970

*Sincerity and Authenticity*. London: Oxford University Press, 1972

*The Opposing Self: Nine Essays in Criticism*. Oxford University Press, 1980

Tyack, D. B., *Turning Points in American Educational History*. Waltham, Mass.: Blaisdell, 1967

Veblen, T., *The Higher Learning in America: A Memorandum on the Conduct of Universities by Business*. New York: B. W. Huebsch, 1918

*The Theory of the Leisure Class: An Economic Study of the Evolution of Institutions*. New York: Macmillan, 1899

Vesser, H. Aram, ed., *The New Historicism*. London: Routledge, 1989

Volosinov, V. N., *Marxism and the Philosophy of Language*. New York: Seminar Press, 1973

*Freudianism: A Marxist Critique*. New York: Academic Press, 1976

Walker, Marshall, *Robert Penn Warren: A Vision Earned*. Edinburgh: Paul Harris Publishing, 1979

Wallerstein, Immanuel, *The Capitalist World Economy*. Cambridge University Press, 1979

*Historical Capitalism*. London: Verso, 1983

Warren, A. and René Welleck, *Theory of Literature*. Harmondsworth: Penguin, 1973

West, Paul, *Robert Penn Warren*. Minneapolis: University of Minnesota Press, 1964

White, Hayden, *Metahistory*. Baltimore: Johns Hopkins University Press, 1973

*Tropics of Discourse*. Baltimore: John Hopkins University Press, 1978

Wiebe, Robert H., *The Search for Order, 1877–1920*. New York: Hill and Wang 1967

*The Segmented Society: An Introduction to the Meaning of America*. London: Oxford University Press, 1976

Wiener, Jonathan M., *The Social Origins of the New South: Alabama 1860–1885*. Baton Rouge: Louisiana State University Press, 1978

'Class Structure and Economic Development in the American South 1865–1955', *AHR* 84 (1979) pp. 970–1006

Williams, T. Harry, *Huey Long*. London: Thames and Hudson, 1970

Williams, Raymond, *Culture and Society 1780–1950*. Harmondsworth: Penguin Books, 1961

*Communications*. Harmondsworth, Penguin, 1962

*The Long Revolution*. Harmondsworth: Penguin Books, 1965

*Modern Tragedy*. London: Chatto and Windus, 1966

*Television: Technology and Cultural Form*. London: Fontana, 1974

*Keywords: A Vocabulary of Culture and Society*. London: Fontana, 1976

*Marxism and Literature*. Oxford: Oxford University Press, 1977

*Politics and Letters*. London: NLB, 1979

*Problems in Materialism and Culture*. London: Verso, 1980

*Culture*. London: Fontana, 1981

*Towards 2000*. London: Chatto and Windus, 1983

Willis, Susan, 'Aesthetics of the Rural Slum: Contradictions and Dependency in "The Bear"', *Social Text* 2 (Summer 1979) pp. 82–103

Wimsatt, W. K., *The Verbal Icon: Studies in the Meaning of Poetry*. New York: Noonday, 1958

Wimsatt, W. K. and Cleanth Brooks, *Literary Criticism*. New York: Alfred A. Knopf, 1957

Wingard, Joel, 'Folded into a Single Party: Agrarians and Proletarians', *SR* 16 (1980) pp. 776–81

Winters, Yvor, *In Defence of Reason*. London: Routledge and Kegan Paul, 1960

*The Function of Criticism*. London: Routledge and Kegan Paul, 1972

Woodman, H. D., *King Cotton and His Retainers: Financing and Maintaining the Cotton Crop of the South 1800–1925*. Galway: University College Press, 1973

'Sequel to Slavery: The New History Views the Post Bellum South', *JSH* 43: 4 (November 1977) pp. 523–54

Woodward, Comer Vann, *The Burden of Southern History*. Baton Rouge: Louisiana State University Press, 1960

*The Strange Career of Jim Crow*. New York: Oxford University Press, 1966

*The Origins of the New South 1877–1913*. Baton Rouge: Louisiana State University Press, 1971

*American Counterpoint: Slavery and Racism in the North/South Dialogue*. New York: Oxford University Press, 1983

*Thinking Back: The Perils of Writing History*. Baton Rouge: Louisiana State University Press, 1986

Woolf, Janet, *The Social Production of Art*. London: Macmillan, 1981

Worpole, Ken, *Dockers and Detectives: Popular Reading: Popular Writing*. London: Verso, 1983

*Reading by Numbers: Contemporary Publishing and Popular Fiction*. London: Comedia, 1984

Wyatt-Brown, Bertrum, *Southern Honor: Ethics and Behaviour in the Old South*. New York: Oxford University Press, 1982

Young, Thomas Daniel, *Donald Davidson*. New York: Twayne, 1969

*Gentleman in a Dustcoat: A Biography of John Crowe Ransom*. Baton Rouge: Louisiana State University Press, 1976

*Waking the Neighbours: The Nashville Agrarians Reconsidered*. Athens: University of Georgia Press, 1982

Young, Thomas Daniel and John Tyree Fain, *The Literary Correspondence of Donald Davidson and Allen Tate*. Athens: University of Georgia Press, 1974

Young, Thomas Daniel and John J. Hindle, *The Republic of Letters in America: The Correspondence of John Peale Bishop and Allen Tate*. Lexington: University of Kentucky, 1981

Zinn, Howard, *A People's History of The United States*. London: Longman, 1980

# Index

Adorno, T. W., 112–13
Althusser, Louis, ix
Arac, Jonathan, 150–1
Aristotle, 42
Arnold, Matthew, 117
Atkins, Floyd c., 25, n. 29

Barthes, Roland, ix, 9
Baudelaire, Charles, 53
Beardsley, Monroe, 5, 77
Bleich, David, 8
Belsey, Catherine, 7
Berman, Marshall, 15–16, 152—3
Bishop, John Peale, 26
Bloom, Harold, 97, 137
Bolenius, Emma Miller, 87 n. 15
Bourdieu, Pierre, 18, 151 n. 30
Bradbury, J. M., 21 n. 8
Braverman, Harry, 21 n. 4
Brooks, Cleanth, 5, 10 n. 20, 19–20, 67, 69,
    76–8, 81–9, 98, 99, 122
Brooks, Van Wyck, 120
Brown, Ashley, 48 n. 12
Bryan, William Jennings, 21
Burke, Kenneth, 72

Cain, William E., 137–8, 144
Caldwell, Erskine, ix
Callan, Norman, 87 n. 15
Chandler, Alfred, 21 n. 2
Cheney, Frances Neal, 48 n. 12
Coleridge, Samuel Taylor, 127
Conrad, Joseph, 129
Cooper, James Fenimore, 133
Cowley, Abraham, 60 n. 18
Cox, Sidney, 99
Crane, R. S., 86
Culler, Jonathan, 8, 137
Cutrer, Thomas W., 72 n. 1

Dante, 52, 122–3
Davidson, Donald, 25, 26–8

Davis, Jefferson, 115
Davis, Mike, 126 n. 4, 149–50, 152–3
de Man, Paul, 86, 92, 93
Degler, Carl, 21 n. 4
Derrida, Jacques, ix, 117–18
Descartes, René, 119
Dickinson, Emily, 46–7, 56
Dostoevsky, Fyodor, 118
Dreiser, Theodore, 7, 134

Eagleton, Terry, 4–7
Eco, Umberto, 17
Eliot, T. S., 21, 50, 53, 62, 76, 78, 106
Emerson, Ralph Waldo, 47
Empson, William, 122
Ewen, Stuart, 21 n. 3.

Fain, John Tyree, 24 n. 22, 28 n. 48
Faulkner, William, ix, 17
Fekete, John, 11–15, 29, 30, 69, 75, 91
Fish, Stanley, 8
Fitzhugh, George, 13, 17, 24
Foerster, Norman, 44
Foucault, Michel, 16, 146 n. 2
Freedman, Estelle B., 21 n. 4
Frye, Northrop, 4–5, 7, 8

Garnham, Nicholas, 18 n. 21
Genovese, Eugene, 12–13, 15, 24
Gitlin, Todd, 153
Godden, Richard, ix, 17–18
Grady, Henry, 124
Graff, Gerald, 16, 86, 139–40, 141–2, 144
Gramsci, Antonio, 150, 151
Gray, Richard, 17, 143 n. 15

Hall, Stuart, 148
Hanes, Ernest, 87 n. 15
Hartman, Geoffery, 5
Hawkes, Terence, 7, 8–10, 142 n. 10, 145
Hawthorne, Nathaniel, 56
Hegel, Georg W. F., 92, 109, 111

216